T0130877

Animals, the Law and Veterinary Medicine

A Guide to Veterinary Law

Fourth Edition

Animals, the Law and Veterinary Medicine

A Guide to Veterinary Law

Fourth Edition

Orland Soave

Austin & Winfield, Publishers
Lanham • New York • Oxford

Copyright 2000 by
Austin & Winfield, Publishers
4720 Boston Way
Lanham, Maryland 20706

12 Hid's Copse Rd.
Cumnor Hill, Oxford OX2 9JJ

Library of Congress Cataloging-in-Publication Data

Soave, Orland A.
Animals, the law and veterinary medicine : a guide to veterinary law / Orland
Soave.—4th ed.
p. cm.
Includes bibliographical references and index.
1. Veterinary hygiene—Law and legislation—United States. 2. Veterinarians—
Legal status, laws, etc.—United States. 3. Animal welfare—Law and
legislation—United States. I. Title.
KF3835.S67 2000 344.73'049—dc21 99-087960 CIP

ISBN 1-57292-149-8 (cloth: alk. ppr.)
ISBN 1-57292-148-X (pbk: alk. ppr.)

TABLE OF CONTENTS

Chapter Three

Chapter Four

Chapter Five

Chapter Six

ACKNOWLEDGEMENT

As in the previous edition, I have had free access to the Stanford University Lane Library as well as other University Libraries. The support, help and suggestions of library staff have been essential in finding references and collecting appropriate material for inclusion in the book. I sincerely appreciate library support, without which authors would not be able to produce a product.

THE AUTHOR

Orland Soave, B.S, DVM, LL.B, is the Director Emeritus of the Division of Laboratory Animal Medicine of Stanford University in California. He is the author of over one hundred scientific papers and four books. He was president of the American Association of Laboratory Animal Science and the American College of Laboratory Animal Medicine and Editor of the Journal, Laboratory Animal Science. He served as a consultant to the National Institutes of Health and the Food and Drug Administration in Bethesda and Rockville, Maryland.

PREFACE

How do I get into trouble?
How can I stay out of trouble?
What constitutes the practice of the profession?
What should my relationship be with clients?
How do I relate to the public and the animals I serve?

Essentially, these are the things a veterinarian beginning a career in veterinary medicine, or engaged in the profession, wants to know. The aim of this book is to provide answers to these questions. I hope it succeeds.

If we include "Veterinary Law, (Saunders), "Veterinary Medicine and the Law, (Williams Wilkins), and "Animals, the Law and Veterinary Medicine," (Austin Winfield), this represents the third revision, (fourth edition) of the original work spanning over 20 years time.

The current edition includes many additions to the sections on history, malpractice and negligence, recorded cases, business ethics and manners, animal patent law, copyrights and trademarks, and insurance for animals.

In the author's opinion the present text will be better suited to the teaching of jurisprudence, for practitioners of veterinary medicine, persons engaged in all aspects of agriculture involving animals, animal interest groups, and the legal profession.

Orland Soave, DVM, LL.B.
Stanford University
June 1999

CHAPTER ONE
HISTORICAL BACKGROUND

Origins of The Law

Information on the origins, growth and development of our legal system is interesting and provides an understanding of how the laws of the United States came into being, how the court system works and why we need rules and regulations to govern our daily lives.

Unwritten laws, originating as customs, mores and the responsibilities of one person toward another and the tribe, date back to the beginning of civilization and these operated to control family and social life. Rules relating to marriage, property ownership and criminal acts became accepted ones necessary for living in family groups and were passed from one generation to the next. As family clans banded together in groups forming communities, laws continued to develop and expand to govern the conduct of people dwelling in close contact with one another. Laws were necessary for the survival of civilization in a controllable form.

Two systems of law have survived and continue to be practiced in Western civilization today: Roman Civil Law and English Common Law. Roman Civil Law began 3000 years ago with the establishment of the Twelve Tables — clay tablets engraved with the rules Romans felt were necessary to protect daily life, including trade, the conduct of business and criminal acts. For centuries Roman law has formed the basis for codes of law in European states and some other parts of the world. (Cuschan)

Roman law evolved from customs of the populace originating from daily acts which were set down in written codes becoming a system of law used by the judiciary. Disagreements and disputes were resolved based on what was considered right at the time — a rule was laid down to be followed with similar disputes in the future. In totality, Roman law represented formalism, rigidity, and strict application, with limited flexibility. Written codes were divided into public and private law and included the law of persons, property, succession, obligations and procedures. (Van Wemelo)

Roman law reached the British isles when the territory was occupied by Roman legions in the second century A D. By the 9th and 10th centuries the Anglos and Saxons destroyed the remains of Roman civilization and instituted their own customs and rules for living, dying and doing business, setting down the foundations for the development of English Common Law. The system supports individualism and the belief that an individual's rights must be protected by the government. Unlike the Roman law it is not an inflexible written and coded law but is based on precedents set by court decisions throughout the years making it fluid and ever-changing to meet the needs of contemporary society.

The Norman invasion of the British Isles in the 11th century brought unification and stability to England. The Normans brought with them some of their legal beliefs concerning property ownership and succession along with a system involving legal tribunals, but they also adopted many Anglo-Saxon customs. The major Norman contribution was the establishment of a stable, on-going government — the idea of the existence of a state or nation giving cohesion and order to the law. Law and state became one because without an organized state to support interpretation and give force to rules of law these would be useless as a means of governing the peoples personal and public interactions.

The state cannot give force and direction to the law without the ability to communicate; oral or written publications of announcements, decrees, statutes and codes for the control of daily life. The application of the law gained more force and attention when written and circulated throughout the land. Communication by word-of-mouth was not dependable and did not leave records for future use.

The Norman conquest also brought to the land a strong and established church which was instrumental in spreading the written word, leading to a civilized and settled urban and rural life for the populace.

The quintessential factor in the foundation of the English Common Law was the formulation and presentation of the Magna Carta and its signing by King John in 1215 A D. This document is and remains a milestone in the origin and development of English law. Here for the first time limits were placed on the lords of England and on the authority of the king for the protection and benefit of all the citizens of the country. This document was the foundation and the beginning of the English Common Law. Since this time, with the development of the court and jury system and the concept of the inalienable rights of the individual, the English Common law became the single most important inheritance the American colonies received from England.

The Magna Carta was the source of the basic concept of the law for the colonies. The idea of a written constitution for the United States stemmed from this document. The Supreme Court of the United States in over 100 decisions in the past 25 years has referred to our dependence on the Magna Carta with respect to the due process of law, trial by jury of one's peers, protection against excessive bail or fines and cruel or unusual punishment. In reality, the Magna Carta is an early version of the United States Bill of Rights. (23 TN Bar J. Jul/Aug 1978 p. 40)

English Common Law
in the United States

The American colonies were founded on charters granted by the King of England, hence the legal system of the mother country naturally followed the colonists into America. The charter of the Territory of Virginia provided that their citizens would have charters and that these must not be contrary to the laws and statutes of England.

The English Common Law, not bound by written codes, made it adaptable and flexible in its interpretation and application to the legal needs of the colonies. Freer living and business conditions were practiced in America which liberalized the common law and resulted in a greater degree of equality among the population compared to England. One factor that contributed to this increased freedom was that few of the English nobility emigrated permanently to the colonies. The majority came as administers for specified periods of time

With evolution the common law became divided into constitutional, criminal, commercial and private law. The latter contains rules that govern relations between individuals, the laws of persons and properties.

As indicated, it is of primary importance that the common law is not written in rigid rules to be strictly followed as is statutory law, but is based on precedents set by the decisions of the courts. With the passage of time and changes of customs and viewpoints, courts of law developed and established new precedents applicable to the issues of law relative to changing periods. This keeps the law flexible and sensitive to the circumstances and needs of the public in an ever-changing society.

Statutory Law

Statutory law represents the decisions of a legislature or law-making body, separating it from the common law which can only evolve from court decisions. Statutory law is recorded in statute books separated into codes or sections for ease of use. Generally statutes define and describe the responsibility and relationships between private persons and the government. They make the duties in personal relationships more positive and certain where the common law is not specific or requires workable and applicable definitions of personal and public interactions; marriage, divorce, animal control, protection of the health and welfare of the public. Statutory law often follows the principles of the common law only making these more positive and specific. An important difference between the two being that statutes are passed by a legislative body as written laws and apply to the relationships of persons and the government. They are legal principles adopted by individual states and incorporated into their constitutions, under which they function. To protect the federal government and the public there is a legal precedent with respect to state statutes and local ordinances that these are not binding if they violate the constitution of the United States. (Edmunds)

The United States legal system was provided for in the Constitution, Article III, section 1, "The judicial powers of the United States shall be vested in one Supreme Court, and in such inferior courts as the Congress may from time to time ordain and establish. Section 2, the judicial power shall extend to all cases in law and equity arising under this constitution, the laws of the United States to controversies between two or more states, between a state and a citizen of another state."

Lawyers for Animals

Prior to Biblical times animals were held responsible for their actions causing damage to human beings or their property. This historical information is interesting as it relates to the evolution of human-animal interactions.

In ancient Greek cities there were temples of fire called Prytaneum which served as public halls where the citizens gathered, foreigners were entertained and court trials were held in the open air of the courtyard in order that condemned prisoners breath would not contaminate the judges or viewing public. Trials of animals accused of injuring or killing human beings were also held here. Animals causing a crime were considered to have disturbed the peaceful equilibrium of the community and had to be punished otherwise misfortunes such as floods, droughts, plagues or reversal of fortunes would befall the community. Killings and injuries by animals were tried by official tribunals and the law of Lex Talionis was applied, a law of retaliation; blood for blood, an eye for an eye; the animal was physically punished.

In ancient Persia animals were dealt with as responsible beings and in the religious laws if a vicious dog was not muzzled and it injured a man or sheep it must be tried and punished for its acts. If found guilty the punishment was a progressive mutilation of the animal corresponding to the numbers of persons or animals bitten and wounded or killed. This began with the loss of ears and ended with the amputation of the tail

In the early nations of Greece, Rome, the Teutons, Celts and Slavs an animal which did damage to persons or property had to be surrendered to the injured party or his relatives to be dealt with as they saw fit. Beginning with the 9th century in Europe available records show that domestic animals were tried in criminal courts and if found guilty were usually put to death.

A fascinating case is one where a distinguished French lawyer of the 1500's made his reputation as a man of talent by representing a group of rats. The Ecclesiastical court of the province accused the rats of wrongfully and wantonly eating and destroying the local citizen's barley crop. The Bishop's deputy cited the accused rats and ordered them to appear in court on a specified date and time. The fledgling attorney above was appointed by the court to defend the rats. It was the custom of the times to have the court appoint an attorney to defend accused animals.

The lawyer knew his clients had bad reputations and were undoubtedly guilty. He had to find some legal loophole for his clients to escape. First, he pleaded to the court that his clients, the defendants, were scattered over a large part of the province, living both in villages and the countryside. For this reason a single summons could not be used to notify all of the rats of the charges against them and of their day in court. He succeeded in obtaining a delay while citations were published and sent to all of the parishes for the priests to place notices of the charges in all of the areas inhabited by the accused rats.

At the trial the defense attorney excused the non-appearance of his clients at court on the grounds that to appear they had to travel a great distance exposing themselves to their mortal enemies, cats who would lie in wait for them on every path and road. The young lawyer reminded the court it was a general rule of law that if a person cited to appear in court could not come in safety he could, due to the danger involved, refuse to obey the order. The point of law was argued at length by the lawyers for both sides. The result was that the rats were acquitted and the French defense attorney became a prominent magistrate

Noxious wild animals such as rats and locusts were usually tried in Ecclesiastical courts and punishment was either death or banishment and excommunication from the parish or provence by a formal religious decree. The authority of the church to punish animals for their offenses under religious law presupposed a contract between God who made the laws and all the creatures He created who should be subject to the rules of the law.

Trials involving animals were conducted in accordance with all the requirements of legal protocol and procedures. A town or district that was disturbed by any type of animal could appeal to the criminal or ecclesiastical court who would institute an investigation and if sufficient grounds were found for a trial a lawyer would be named to defend the animal(s). A summons was served by an official who would go around the district and read the summons aloud in a strong voice in places the animals frequented. The culprits were summoned to appear in court three times and if they did not a judgment by default was made and a warrant issued to the animals to leave the district in a specific period of time. If they did not do so they were excommunicated or pronounced evil spirits by judication or ceremony.

In Basel Switzerland in 1474 a cock was tried for laying an egg. Superstitious tales associated cock's eggs with witches who used these to make magical preparations, therefore they were very valuable. The defending lawyer claimed the laying of an egg in this case was involuntary and not premeditated, consequently the happening was not punishable by law and his client was innocent since no evidence was presented that the cock was under the influence of Satan. The court found the cock guilty on the evidence of the presence of an egg. The cock was condemned and burned at the stake in the town square in front of a large crowd.

Why force capital punishment on animals? In the minds of citizens of Medieval times there were several reasons for this; an animal that has killed or injured a person or damaged his property may do so again. By punishing the culprit the court has protected its citizens from a repeat occurrence. Punishments were also aimed at the owners of animals. Depriving them of their animals through a death sentence or fining them for the animal's actions was intended to make an owner more careful in the maintenance and confinement of his charges. Domestic animals in past times could be arrested, tried, convicted and executed; the same as their owners. They were considered a part of the family and entitled to the same legal protection and control by the courts. Domestic animals were tried by civil courts whereas wild animals, unowned creatures of God, were tried by religious ones. Insects and rodents could not usually be seized, imprisoned and tried, consequently, a method of controlling such noxious creatures was to excommunicate them and place a curse on their bodies and souls. One custom was to capture some of these wild animals, bring them before an ecclesiastical court and condemn them to death as a symbol of how the entire population would be dealt with if it were possible.

Swarms of insects and hordes of rodents were believed to be released by Satan, the devil, who used these creatures to punish sinful man. Many types of beasts and birds were classed by the church as devils in disguise. Another method used to control pests was to place a price on their heads This approach was used to attempt to eliminate a plague of locusts occurring in Rome in 880 A D; history says it didn't work. Similarly, today we place monetary bounties on undesirable animals such as wolves, coyotes or mountain lions.

The ancient Greeks believed that a murder or crime committed by man or animal had to be dealt with legally or the "Furies" would be aroused and bring a pestilence to the land. The Furies were three terrible female spirits in Greek and Roman mythology whose charge was to punish all doers of unavenged crimes. Later, the church in Medieval times supported and taught the same belief but substituted demons and evil spirits for the Furies. Superstitions helped the church to control its believers

In 864 A D a judicial council of the church decreed that bees, causing death of a human being through their stings, should be suffocated in their beehive before more honey could be produced because this would be tainted by the demon and not be fit for human consumption.

Pigs in the Middle Ages were allowed to roam free and they were aggressive, fierce creatures. Several records show these animals were tried by the courts and often hung for maiming or killing children. In 1266 near Paris a pig was convicted of having eaten a child and by order of the court was burned in a public ceremony. In 1394 another pig was found guilty of murdering a child and was hung by the neck until dead. In 1403 another pig was executed for the same crime. Records from France show that to the middle of the 1700's at least 92 animals were tried and executed on criminal charges, the last being a cow that had killed a young boy in 1740.

Accused beasts and human beings were often thrown together in the same prison and given the same treatment; chains, beatings, bread and water. A jail-keepers records of the time show he was paid about 4 dollars for providing bread and keep for several prisoners including one pig kept in jail for one month before it was hanged for killing a child. The board for a pig was the same as for a man; four cents a day.

In 1457 a sow was convicted of flagrantly murdering a five year old boy and sentenced to hang from a tree. Her six suckling young were stained with blood and included in the indictment. Due to a lack of proof they had assisted the mother in the murder they were acquitted and returned to their owner who had to pay bail to get the piglets back.

Where locusts invaded vineyards in a province of France the priest of the area proclaimed, "In the name and by virtue of God, the omnipotent, Father, Son and Holy Spirit, and of Mary, the most blessed Mother of our Lord Jesus Christ, and by the authority of the Holy Apostles Peter and Paul, we admonish by these presents the aforesaid locusts and grasshoppers under pain of malediction and anathema to depart from the vineyards and field within six days from the publication of this sentence and to do no further damage. If, on expiration of this period, the animals have refused to obey this injunction, they are to be accursed and excommunicated."

More recently, animals have been tried and sentenced for their actions. In 1916 a circus elephant trampled a man to death. The authorities involved decided the elephant should die on the gallows for this action. The animal was taken to a railroad yard where there was a 100 ton derrick, a chain secured around the neck, the elephant lifted into the air and hanged until dead.

In 1924 a male Labrador retriever belonging to the Governor of Pennsylvania seemed to suddenly go berserk and killed the family cat. The governor presided at a hearing and trial. The dog had no counsel but with overwhelming evidence was sentenced to life imprisonment in the state penitentiary. It lived with the prisoners, was befriended, lived a happy life and died of old age

In 1963 75 carrier pigeons smuggled bank notes from Greece and Egypt into Libya under the supervision and direction of an international gang of smugglers. Captured by Libyan police the court ordered the pigeons to be killed on the grounds they were so well-trained to let them loose would be too dangerous. Convicted smugglers were only fined.

Jewish Law on Clean and Unclean

Jewish laws relative to clean and unclean animals have received considerable attention for centuries without a definitive solution. Why did God decree that some foods could be eaten and other not? Suggestions have been put forth but none have withstood the test of time. Why can sheep and locusts be eaten but pigs and mice forbidden? What is the reason for dividing land animals into cloven hoofed, cud chewers which are clean while some other animals are not? Four explanations have been postulated for these laws:

1. They are arbitrary and the rationale is known only to God

2. A cultic explanation holds that the unclean animals are those used in pagan worship or are associated with deities against the beliefs of Israelites.

3. The hygienic theory contends that the unclean creatures are unfit for food because they are insanitary, are carriers of disease or are predators eating other animals

4. A symbolic interpretation states that the clean animals furnish examples of how man should conduct his life; chewing the cud

reminds man to pause and think about life and to meditate on the customs and laws and to lead a righteous life. Sheep are clean because they are a reminder that the Lord is man's shepherd, protector and leader. The pig is a dirty animal with repulsive habits eating anything including filth. Predators kill and eat others hence are poor examples for an exemplary life.

In Medieval times animals were given some legal rights and their day-in-court. In spite of the appointment of attorneys to defend them, they were usually found guilty and lost their case. Today, there are individuals and associations who champion the position of animals in society and feel they should have some degree of moral and legal rights. There are groups of attorneys who will defend animal causes and welfare groups who champion the position of animals in our current society.

CHAPTER TWO
MALPRACTICE AND NEGLIGENCE

In recent years there has been an increase in the number of malpractice suits against veterinarians. Up to 5 percent of active practitioners become involved in a lawsuit each year. Engaged in a malpractice case is undesirable because the solution may be time-consuming and expensive. The reasons for the increased number of cases are more people, more animals, more lawyers, public sensitivity of and awareness of personal legal rights, animal welfare and rights movements, and increased competition among veterinarians.

Tort and Contract Actions

Law suits against veterinarians for malpractice and negligence are tort actions, a wrong has been committed against another person or persons. Tort actions must be tried in court in a shorter time from their commission than civil actions, for example breach of contract. Tort actions in most instances must be brought into court within one year of their occurrence as opposed to breaches of contract where as much as four years may be allowed for their appearance in court. (West's Calif Codes, St, Paul MN 1992)

Contract and tort actions have significant legal differences. In contract actions the parties have agreed to perform a specific act or acts and the parties to the contract know their duties and liabilities with respect to one another. A veterinarian contracts with a builder to construct an animal clinic in a fixed amount of time following a given set of plans, for which the veterinarian will pay an agreed upon sum. In tort actions no mutual agreement has been made, no meeting of the minds has occurred, no elements necessary for a valid contract have been agreed upon. A tort action is based on the premise that every person owes a duty to another person to conduct themselves in such a manner that no one will be injured by their actions; A Golden Rule concept. A veterinarian who fails in a duty to a client, to bring to the case the acceptable professional skills has injured the client and committed a crime against the client, or his property and he is therefore liable for the resulting damages. When a client brings an animal to the veterinarian for treatment he must handle the animal in a reasonable manner, using the proper skills to make a diagnosis, employ acceptable treatment and follow the animal until recovery or dismissed from the case. A tort action is separate and distinct from a contractual one.

Historical Background

The earliest systems of law contained provisions for dealing with medical malpractice. Five thousand years ago in ancient Egypt the healing arts were too important to be placed under the control of the general public. This was restricted to a class of priests, called image bearers, who were required to make a complete and thorough study of the standard Egyptian works on medicine. Of the 42 books of Hermes, 6 dealt with the human body, diseases of the organs, of the eyes and diseases peculiar to women, and of the remedies for disease.

If the medical man followed the rules of the sacred books and did not save the patient he is held free from guilt. If any action is performed contrary to the rules of the books the physician is liable for capital punishment. One rule in the books forbade a medic to purge his patient before the 4th day of treatment, but the medical man who deviated from the rules and cured the patient was spared punishment. But if he experimented with new treatments and the patient was not cured or died, the medic was killed.

A breach of the teachings of the books of Hermes was sacrilegious and most physicians became highly specialized in order to know all the books contained on a given subject in order to save their heads. Each medic limited himself to a single disease or condition and become noted for this type of specific knowledge, treating only the eyes, the head, teeth, abdominal pains, respiratory or intestinal disease.

In China the oldest medical code dates back to the 7th century BC. A current edition of the code, TaTsing Lee of 1647 A.D., deals with the practice of medicine; in section 297 it says, "When an unskilled practitioner of medicine or surgery administers drugs or performs operations with the puncturing needle contrary to the established rules of practice and thereby kills the patient the magistrates shall call in other practitioners to examine the nature of the medicine or of the wound which was the cause of the fatality and if it appears this was due to an honest error without intent to injure the patient, the practitioner shall be saved from being killed but shall be banished from the practice of medicine forever." An early example of the use of expert witnesses and the loss of license to practice. The penalty for intentional negligence was beheading of the medic.

In ancient Greece liability for malpractice did not exist. Plato (400 B.C) said, "As regards to physicians they are free from all legal responsibility for the death of their patients unless they themselves have brought about the fatal issue." In the same era Hippocrates is quoted, "Of all the professions medicine is the only one in which incompetence entails no further punishment than disgrace." A practitioner doing his best as judged by his peers is relieved from medical responsibility.

Roman medical law contained provisions for both contract and tort law. If a physician treated a persons slave and the slave died the physician could be held for damage to property and pay for the cost of the slave. When treating a peer negligence could be held against the doctor. (Trans Med Legal Soc 1909-1910,1 .98)

The first recorded case in England against a physician was brought in 1374 before the King's Bench. This involved one J . Mort a surgeon tried before the court for the treatment of a wounded hand. Negligence was not proved but the court indicated if negligence was the case a remedy could be provided for the wronged person. (Temple Law O vol. 30, 1957)

The first malpractice case in the United States against a veterinarian was Connors v Winton, 8 Indiana 315, 1856. Connors was the owner of a horse valued at $125 which had a swelling on the hock joint. Winton, a veterinary surgeon, stated he could relieve the horses pain and lameness by lancing the joint. This he did so unskillfully and negligently that the horse became permanently disabled and worthless and eventually was killed. Connors had spent $25 in expenses and placed the value of the horse at $200. Winton, the veterinarian, had acted as a friend without compensation. The court said he was still liable for his actions and not being a farrier was irrelevant. He assumed to perform a delicate operation and did so in ignorance and negligence and was therefore liable.

In an English case of 160 years ago the court stated a veterinary surgeon is a professional person and the general principles of negligence as they affect other professional persons and in particular medical practitioners, are applicable to him. Thus a veterinary surgeon by the nature of his calling holds himself out to the public as being possessed of the skill and knowledge of that calling. It has been said that a medical man, and the same principal will apply here, owes a threefold duty of care to anyone who consults him professionally; 1. a duty of care in deciding whether he should take the case, 2. a duty of care in deciding what treatment is appropriate, and 3. a duty of care in administering the treatment. A breach of any one of these duties would constitute negligence. (Lamphier v Phipos, 8 C & P475, 1838.)

Duties and Liabilities
of Veterinarians

Most lawsuits against veterinarians occur because malpractice or negligence has been alleged by the client. Malpractice is a dereliction of a professional duty, intentional, criminal, or negligent by the one providing professional services that results in an injury, loss or damage to the one receiving these services.

The major determining factor is the failure of one providing professional services to exercise the degree of care, skill and learning that would be brought to the case by the average, reputable member of the profession to each case brought to him or her for services. Such a failure can result in an injury or damage to the person relying on these services. The law says that one seeking the services of a professional person is entitled to receive the benefit of service equal to those provided by any qualified veterinarian under similar circumstances (Ramiro 1989)

Negligence is the omission to do something which a reasonable person would do when faced with a similar problem. Conversely, it is not doing something a reasonable person would do under similar circumstances. Malpractice is bad practice due to a lack of skill or the failure to apply it. The word is used to the negligent performance of all professionals; physician, dentist, attorney, accountant, chiropractor, and the veterinarian; that is, the professions where the public relies on the training and skill of a professional to provide specific results; treatment, surgery or immunization of an animal. When unskilled practice of a profession results in injury to the patient (animal) the client (owner or keeper of the animal) may sue the veterinarian. Malpractice may be willful, negligent or ignorant (ALR 4, 1991)

The words malpractice and negligence are often used together or interchangeably because it is difficult to separate the two because one who is negligent usually commits malpractice and the charge of malpractice implies negligence. Negligence on the part of a physician consists of doing something that should have been done or omitting to do something that should have been done; the failure to exercise the degree of care, skill and diligence of the profession. The courts today consider the principles of malpractice and negligence the same for physicians and veterinarians. However, differences in the requirements of skill between the two professions do exist: (1) veterinarians treat several different species of animals where treatment may vary with the species involved; (2) treatment may vary depending on the use of the animal — food-producing, work animals, companion animals; (3) animals do not communicate verbally to define their problems; (4) the level of care may depend on the value of the animal, is the treatment worth the expense or will the treatment interfere with the intended use of the animal; (5) euthanasia is legally and universally available to the veterinarian, not the physician. (Southall 1971, Staples 1910, King 1990, Brochett 1964)

Liability for Malpractice

To be liable for malpractice and negligence it must be established that the veterinarian owed the person suing a duty and that negligence occurred in the performance of this duty. Courts have ruled many times that one who practices veterinary medicine, accepts a case, cares for and treats an animal has assumed and owes a duty to the client. The duties being to have the required training and to exercise the degree of care and skill required by the profession and to apply these to any and all cases accepted for treatment. A veterinarian's duty to the public is to practice the profession in a careful and responsible manner so that the public will not be injured by the actions of the veterinarian.

A professional engaged in treating animals is required in performing the duties of employment, to use such reasonable skill, diligence and attention as may be expected of careful, skillful and trustworthy persons in the profession. If these qualities are not possessed or exercised the veterinarian is answerable to the clients and courts can award damages for this lack of care and skill. (Conner 1856, Kelliher 1890, Kervow 1953)

In cases of malpractice and negligence an alleged breach has occurred in the duty to exercise reasonable care and skill by the veterinarian and as a result of this the animal and, indirectly, the client, have been injured. The degree of Doctor of Veterinary Medicine along with a license to practice are coupled with an obligation; with these documents the veterinarian represents to the public that he or she possess the necessary qualifications to practice the profession along with the ability and experience to deal with problems that fall within the scope of this training in a satisfactory manner, without doing harm to clients or patients. The law requires of all licensed professionals that they possess the skill and exercise the care practiced by all persons in that profession in general.

The reason that the veterinarian owes a client a duty and is required by law to exercise ordinary care and skill in the practice of the profession serve two purposes; to protect the unwary public and to discourage non-qualified persons from representing themselves to the public as qualified veterinarians.

In most instances for a person to recover damages in a law suit for malpractice and negligence a demonstrable injury must have occurred to the plaintiff (client). A veterinarian may be guilty of malpractice and negligence but if no injury occurs to the client, recovery will not be allowed in a court of law. (Corpus Juris 1966)

Negligence is the most common wrongful conduct of a veterinarian. In these cases the client, or plaintiff, must establish in court that the defendant veterinarian owed the client a duty, failed in performance of this duty, and demonstrable harm resulted from the alleged negligence of the veterinarian. (Turner 1988)

In Moreland v Lowdermilk the owners of a horse that died brought a lawsuit against the veterinarian who had treated the horse. The veterinarian filed a countersuit for fees for the services rendered. The court held that testimony by experts in equine medicine disagreed on the proper treatment for thromboembolic colic and failed to prove the proper degree of care and skill was lacking in this case to amount to malpractice. An underlying cause of the death of the horse was the failure of the owner to maintain an effective de-worming program. The decision of the court was that the veterinarian was entitled to receive a reasonable fee for services rendered plus attorney's fees. (Moreland 1989)

A dog owner brought a malpractice suit against a veterinarian charged with the failure to properly diagnose the presence of a fracture of the spinal column in the dog. The owner won the case and was awarded $400 in damages plus court costs and attorney's fees. Evidence of witnesses stated that with proper equipment and attention to the case the average responsible veterinarian would not have missed the diagnosis.

A veterinarian filed a complaint against a state department for the revocation of his license for the charge of gross malpractice. A dog was brought to the veterinarian on a week end and the diagnosis was an involvement of the lungs and the animal was treated with an acceptable drug. Pyometra was also diagnosed and the dog's uterus removed to remedy this problem. The dog died and at autopsy its uterus was completely normal. The charge of malpractice was upheld (Turner 1989)

A racehorse owner brought suit against a veterinarian to recover damages for the death of a racehorse. The court entered judgment for the veterinarian and the decision was appealed. The appellate court held that the evidence was sufficient to support the finding that the veterinarian was not negligent in administering vitamin E to the horse for anhydrosis, the veterinarian breached no duty to warn the racehorse's trainer of possible fatal reactions in the administration of vitamin E since reactions are estimated as being less than 1 in 25,000. (Massa 1974)

Responsibilities and Obligations of the Veterinarian

When a client seeks the services of a veterinarian and the veterinarian agrees, either verbally or by implication to accept a case, the obligation and responsibility entered into is to use the ordinary and reasonable degree of skill and care expected from the average licensed professional in the handling and management of the case. If standard of care does not occur, the client may sue the veterinarian for negligence or malpractice, as opposed to a suit for breach of contract because charges of malpractice and negligence are usually more damaging than ones for contract abuse. However, keep in mind that the client has an election of remedies and may sue for negligence or breach of contract. If a veterinarian should state on the telephone that he will go to a client's home to care for a sick or injured animal and fail to appear, he would be liable for a breach of contract since a specific agreement was made with the client to come and give professional services. The measure of damages in this case would depend on the amount of injury suffered by the client due to the veterinarian's failure to appear, as agreed upon. If the animal should die, damages could be the value of the animal or, if sentimental value is allowed even more.

A careful veterinarian never guarantees to cure an animal. If he or she should be so foolish to do so, make a positive statement that an animal will recover, he or she has contracted to cure the animal and can be held to such an agreement if the patient should not recover or die. Psychologically, it often seems rational and expedient to placate a client and say, "Oh, don't worry Shep will recover and be all right." Never get into such a situation no matter how minor an animal's ailment appears to be.

A veterinarian was called upon to castrate a colt. Before performing the operation the veterinarian assured the owner the animal would be well in 3 days. The colt did not recover from the surgery and died; the veterinarian was held responsible for his guarantee of a cure. On a warranty of a cure the veterinarian is responsible whether the loss or injury to the animal is the result of negligence or due to some other cause. Conversely, a veterinarian does not, in the absence of an express contract to do so, undertake to perform a cure. He cannot be held legally for not producing a cure unless negligence occurs in handling a case. (Lyford 1900)

In one case a veterinarian was called upon to treat a sick mare. After a few days of treatment the animal died. The farmer brought a law suit against the veterinarian, claiming he was incompetent and used the wrong type of treatment. The court ruled that when a veterinarian is employed to perform a service he brings to the job the degree of care and skill ordinarily expected from the profession and he does not contract to perform a cure. Unless the plaintiff, or the supposedly injured farmer, can prove the veterinarian was negligent he cannot recover in a lawsuit simply because the treatment was not successful or the animal died.

Most of the court cases against members of the profession are aimed at a lack of the duty of a rational and normal level of care given to the patient as is required by law. In the absence of specific contracts the veterinarian does not insure a cure when treating an animal. Whether he does or does not make a contract for a cure is for a jury or judge to decide. (Broom 1893, Williams 1891)

Referral of patients to another professional are another legal problem. Does a referral relieve the first or original veterinarian from total responsibility? In referrals to a specialist for a specific purpose, eye surgery, an animal's primary care continues to remain with the referring veterinarian, unless other arrangements are made that are satisfactory to both the client and the veterinarian involved. In making referrals the primary veterinarian should be certain all areas of responsibility are understood and made perfectly clear to the client.

If a client does not follow instructions given for home care or care by owners of animals, or does not return an animal for follow-up examination and treatment, this can be a defense for a veterinarian in the case of a lawsuit. This may be very important if the charge is abandonment of a case. A client that does not follow instructions would have a difficult time in a charge of abandonment. Failure of a client to pay a fee for services rendered does not allow a veterinarian to unilaterally terminate a contract for treatment of an animal nor to abandon a case until arrangements are made that are satisfactory to all of the parties involved.

In support of this statement is the case where a track veterinarian attempted to draw blood from the jugular vein of a race horse for chemical analysis. The needle broke off of the syringe and lodged in the surrounding neck tissues. The track veterinarian could not find and remove the needle. He recommended calling another veterinarian who had better equipment and left the case. Several hours later the second veterinarian appeared and attempted to find the broken off needle, but could not. The needle part migrated and reached the horse's lung, ending its racing career. Charges against the first veterinarian were for abandonment of the case and gross negligence; he was found guilty

An important duty of veterinarians is to inform clients of the results of the diagnosis and of laboratory tests, especially if the client must use such information to decide on how to proceed with the case; elect surgery, prolonged and expensive treatment, poor prognosis, euthanasia and loss of a loved animal. Veterinarians must use good judgment and assess client's susceptibility to the acceptance of bad news. Some clients become very upset when they receive blunt, terse and inadequate statements regarding their animal's condition and what may or can happen to them. (Restrip 1989, Hannah 1993)

Clients have the right to decide what shall be done to their animal, based on the doctor's assessment of the case and the information presented to them. If a veterinarian does not sufficiently inform clients of the medical situation he or she may be liable for fraud, deceit, misrepresentation, conspiracy or negligence. Communication with clients so that they can decide on how to proceed with a case may be as important as the diagnosis of the situation itself. (Phillips 1974)

Another duty of the veterinarian is to adequately instruct the client as to follow-up treatment when an animal leaves the hospital and the supervision of the veterinarian. A judge said in Cosby v Grand View Nursing Home "it is the duty of a physician, even if personal attention is no longer needed, if a case requires, to give the patient instructions as to future care. If this is not done the doctor could be held liable."

If laboratory tests are necessary for a definitive diagnosis to be made these should be done. If they are not performed and careful, responsible veterinarians would have done so in similar situations, their omission could constitute negligence. For example, a physician diagnosed diabetes in a patient based on a single laboratory test. This patient was treated for the disease for 5 years with no further laboratory tests performed. After 5 years further tests showed the patient did not have diabetes. The physician was found to be grossly negligent for not having periodic laboratory tests performed.

X-rays for the diagnosis and therapy of disease are commonly used in animal hospitals. Careless operation of x-ray equipment could lead to a lawsuit. In human medicine a radiologist is liable for damage that occurs to a patient if he has been careless in arriving at a diagnosis or if the equipment is not accurately calibrated. This would also be true in veterinary medicine where an animal is injured through the negligent use of x-ray equipment. The doctor in charge is also responsible for the actions of an x-ray technician and a technician's negligent use of equipment would render the veterinarian liable for the technician's carelessness. (Bangess 1981)

A practitioner who uses x-ray equipment should have this checked periodically to insure proper function, protection against scattered radiation and calibration for the amount of radiation delivered to subjects. Shielding recommended by manufacturers must be used to protect the users. Animals, clients, and employees can be injured by x-ray machines and if not properly supervised a veterinarian could be liable for negligence.

Acceptance of a Case

There is no obligation on the part of a veterinarian to accept a case. Even in an emergency he is not bound to care for or treat a sick or injured animal — this is true legally but perhaps not morally. However, once an animal is accepted for treatment the veterinarian cannot leave or abandon the case without being liable either for a breach of contract or negligence. A veterinarian was caring for a horse that was critically ill. He treated the horse and agreed to return the following morning and give the animal further follow-up care. He did not show up the next morning; in fact, never did return. The court found that the veterinarian had abandoned the case and was negligent in so doing, saying "abandoning the treatment of an animal when the veterinarian had previously undertaken to care for the animal renders him liable for abandonment. Duties of the veterinarian to the client are not terminated until the contract is completed and his services longer needed. His services may be revoked by dismissal by the client or terminated by the mutual consent of the parties involved in the contract. The contract may also be terminated when the veterinarian dies and has no partner to assume the case. (Bellance 1928)

Sometimes it is a debatable question as to when a cure has been reached and the services of the veterinarian are no longer needed. If a client can show that the services of the veterinarian were still required, in spite of termination, the client may recover for abandonment.

Accidents

There are over 2000 malpractice and negligence cases brought to court against veterinarians annually in the United States. About 20% or 400 involve injuries to human beings caused by animals under the care of a veterinarian. Some examples emphasize the importance of this problem.

A veterinarian sold flea dip to a client in a bottle that was not child-proof and contained no danger-warning on the label relative to potential toxicity. The client's child drank the liquid and suffered permanent physical damage; the award was $275,000. (Bartlett 1981)

An owner of a cat brought the animal to a veterinarian for treatment for urethrolithiasis. She held the cat during the treatment procedure and was severely bitten, a tendon in her hand being severed. The cat owner sued for medical expenses and loss of wages due to absence from work. The court awarded the cat owner damages finding the veterinarian owed a duty to the client to exercise reasonable care to prevent the cat from harming the owner while the animal was in the care of the doctor. On appeal the decision was reversed, the judge saying the veterinarian was not responsible for the injury because due to the actions of the cat the owner should have known the animal was in distress and pain and might react by biting. Volunteering by the client to hold the animal amounted to contributory negligence. (Branks v Kern 359 SE 2d 780,1987)

Veterinarians should take preventive precautions to minimize damages to clients by their animals; use proper and adequate restraint, tell owners of possible animal's reactions, aggressiveness, biting, clawing. The safest approach is to keep owners away from their animals when being treated. Whenever possible use your own employees. (Hannah 1990) Another example is one where a veterinarian's assistant was attempting to collect blood from a horse. The animal jumped suddenly with the prick of the needle, forcing the syringe to fly out and puncture the owner;s eye. The court awarded the injured person $250,000. (King 1990)

A surviving widow brought a wrongful death action against a veterinarian who had dispensed a poisonous dye which the husband accidently drank. The woman plaintiff failed to prove that inadequate labeling on the bottle containing the dye was the proximate cause of death of her husband. The veterinarian was not liable under the state's hazardous substance act and the dispensing of the dye was within the scope of the veterinarian's professional activities and the product was clearly marked as to its contents, "For Animal Use Only." The deceased was working in the field and had a similar-looking jug containing water. He drank the dye mistakenly thinking it to be water, even though the dye was colored. (Breece 1940)

Generally, when a veterinarian or assistant is injured by an animal under treatment, damages are not awarded. the veterinarian and staff have accepted the case and due to their training are familiar with the risks involved. Dangerous animals may alter the situation and render owners liable for damages caused by a known vicious animal.

Restraint of Animals

Handling and management of animals before and during examination and treatment are a necessary part of the treatment process. Carelessness in the restraint of animals can result in a negligence or malpractice suit. If the attending veterinarian notices the actions employed are frightening or exciting an animal making treatment difficult, impossible or dangerous, the procedures should be stopped, the animal allowed to calm down and then employ sedation, an anesthetic or a different method of restraint. Continuing to attempt to treat an unmanageable animal can result in injury to the animal, to individuals handling the animal and perhaps end in a lawsuit. (ALR 1981, Turner 1988, Johnson 1992)

A mule was seriously injured during the course of an operation because of the employment of a poor method of restraint. The court held it was immaterial whether the injury was caused by the negligence of the veterinarian, or his assistant, because it is the duty of the attending veterinarian to be certain that the mule, or any animal being treated, to be properly restrained before beginning an operation (Beck 1916)

A veterinarian was called upon to castrate a yearling colt. The colt was running free when the veterinarian arrived at the farm so he helped round it up from the pasture. The horse was restrained through the administration of succinyl-choline and castration was performed. Upon completion of the surgery the horse could not rise and died in a short time. The veterinarian was sued because of the lack of resuscitation equipment which the label on the drug recommends with its use. The veterinarian lost. (JAVMA Jan. 1, 1974)

In preparation for the castration of a 2-year old thoroughbred stallion a veterinarian gave the animal a tranquilizer and then applied a casting harness. In casting the horse it slipped on ice covered with snow on a hard surface. As the horse fell his rear legs spread outward, causing a fracture of the pelvis. Treatment and the use of a sling did not result in recovery and the horse died from complications. The owner accepted settlement out-of-court. (JAVMA Mar 15, 1974)

In another lawsuit a veterinarian was called to treat a spavin in a horse. He threw the animal so negligently that the procedure caused a rupture of the diaphragm and it died. The throwing, or the restraint, of an animal is considered by the courts to be a part of the treatment.

Negligence and lack of skill in applying restraint to animals can result in the loss of lawsuits.

Beginning with the time the veterinarian approaches an animal to be examined or treated, the responsibility of the veterinarian begins and his or her liability for the care of the animal starts. A veterinarian, through training and experience, is considered to be an individual who knows animals, their propensities and reactions under various circumstances, including the use of proper restraint. Actions or methods of treatment likely to alarm or frighten an animal should be known and recognized by the trained veterinarian.

Practitioners should be aware and familiar with the contents of drugs and the products they use and dispense. In one case cited below a veterinarian injected animals with a product that was not safe nor recommended or manufactured for the use that it was given. The court held the veterinarian liable on the grounds that a person using a product warrants that it is safe and suitable for the purpose for which it is given. The professional should know the pharmacological action of products used and when to use them and on what species of animals.

This may be a difficult responsibility to accept. This means the user must know the action, reactions, toxicity, species of animals for which a product is intended and possible adverse effects. In realty, a practitioner is forced to rely on the integrity and dependability of manufacturers to adequately test their products, label these correctly and dispense directions for their proper use.

Manufacturers have been held to be liable as warrantors of the products they make for use by professionals for the public. (see product liability) This means a manufacturer insures there is nothing inherently dangerous or harmful in their products and they will, within reason, perform the function for which they were intended.

Regardless of a manufacturer's liability for their products, a veterinarian is still liable for injury to animals from the improper use of drugs, vaccines or any products used for the treatment of animals. To allow otherwise would free the professional from treatment responsibility and place the public in a compromising position. The warranty of products extends to all types of items. It represents a guarantee, express or implied, that a product used, sold or given away free will perform the function for which it is used. For example, a producer of animal feed insures that their product is edible, not harmful and contains the ingredients listed on the label or package. (North Miami 1986, Dodd 1943, Barney 1890, Kushn 1860)

Damages

Damages are a monetary award which the law gives to a party or parties that have been injured by the actions of another person or persons. This is compensation for some wrong, such as a breach of contract, misdemeanor or felony wherein the injured party has suffered due to an act of commission, omission, or negligence of another responsible person.

* Compensatory damages are those which will Compensate the injured party for the damages sustained and no more.

* Consequential damages are those that arise not from the primary damage but as an incidental result of it -- for example, a dog bites a person and the law requires quarantine of the dog; it escapes from the veterinarian's care and the person bitten must undergo antirabies treatment. The pain and expense is consequential to the escape of the dog and the veterinarian is responsible not for the damages from the bite but from the consequences following it.

* Exemplary or punitive damages are damages awarded to the plaintiff over and above those that would Compensate for the injury or property loss. They are given because the wrong done was aggravated by circumstances of violence, malice, fraud, negligence or wanton and wicked conduct on the part of the defendant. These are intended to give solace to the plaintiff for mental anguish, damaged feelings, shame, degradation or other pain and, at times, to punish the defendant's evil behavior and make an example of the guilty one.

Burden of Proof

Where a plaintiff brought an action against a veterinarian for the death of his sheep, it was his responsibility to prove the defendant was negligent in administering worm medicine to the sheep. A farmer bought some lambs and had them examined by a veterinarian who stated they were healthy but should be wormed. Later, he wormed the sheep, stayed for dinner with the farmer and examined the sheep afterwards. A few were dead and the rest prostate on the ground, exuding froth from their mouths. Several lambs died and the farmer brought a suit for negligence in administering the worm medicine. (Erickson 1931)

Expert testimony supported the fact that the worm medicine containing the ingredients listed on the label, if improperly given, death from strangulation would result. To prove negligence of the veterinarian the plaintiff showed the medicine was of standard manufacture and contained the products listed on the label and was not faulty.

Evidence submitted to the trial court was sufficient to prove negligence on the part of the veterinarian and that his action was the proximate cause of death of the sheep. To receive damages the farmer had to prove the veterinarian's lack of care and his negligence in worming the sheep was the actual cause of death of the animals.

This case emphasizes the fact that the plaintiff, or person injured and initiating the lawsuit, must prove to the court that negligence occurred. The same doctrine exists in physician-patient law. The law presumes the physician performed his duty properly and the patient, if injured, must prove a lack of reasonable care and skill occurred on the part of the physician. In malpractice actions against physicians and veterinarians there is no presumption of the presence of negligence due to an honest error of judgment in making a diagnosis. (Hanners 1931, Pendergraff 1932)

Placing the burden of proof for malpractice and negligence on the plaintiff (accuser) is logical and reasonable. Otherwise the defendant professional would be in the position of being guilty and have to prove innocence. Even if a plaintiff proves the presence of malpractice or negligence, if no injury or damage has occurred, no recovery is usually allowed.

In an instance of gross malpractice a 9-month old Gordon setter was taken to a veterinarian for treatment. The animal was kept in the hospital for 6 days At this time the veterinarian told the client the dog had a floating kidney, which he had reattached, and the other kidney was enlarged and should be removed. He said the animal had a hiatus hernia which he had repaired and a portion of the liver was removed. The dog did not improve and was taken to another veterinarian. The animal died and an autopsy was performed by a veterinary pathologist. No sutures or scar tissue were found. Expert witnesses testified there should be some evidence present following such extensive surgery as described by the first veterinarian, who was found guilty of malpractice and negligence of a gross nature. (Eastep 1975)

Contributory and Comparative Negligence

In negligence cases if the injured party, or plaintiff, contributed directly to the cause of injury recovery is usually not allowed. This is based on a common-sense fact that if the injured party was partially responsible for an injury he should not be allowed to recover damages. Conversely, even if the suing party (plaintiff) was also negligent, along with the veterinarian, he can only recover damages if his wrongdoing was not the direct and major cause of the loss (Breece 1940)

An example of a case of contributory negligence is where a veterinarian was called to vaccinate a group of cattle. The owner of the farm helped the veterinarian drive the animals into a barn. The barn was too small for the number of animals and during the vaccination the cattle became frightened and trampled one another, killing 6 animals. The veterinarian based his defense on the fact that the owner of the farm helped him drive the animals into the barn and was therefore guilty of contributory negligence. The court held that the veterinarian was supposedly trained and competent in his work and as soon as he observed his actions were exciting the cattle he should have stopped vaccinating the animals and used some other method of containing the cattle. It was considered that the veterinarian's actions were the main reason for the loss and the negligence of the farmer, if any, in allowing the veterinarian to handle the animals as he did was not sufficient to remove any of the blame from the doctor.

In another malpractice action a client did not return for a re-examination of his animal as directed by the veterinarian. The court said this amounted to contributory negligence on the part of the client and any damages given for malpractice should be reduced in an equitable amount due to the failure to return the animal for examination and treatment. The client had contributed to his injury. (Turner 1988)

As defined previously negligence is the failure to exercise a degree of care which a person of ordinary prudence, or a reasonable one, would exercise under similar circumstances. Contributory negligence is conduct on the part of a plaintiff which falls below the standard to which he should conform for his own protection, and which is a contributing cause legally, along with the negligence of the defendant, in bringing about the plaintiff's injury.

In comparative negligence the damages or compensation for injury are shared proportionally between plaintiff and defendant based on the relative negligence of both parties. Damages are decided by the court and may fall into any percentage as the court determines; 50/50, 25/75 etc., depending on the degree of guilt of the parties in causing the injury; the relative negligence of each. Comparative and compensatory negligence are mostly controlled by state laws and these may vary depending on the state.

Proximate Cause

For professionals to be held liable for negligence their actions or omissions must be a direct cause of the injury complained of, or at least be so closely related to the injury that it could not have occurred without the negligent act or omission. This is the proximate cause rule and is the basic test applied to determine if culpable or actionable negligence has occurred. To recover for negligence it must be proved to the satisfaction of the court that the negligent act in question was the proximate cause of the injury or death of the animal(s).

Negligence was charged against a veterinarian based on an error in diagnosis; the use of the wrong vaccine and improper methods of vaccination. The accusing farmer noticed sick hogs in his herd and called a veterinarian who advised vaccination against cholera on the feeling the animals might have this disease. Two months after vaccination 93 hogs had died. The plaintiff farmer maintained the veterinarian had introduced blood poisoning into the pigs. The court held that the hogs could have died from any one of the naturally-occurring malignant diseases of swine present in the area. Judgment was given in favor of the veterinarian on the grounds that the plaintiff failed to show that the veterinarian's actions were the primary cause of the death of the hogs.

The proximate cause rule is illustrated in another case. A horse was brought to a clinic for lameness, was examined and returned to the owner's farm. At a later date the animal was returned to the clinic for a series of x-rays as it had not improved. A bone spur was found in the foreleg and surgically removed. When the horse was loaded on a trailer to be taken home it became frightened and unmanageable and was given a tranquilizer. Once in the trailer the horse threw itself against the sides of the vehicle, tearing out the sutures in the leg and injuring itself. The owner, after the horse was returned, maintained it had become a killer animal, completely unmanageable. Suit was brought for the horse's change in temperament and the loss of its services. The plaintiff was unable to prove satisfactorily that the veterinarian's alleged poor care was the direct and proximate cause of the horse's personality change. (Erickson 1931, Hanners 1931, Pendergraft 1931, Hohenstein 1943, Bekkemo 1932, Breece 1940, Prahl 1870, Southall 1971)

Locality Rule

Acceptable standards for professionals were previously gauged by the courts by the level of skill, care and training of persons in the same type of endeavor practicing in the same geographic area or locality. This locality rule is now disappearing for several reasons; rapid international communication, continuing education programs, information retrieval systems, human and veterinary medicine on-line have all contributed to the legal concept that all men are created equal. The trend today is for the courts to disregard the locality rule and consider a national standard of training and care for the average practitioner in his field of endeavor, regardless of geographical location. (Brune 1968)

An example of this philosophy is the case where an anesthesiologist gave a higher dose than recommended of a drug for a spinal anesthesia. This was the customary dose in the general area, but not elsewhere, nor was the dose recommended by the manufacturer. The court said that different standards of professional conduct in different localities no longer applied. The standard of care should be that of the average practitioner in the field in general, not locally. (Nichols 1931)

The locality rule was promulgated and developed when communication in the medical professions was limited and knowledge spread slowly to the outlying communities. The rule grew to protect professionals who had limited access to current information. Today, most professionals must be able to meet a national standard (Hannah 1989)

Specialties

Veterinary medicine now has specialties for specific areas within the profession; pathology, surgery, ophthalmology, etc. Practitioners should use caution in holding themselves forth as specialists because the standards of care, knowledge, and expertise required from specialists are greater than for those of a general practitioner. A specialist's responsibility to clients is greater than the generalist and they rely on this superior skill.

In Smith v Guthrie the court held that a general practitioner may not be held to the same standard of care as a specialist and it was improper to ask an expert specialist what he would have done under similar circumstances faced by a general practitioner. (Ardoin 1978, Carter 1988, Smith 1977)

Another specialist case is one in which a horse was treated for a stomach disorder and subsequently its tail had to be amputated. The court found that a horse treated for gastritis does not lose its tail under ordinary circumstances and the professor (at a veterinary school), due to his expertise as a specialist, was required to meet more than the community standard of care. The award of $30,000 was not an abuse of discretion by the court. The horse's tail was tightly bound to keep it out of the way of the rectum, as a result it underwent necrosis and had to be amputated. (Carter 1988)

In a discussion of specialists, the general practitioner, when faced with a difficult case, beyond the area of his expertise, should refer it to a specialist in the appropriate field. (Hannah 1990)

Gratuitous Services

No fee, no professional liability! Do not get caught in this false belief. The duties and responsibilities of the veterinarian toward the client are not relieved, lessened, or altered if no fee is received for services. The veterinarian who undertakes to treat an animal may be just as liable for negligence notwithstanding the fact the undertaking was gratuitous. (Nichols 1931)

A student of veterinary medicine, during vacation, castrated animals for some farmers near his home. He was called by the plaintiff to castrate his horse. After this was done the farmer brought him another horse with a sweeney on the shoulder and asked the student to treat it. The student emphasized, in front of witnesses, the fact that he was still a student of veterinary medicine and did not want to treat the horse. He never professed to be a graduate veterinarian. The farmer insisted and finally the student incised the area and injected turpentine solution. He refused payment for his services. Later, the horse's shoulder became inflamed and required additional treatment, involving expense.

In an excellent summary of the case the judge said the right to recover damages in this action is based on the theory the defendant (student) failed to discharge a legal duty owed to the plaintiff, resulting in injury to an animal. If the student had held himself forth as a competent veterinary surgeon he was duty bound to bring to the case the skill, learning and care which characterized the profession generally. His duty would be none the less because he performed the service without a charge. However, if he did not hold himself forth as a graduate veterinarian and undertook treatment only on the request of the plaintiff and he performed the services honestly and to the best of his ability, then his duty to the plaintiff is discharged and he is not liable.

The services of veterinarians are often requested to be donated gratuitously for functions such as fairs, livestock exhibits, and dog shows. At such gatherings he may be asked to examine and/or treat an animal or animals, without a fee. If professional services are given the standards of professional care and skill are still in effect, fee or no fee. To permit a different rule would allow two standards of care, one where a fee is collected and one where services are given for no fee. This would be having double standards and two levels of professional skill.

Wrong Diagnosis

A wrong diagnosis, or the failure to correctly diagnose an abnormal condition, in an animal does not render the veterinarian liable for malpractice or negligence. However, if he is negligent or careless in making a diagnosis of a condition that the average practitioner should be able to diagnose, he may be required to answer legally for this negligence. (Branks 1986)

A veterinary surgeon has been held liable when it was proved he had made a gross error in arriving at a diagnosis. A farmer noticed his pigs appeared to be sick and one was dead. He called a veterinarian the next day when 10 animals were dead. The veterinarian autopsied 5 of the dead pigs and arrived at a diagnosis of necrotic enteritis. Four days later, after more losses, the farmer called in a second veterinarian who diagnosed the problem as being cholera. In court evidence was presented to show the defendant, or first veterinarian, did not open the thoracic cavity of the pigs at autopsy and did not examine the tissues which could have shown evidence of cholera. The court held the defendant to be negligent in arriving at his diagnosis. If he had made a more thorough examination of the pig's tissues and still made a wrong or faulty diagnosis, he would not have been liable.

A veterinarian must guard against being hasty and careless in arriving at a diagnosis and use reasonable care and skill in the treatment of animals, neglecting no essential part in the handling of a case.

Judgment Errors

Errors in judgment in caring and handling animals does not, in the absence of negligence, make a professional liable for malpractice. Proof that a diagnosis was wrong will not result in a malpractice verdict. Similarly, evidence that a treatment was not successful does not constitute negligence by itself.

Methods of treatment and surgical techniques may vary due to professional training, equipment, locale, species and value of the animal and resources. Two professionals may treat a similar case differently yet each effect a cure. Treatment depends on the diagnosis made. Despite modern aids, diagnosis and treatment are often a matter of opinion based on training and experience. A practitioner should not have to answer in court for an honest error in judgment. To be liable for honest errors would place practitioners in the healing arts in such high jeopardy they would hesitate to arrive at a diagnosis for fear of being wrong and be accountable for their honest mistake.

Although honest mistakes are forgivable, deviations from accepted methods and techniques are not. The use of treatments still in the research or developmental stage and not used by responsible practitioners, could render the user of these liable. This also applies to the use of non-approved drugs.

Sovereign (Government) Immunity

This doctrine involves preventing persons from bringing a lawsuit against the United States government without its consent when the government is engaged in its legal activities. It is based on the aged English concept that, "The King can do no wrong." The modern concept is that there can be no legal action against the authority that makes the laws which give rights to the public. Statutes and judicial decisions in recent times has changed this doctrine.

The doctrine is of importance to federal veterinarians in carrying out their daily functions. When are they liable for injuries to parties when performing their duties?

Employees of the government are those of all federal agencies, including the military, when acting in an official capacity, either permanently or temporally, with or without compensation. The United States is liable to other parties in tort actions the same as a private individual. Before a judgment can be made against a government employee it must be shown that the person responsible for an act or omission of one giving rise to a lawsuit was indeed a federal employee, that such act or omission was within the scope of such a person's employment and the act was either negligent or wrongful or both.

The failure of a public official to comply with laws and regulations under which they inspect, treat or destroy animals may subject them to litigation. Government employees must obey the law and all regulations under the law. (Hannah 1994)

Case Reports

A registered practitioner may have his name removed or suspended from the registers by the Council of the Royal College of Veterinary Surgeons if he has been convicted, either before or after registration, and either in this country or elsewhere, of an offense which if committed in England would be a misdemeanor or higher offense, or if he has been shown to have been guilty of any conduct disgraceful to him in a professional respect. (Vet Surgeons Act 1881, ss 16, 19.)

The professional duty of a veterinarian begins with obtaining the history of the animal, followed by a physical examination. It is the responsibility of the professional to properly diagnose the nature of the ailment or injury. In Brokett v Abbe, (206 A 2nd 447, 1964) a veterinarian was called to determine if a cow was pregnant. He used a punch test instead of a rectal one, recognized as the reliable means of determining pregnancy. As a result of the test he told the owner the cow was not pregnant and the owner sold the cow for $175 rather than $550 obtainable for a cow with calf.

In Turner v Dr. Benhart, (527 2So 2d 717, 1988) a horse owner brought a malpractice suit against a veterinarian after his horse's death. The court found there was no evidence the veterinarian's treatment fell below acceptable standards. The veterinarian presented expert witnesses who stated the treatment of the horse with bicarbonate of soda was not an unusual or unacceptable practice.

In Appellate v Ohio Veterinary Medical Board (441 NE 2d, 1981) the veterinarian was charged with 34 instances of gross negligence and one of permitting an unlicensed assistant to practice veterinary medicine. Where expert testimony was not presented, the Board stated that expert testimony regarding reasonable standards of practice is not mandatory in medical discipline proceedings before the State Veterinary Medical Board. Defendant veterinarian was found grossly incompetent, license suspended for one year.

In Purvis v Board of Veterinary Medicine (461 So 2d 134, 1984) a veterinarian appealed a decision by the Board finding him guilty of negligence and incompetence. A Labrador retriever was struck by an automobile and the dog was comatose. The veterinarian examined the animal and diagnosed a concussion and spinal shock and told the owners only time would heal the injury. The owners left the dog at the hospital. The veterinarian treated the animal with antibiotics and intravenous solutions for shock. The owners came to see the dog on a Sunday and were let in by a caretaker. They found the dog covered with feces and urine and the dog was completely immobile. Later in the day the veterinarian came in and gave the dog more fluids and cleaned the animal. He called the owners and told them the dog had made some improvement. On Monday the owners took the dog to another veterinarian who X-rayed the dog and said the it was a quadriplegic and recommended euthanasia. Decision was for the accused veterinarian because the Board did not find the veterinarian's standard of conduct improper.

Masa v Department of Registration and Education 507 NE 2d 814, 1987. A case of malpractice against a veterinarian with revocation of license. The owners of an 18 month old German shepherd noticed the dog had no appetite, went to the veterinarian. The dog's temperature was 105 F. Owners left the dog and the veterinarian later called and said surgery was necessary and the owners replied all right but we would like to breed her so only spay the dog if absolutely necessary and told the veterinarian to save any organs removed. The veterinarian said, "I am not a machine shop, I don't save spare parts." The veterinarian removed the ovaries and uterus; the dog died the next day. The veterinarian's diagnosis was pyometra and he said he had not saved any organs, but actually he had sent them to a veterinary laboratory. On autopsy the dog had pyothorax, pleurisy and pneumonia; no uterine problems were found.

A veterinarian was called to his office to examine a dog struck by an automobile, he pronounced the dog dead. The owner requested burial rather than cremation. The veterinarian took the dog away and placed a card with instructions on it for his assistant. The next day the owner called and said the dog had bitten her child and the police recommended the head of the dog be sent to a laboratory for testing for rabies. The veterinarian found he could not produce the dog because his assistant had mistakenly cremated the animal. The child had to take antirabies treatment and the veterinarian lost the case. (JAVMA April 15, 1965)

An owner took his dog to an animal hospital and requested euthanasia. When asked why the owner said he believed the dog had bitten a child. The dog was observed at the hospital for one day, seemed normal and was euthanized. Obviously the veterinarian was careless and negligent since the animal should have been under observation for rabies for the recommended period of time. (JAVMA April 15, 1966)

Disposal of animals without the owners knowledge is always a dangerous act. If the veterinarian does not have the facilities for holding a carcass, provisions should be made for this when the need arises. Bodies of manageable sized animals can be refrigerated or frozen. The cost is a lot less than a lawsuit.

Through an error five gallons of 50% cresylic acid was dispensed to an owner of a herd of swine instead of the proper preparation regularly used to spray hogs for lice and mange. Eight pregnant gilts and

2 boars were sprayed with the undiluted solution. Five animals died within 24 hours and 3 more within 3 days. In dispensing any product that can be toxic one must be certain of two things; the product is properly labeled and the product is the proper one for its intended use. (JAVMA Feb 15, 1967)

A newly purchased poodle was taken to a veterinarian for examination; it had dry scaly skin and was scratching. After examination with a Wood's light the veterinarian diagnosed nonspecific dermatitis and began treatment with skin conditioners and vitamins. Later, with no improvement, the dog was given several shots and later still, norticosteroid tablets. Weeks later members of the family began to scratch and had lesions on their legs and torso. A physician's diagnosis; sarcoptic mange. Another veterinarian found this to be the dog's problem also. Although a wrong diagnosis does not make a veterinarian liable, in this case acceptable and reasonable diagnostic procedures were not taken. (JAVMA May 15, 1970)

A veterinarian examined a mare for pregnancy by rectal palpation. The mare strained forcibly during the examination and a small laceration was noticed in the rectum. Penicillin was dispensed for use. Two days later on examination the lesion in the rectum had worsened. The mare was sent to a university clinic and surgery was performed but the animal died postoperatively. Fatality due to rectal lacerations is a fairly common occurrence and extreme care should be taken when undertaking this procedure. (JAVMA Oct. 1,1973)

A dog underwent a ovariohysterectomy and although recovered there was a significant amount of bleeding. The dogs health did not improve and 4 months later was taken to another veterinarian who found a palpable mass in the abdomen and on surgical exploration found a gauze sponge in the abdomen - enough said. (JAVMA Dec 1, 1973)

An 18 month old dog was brought to a veterinarian after being struck by a car. The dog was treated for shock, had some abrasions and a small laceration which was sutured. There was a lameness of the left rear leg which was not examined radiographically. The lameness persisted but no x-rays were taken. Examination at another hospital showed a fracture of the head of the femur. Another example of carelessness. With automobile injuries followed by lameness x-rays are always indicated. (JAVMA Jan. 15,1977)

Malpractice Insurance

Many insurance carriers provide for malpractice insurance. Most professional associations underwrite their members by providing comprehensive professional insurance programs. Some things to consider when purchasing malpractice insurance are:

1. Does the Company insure all or only particular portions of the practice?

2. Does your particular state require insurance companies to offer insurance to all categories of a profession?

3. Do some companies specialize in only some categories of coverages

4. Is the company regulated by state law to write malpractice insurance for anyone licensed in the state as a professional?

Factors to consider when applying for malpractice insurance:

1. Claim history of the company. what kind of suits and settlements?

2. Do they insure only qualified licensees and specialists?

3. The nature and methods of their handling of cases.

4. Do they have disciplinary actions; increase charges for appearing in court

5. How does a company handle an applicants disability, impairments,use of drugs and alcohol.

6. Are specialties adequately covered?

7. Do they have a history of cancelling policies after cases involving their clients?

8.   How does the company judge professional competence?

Legally, the professional liability of the veterinarian is broad and many actions or omissions may place one in a compromising position. The individual who maintains a high standard of professional and personal conduct will seldom be in trouble. The primary cause of litigation against the veterinarian is the veterinarian.

In spite of due care in conducting a practice a veterinarian may encounter legal trouble. As a protective measure against loss from a lawsuit, insurance is a practical answer. Veterinarians working as employees for a veterinarian or in group practices should be aware of their liabilities for malpractice and negligence. Group practices may have coverage that protects all of the members of a group; individually, veterinarians should be certain they are protected.

Malpractice insurance may not cover:

1.   Practicing while intoxicated
2.   A guarantee of results
3.   Expired or revoked license
4.   Negligent acts of employees
5.   Contributory negligence of the veterinarian
6.   Gross negligence or a criminal act
7.   The use of unacceptable or improper techniques
8.   Use of experimental or unapproved methods
9.   Extra-label use of drugs
10.   Selling prescription drugs over the counter
11.   Improper or false labeling of dispensed drugs
12.   Improper transportation of an animal in the care of the veterinarian.
13.   Failure to comply with government regulations
14.   Violations of the narcotic act
15.   Conviction of a felony
16.   Theft of an animal in the veterinarian's custody
17.   Intentional fraud.
18.   Injury to a client due to false advertising

CHAPTER THREE
VETERINARIAN CLIENT RELATIONSHIP

Client Relations

Practice good veterinary medicine, have appealing and sanitary appearing premises, a good staff, a hospital safety program, give the proper care to animals, use the concept of informed consent, let clients help in handling their animal only as a last resort, do not promise a cure, tell owner, or keeper of the animal, about the diagnosis, treatment and prognosis, drugs to be used, possible outcome of the case. In summary, have friendly and good veterinary-client relationships, practice sound and skillful veterinary medicine and few troubles will darken your doorstep. (Hannah JAVMA 1996 209;1 859)

A veterinarian should become familiar with the issues that create friction between veterinarian and client. Many of these are due to carelessness or thoughtlessness. Practitioners will find it to their advantage to guard against compromising situations which may cause clients to develop doubts regarding the professional qualifications of their veterinarian.

The present high level of education and rapid communication resources places medical knowledge within easy reach of the professional, and is also available to the general public. Consequently, the professional must be armed with up-to-date knowledge and developments to not be found lacking in qualifications and ability to handle medical problems presented to the practitioner.

Complaints against veterinarians for negligence or malpractice are often due to poor public relations; not taking time with a client to fully and clearly explain the animals medical problems. Giving clients the "rush" treatment is a good way to lose them. Clients who get the feeling they are being hurried, given superficial attention and rushed out of the doctor's office become good candidates for lawsuits.

With experience, a practitioner begins to "feel" when he has gotten through to the client. Psychologically, a practitioner of experience can tell almost immediately when they are getting through or reaching a client and the client appears to trust them. The use of plain, simple language is important; do not confuse clients with complex medical terms or diagnoses.

Clients are an essential part of the practice of veterinary medicine without which no income would be realized. Client and veterinarian have an important interest in the animal; the client a dear pet or valuable working animal and the veterinarian a case to be handled in a professional manner and a source of income.

Contracts

The veterinary-client relationship involves the principles of contract and tort law. Every day of our lives we enter into some type of contractual agreement without giving a thought to the legal implications attached to such actions. The purchase of goods in a store involves a contract of sale; I will buy that coat and the clerk agrees to sell it to you and you must pay for the coat. Writing a check to a person requires the use of a negotiable instrument, the check which is an agreement to pay; a type of contract. As routine as such actions appear to be, they are governed by legal doctrines and precedents of long standing and the rights and duties of the parties concerned with these transactions are protected by the law and courts.

The origins of contractual agreements are lost in antiquity; an agreement of two persons to perform a certain act and the shaking of hands to bind the contract was enforceable before written history. If one of the parties did not perform their part of the agreement the penalty could be death. Today, we think of contracts as being formal, legal documents and more complicated than in past times, but many are not and are still cemented with the shaking of hands or the nodding of the head. The implications of contractual relationships should be understood by all adults, not only in the context of veterinary medicine.

There are two kinds of contracts - express and implied. An express contract may be in writing or agreed upon orally by the parties concerned. A contract is an express one because the terms contained in it are expressly stated and agreed upon by all parties. A client calls a veterinarian to come to the farm and castrate a horse. The veterinarian comes to the farm, evidence in itself that he has agreed to do the job, tells the client the fee, the client agrees or, if he has the service performed with no mention of a fee, the law considers the requirement to pay is present. Most of the contractual agreements between veterinarian and client are oral and expressed as statements or requests; " spay my dog, " the doctor does it; a contract exists.

The second type of contract is an implied one; implied from the actions and statements of the parties concerned. It is called an implied one because the parties to it do not make express or definitive agreements beforehand as to the duties required of each of the parties. For example, an injured animal is brought to a veterinary hospital and left for emergency treatment. No discussions regarding treatment or fees have occurred. There is an assumption on the part of both parties, the one bringing in the animal and the veterinarian, that the veterinarian accepts the case, will employ acceptable professional skill to care for the animal and the client will be liable for the reasonable value of the services rendered. This is an implied contract because each of the parties expect some type of performance from the other without a written or express agreement. The law will accept this as a contractual agreement.

To believe a contract, to be enforceable, must be in writing, notarized or otherwise blessed, is in error. An oral agreement is binding, subject to some statutory requirements; a meeting of the minds of the parties involved, an understanding of what the agreement contains, and fraud or deception has not occurred in the making of the agreement. A basic underlying principle in contracts is the intent of the parties; did they intend to enter into some type of agreement where each must perform, or not perform some act, did they understand what was being agreed upon? Intent and mutual agreement is usually assumed in implied contracts and, even in express ones, all the elements of agreement are often not present, some being implied. The essential point to emphasize is that verbal and implied contracts are as binding on the parties as are express, written ones, and the law will interpret them as being contracts.

An essential element of a contract is consideration. Consideration is the surrendering by each party to the contract, or the promise to do so, of some right he or she legally possesses or is entitled to possess. A client calls for the services of a veterinarian and it is assumed by the law that the client will pay a reasonable price for these. The veterinarian, in accepting the case, promises (a presumed one) to use the degree of care and skill attached to the profession; each party has agreed to surrender, or give up, something that belongs to them that they are not required by law to give up; the client money and the veterinarian, services. Consideration is not always money, it can be items of personal property; the farmer pays the veterinarian with some farm products or the dog breeder with a choice puppy from the litter of a purebred dog. The essential element in consideration is the implied agreement of all parties to give up something they are legally entitled to possess

Capacity to enter into a contract is necessary to make it valid and legally binding. Capacity refers to the mental ability to understand the agreement being made and entered into and the responsibilities required from each party under the agreement. Mentally deficient and insane persons are not normally acceptable parties to a contract. Contracts with intoxicated persons are often held valid because the contracting individual has placed himself in the inebriated position voluntarily.

Agreements or contracts with minors should be entered into with caution. Usually, minors cannot be held to their contractual agreements except for those made for items necessary for their health or survival. In some jurisdictions minors may enter into contracts for automobile insurance and educational services, such as technical courses aimed toward employment. Some states have lowered the contractual age for minors from 21 to 19 years. A minor may, upon becoming of legal age, ratify or void contracts entered into as a minor.

Quasi Contracts

A client is bound by law to pay for services given to his or her animal, whether the services are professorial or otherwise. Such a responsibility may arise even when an individual without the authorization of the animal's owner brings an animal to a veterinarian for services. The law of quasi contracts states that no person should be enriched at the expense of another person. Therefore, animal owners are obliged to pay for services rendered even though they did not authorize and were not present when the services were given. The legal theory is that the owners of animals have benefited from the services of the veterinarian and should be required to pay for these. In these cases, the law assumes an agreement existed, or would have existed under the circumstances existing between the parties.

Informed Consent

It is a legal duty of the veterinarian to give sufficient information to clients to allow them to make a rational decision on whether to proceed with the care of an animal. Informed consent means the owner understands what the animal's problem is, what can be done to remedy it, the risks and dangers of the treatment and how much the fee will be. Failure to adequately inform a client of all of the medical aspects of a case may constitute negligence or fraud on the part of the veterinarian. In human medicine there is an exception to this rule; if a patient asks specifically not to be told about the risks and dangers related to treatment, he or she has the right to have this information withheld. This would probably be true in veterinary medicine if a client makes a positive statement to the effect, "Do not tell me about the dangers involved, I do not want to know, just go ahead with the treatment."

Unnecessary or non-requested treatment also falls under the informed consent rule and a veterinarian may be liable to a lawsuit if he performs a procedure or a treatment on an animal not previously agreed upon, unless such an action is necessary to save the animal's life. The veterinarian must inform and warn clients about the use of a dangerous procedure, toxic drugs or experimental or developmental methods not commonly employed.

At times problems between veterinarian and clients arise because a doctor-client relationship was not satisfactorily consummated, or the relationship broke down due to poor communication. In some instances veterinarians have a method of hospital management that protects them, or keeps them away, from contact with the public, giving the impression the veterinarian is too busy or important to spend much time with the client.. An attorney is quoted as saying, "You can avoid your patients, you can give them only a minute or so, you can have your receptionist do the talking, but remember for every dissatisfied patient, there is an attorney who will listen and sympathize with the patient's problems. (Conn Med 1975, Cazalet 1977, Price 1979)

In human medicine information given to a physician by the patient or others involved in the case, is considered in law to be privileged information between physician and patient, not to be carelessly given to other parties. Patients may want their health status confidential for several reasons; sensitivity, embarrassment, to protect others and for various legal reasons. A similar doctrine has not been followed in veterinary medicine. In a court decision a judge said, "The following are not physicians or surgeons within the statute of privileged communication between physician and patient; chiropractors, veterinary surgeons...." (Amer Juris 1976)

An early case defined privileged communication and veterinarians in 1898. The court decided that the testimony of a veterinarian should not be excluded from being presented to the court under a statute defining privileged communication for the medical profession, but not specifically veterinarians. (Hendershot 1898)

Recently the State Legislature of Georgia added a provision to its Public Records Law stating that medical, veterinary and records of similar fields, when the disclosure of the information would be an invasion of privacy are confidential. (Geo Stat 1986) The Legislature of the state of Kansas has amended their Veterinary Practice Act, adding, " No veterinary licensee under the Act shall be required to disclose any information concerning the veterinarians care of an animal except on written authorization or other waiver by the veterinarian's client or an appropriate court order. "

The ethical ideals of the veterinary profession imply that a doctor of veterinary medicine and the veterinarian's staff will protect the personal privacy of clients. (Hannah 1991)

Termination of Contracts

Termination of duties required by a contractual agreement end when each party to it have completed all the duties they were required to perform under the contract. Therefore, a contract between a veterinarian and a client ends when the animal is cured to the reasonable satisfaction of the client, or the animal dies or is terminated, and the owner pays the fee requested by the veterinarian. Contracts may also terminate by mutual agreement of the parties involved. A client leaving an animal for treatment may discharge the veterinarian from the case even though the animal is not cured or the treatment incomplete. The veterinarian is relieved from responsibility by the client's statement or actions that the services of the veterinarian are no longer needed. In this case the veterinarian relieves the client of further obligation by establishing a fee for the service given up to the time of discharge. When the fee is paid the contract is terminated. If a veterinarian wishes to leave a case he must give notice in a reasonable amount of time to allow the client to seek and find the services of another practitioner. In these cases the veterinarian should make it clearly understood that he or she is ending responsibility but, if true, inform the client that the animal should receive further treatment. A common problem with termination of a contract for the care of an animal before treatment is finished is the failure of the client to pay the requested fee. A client is liable for the services rendered up to the time of termination, barring any illegal acts that might have occurred; negligence, fraud, default, abandonment of the case. A court has stated the duties of the veterinarian are not terminated until the contract is revoked by his dismissal, terminated by mutual consent, or his services are no longer needed. (Bolles 1928)

Contracts for personal services usually terminate with the death of the party who is to perform the service. If the veterinarian treating an animal dies before completion of the treatment, the agreement automatically ends. If a client dies his personal property passes to his heirs through an executor or administrator who is then responsible for debts against the estate and would be liable for fees up to the time of the clients death. Arrangement for further treatment or other disposition of an animal following the death of a client should be made with whoever is administering the estate of the deceased. If heirs should wish to keep an animal and continue to care for it, the veterinarian may be asked to continue to provide services and the heirs become responsible for all costs.

Breach of Contract

A failure to perform any part of the terms and agreements in a contract constitute a breach of contract. Some breaches may be severe enough to violate the entire contract, with other cases only part of the contract may be breached; a partial breach occurs when the possibility exists of fulfilling the rest of it. Where a veterinarian accepts a case and later refuses to treat the animal or the client who has engaged the veterinarian, refuses to pay for the services, a total breach of contract occurs. Partial payment by the client or part performance by the doctor may result in a partial breach of a contract, each party having performed a portion of the contract. Failure to perform the agreements contained in a contract may result in the injured party seeking damages in a court of law for the amount of injury suffered. Damages awarded for a breach of contract are monetary, i.e., money. For the veterinarian damages are usually easy to determine. These being the reasonable cost of the professional services rendered, reasonable being the amount that would be demanded for similar professional services by other practitioners in the same geographical area. In the case of a client the amount of damages may be more difficult to determine; is it the amount to replace the animal, for example a prized bull, the loss of an animal's service - a guide dog or a performing animal or can sentimental suffering be involved? That an animal's value is greater than the normal market value must be proved to the court by the owner or keeper . Occasionally, a court will accept sentimental grief and unusual attachment to an animal as evidence that an award of damages larger than normal should be given. The value of highly trained working, hunting or show animals could be gauged by the amount necessary to purchase, time spent in training the animal to the level of the one lost. Income lost from performing animals must be a consideration in determining the amount of damages awarded. An example could be a race horse whose potential winnings, based on past performance, might be estimated as $250,000, an owner recovering this amount or a part of it.

Animals are items of personal property and a person cannot recover damages for an injury to an animal without proving it's value. Usually, value is placed at the current market value; a $500 dog is a $500 dog, if this is the replacement cost. Special value above the market one must be proved to the court. Damages for sentimental loss or mental suffering due to the loss, are not recoverable. However, in recent years, this concept appears to be changing. One court said, market value means the value of ordinary animals of the same species. A person having expert or special knowledge of the value of a horse may give an opinion that its value was X number of dollars, which may be in excess of the market value. (Julian 1971) Under such circumstances the damages awarded for an injury to an animal could be extraordinary and not just the cost to replace it with one of the same breed, sex, pedigree, etc. With respect to recovery for sentimental loss and emotional stress with the loss of a pet animal a recent legal view has stated, " The measure of damages for a pet is the market value determined exclusively by the pets commercial, cognizable qualities of breed, pedigree, or profitable uses in which the pet may be employed." Arguments that the loss or injury to a pet can produce genuine and verifiable emotional stress may be judged to be similar to 4 other areas where the law allows recovery for stressful damage; loss of heirlooms, intentional infliction of emotional stress, negligent infliction of emotional stress, and wrongful death.

That the concept is receiving support in some courts is illustrated in the following; a client brought an action to court for recovery for injury to a dog and the consequent mental pain and suffering experienced by the owners. The court held for the owners (plaintiff), saying the trial court was correct in including as a part of the consideration of injury, the element of mental pain and suffering of the owners of the dog. The hospital's neglectful conduct causing injury to the animal amounted to great indifference to the property of the owners and the award was not excessive. In this case a dog, after surgery. was placed on a heating pad and left for 2 days, apparently with no care or attention. This act resulted in a severe burn on the whole of one side of the animal. The dog was taken elsewhere for treatment and was eventually put to sleep. (Corboy 1968, Wills 1978) In another case a dog was left unattended while recovering from anesthesia and died. Testimony was allowed by an expert witness who indicated this animal was a superior specimen and recovery for more than the market value should be allowed.

The courts have held that the rights in ownership to a dog do not terminate with the death of the animal and punitive damages, such as punishing for the act of the veterinarian, may still be given against the doctor even though the dog has died. The owner of a dog has the right of action to render compensatory damages for intrinsic value, if any, of a dead dog wrongfully destroyed. A dog with a severe dermatitis died and the owner was told the dog died of natural causes. The owner requested an autopsy of the dog, instead it was cremated. Punitive damages against the veterinary hospital were awarded to the owner in excess of the dog's market value.

Evidence of the contractual nature of the professional relationship can be seen in decisions given in physician-patient law. A patient can bring an action for breach of duty arising from a physician's contract of employment, express or implied. The relationship of physician and patient is one arising out of contract, express or implied. An important part in the veterinary-client contractual relationship is the implied agreement that the client pay a treasonable fee for the services given. (Levine 1967, Scott 1933, Carpenter 1933, Kuhn 1910, Corpus Juris 1996)

What amounts to a reasonable fee is judged from the amount charged for similar services by reputable practitioners in the same geographical area. It has been said in physician-patient law, "In the absence of an express agreement, the surgeon who brings to the services rendered due care and skill earns the reasonable and customary price therefor, whether the outcome be beneficial or the reverse." Without an agreement as to the amount to be paid for the services of a physician, the law will imply a promise to pay the reasonable value of the services. (Ladd 1922, Weinrub 1923)

The right of the doctor to recover for medicine and drugs used in treatment is also supported by the courts. Courts have also stated that unlicensed practitioners should not be allowed to recover for such items. "The physicians right to recover for medicinals he has furnished to the patient is governed by the same principles as those governing the right to recover for general professional services." It has been held several times that where there is a failure to comply with statutory provisions regulating the right to practice medicine, the physician cannot recover for medicine furnished or supplied to the patient. This ruling would probably apply to veterinarians since most practice acts state that an unlicensed practitioner who charges for veterinary services is in violation of the act. (Guist 1908)

If a veterinary practitioner should die leaving unpaid bills owed to him by clients can these be collected and by whom? Usually, in most jurisdictions, a veterinarian's business and credits pass to the heirs who would be allowed to collect the outstanding fees owed for the services of the deceased. The rights of the heirs to collect the money may depend on the terms of the will, if any. If no will exists the probate court may decide who and how outstanding fees can be collected. In partnerships business interests may be separated from personal ones and not pass to heirs, some other type of arrangements made for remuneration of heirs of the deceased.

Another important factor in contract law is the understanding that parties to a contract entered into it in good faith. If a client should mislead, defraud or deceive the veterinarian the contract would be void and no responsibility would rest on the veterinarian. A client may claim to be the owner of an animal and not be or misrepresent the medical history to trap the veterinarian, placing him in a compromising position. The intent to deceive must be present; the person wanted and intended to misrepresent the facts. Ignorance or lack of knowledge is not sufficient to constitute fraud in the formation of a contract. If a client has knowledge regarding an animal that is not commonly known, this should be given to the doctor to aid in the diagnosis and treatment. If an animal is of a vicious nature, the client should tell the veterinarian; if this is not done and the veterinarian or an assistant in injured the client can be responsible for the damages.

Liens

A person who makes, alters or repairs an article of personal property at the request of the owner, or legal possessor of the property, has a lien on the property for reasonable charges, or for the balance due, for the work done and the materials furnished and may retain possession of the property until the charges are paid. The veterinarian shall have a lien, dependent on possession, for their compensation in caring for, boarding, feeding and medical treatment of animals. (West's Calif. Code 1988)

A lien is a claim or charge on property for payment of a debt, obligation or duty. Liens may be created by contract, express or implied. They are the hold or claim on the property of another person as security for a debt. Normally, death of either of the parties terminates the existence of a lien. Once created, a lien continues to exist until two events occur; when the obligation is discharged to the lien holders satisfaction or when the asset disappears. The debt is either paid off of some other arrangement is made to the satisfaction of the lien holder.

A veterinarian claimed a lien on a group of cattle and the court awarded the veterinarian expenses for the care and veterinary services for the cattle he possessed at the time of the foreclosure sale. The cattle owner appealed and the court held that the veterinarian was entitled to a possessory lien only on the 85 head of cattle in the amount of $1,027 for veterinary services, but was not entitled to services rendered for the other 2 to 3000 head of cattle already disposed of by the owners. An example of the importance of possession by the lien holder. (NE Kansas 1985)

Courts have decided that the role of the veterinarian in dealing with animals is similar to that of an agistor, consequently, he has a lien on animals in his care. An agistor is one who keeps and boards animals for another person and for these services the agistor is entitled to keep the animals until paid for his services. A lien is dependent on the continual possession of the animals by the agistor. If the animals are surrendered to the owner or his agent the lien is no longer in effect.

In some cases courts have allowed animals to leave the possession of the lienholder. A veterinarian's right to render for professional care, materials, plus board was not lost by the sale of the horses boarded. Owners of establishments giving care to horses and other livestock shall have a lien on the animals for reasonable fees for board, materials and veterinary services. Some jurisdictions state that part of a lien is the right to sell livestock at public auctions and apply the proceeds to the liquidation of the debt owed. (Ahiswede 1971, Crough 1959, Donegan 1952) Some other states specifically say that veterinarians have a lien on animals dependent on possession for their compensation for the care and medical treatment of animals. Most states hold that the legal concept of a lien for veterinarians is valid. (Corp Juris 1992)

Recovery of fees when animals are abandoned by owners is similar in concept to a lien. "Without any further provisions of the law, when any animal is delivered to a veterinarian, dog kennel, cat kennel, pet grooming parlor, animal hospital, or any other animal care facility and the owner of such animal does not pick it up within 14 calendar days after the animal was due to be recovered, the animal is deemed to be abandoned." Veterinarians having custody of animals must try for a period of 10 days to find the owner of the animal and, if unable to do so, may humanely destroy the animal. A notice is required to be posted in the place of business warning persons leaving animals at the animal facility of the disposition of animals not claimed within a certain time. This code prohibits the use of abandoned animals for scientific experiments or turning them over to a pound or any department of a public agency. (Deering Cal Codes 1973)

An example case further explores liens. A friend of the owner of an animal brings it to a veterinarian for treatment. Under the law, the friend is considered to be an agent, or representative of the animal owner. Under such circumstances most jurisdictions would give the veterinarian a lien on the animal for the amount of services provided and the animal could be retained until a settlement is made for the payment of the fee.

Liens exist in many states for professional services and for boarding of an animal, but the right to sell or otherwise dispose of an animal in the holder's possession is not legal in many states. As noted above, a veterinarian does have the right to dispose of an unclaimed animal in California. In this state the right to sell personal property on which a lien is claimed is given, by statute, to agistors, (boarders of livestock) with the right to convert this personal property (animals) into money. (Quist 1908)

Bailment

A contractual agreement exists for professional services when a client brings an animal to a veterinarian for treatment. Another legal aspect exists in boarding an animal for a person when no professional services are given to the animal. This is considered legally as a bailment. A bailment is a kind of contract where one person keeps an item of personal property for another without changing it or applying professional skills. It is the holding of another's property in trust. The difference between a contract for professional services and a bailment is when professional services are given to an animal the veterinarian has expended his skill and labor in treating the animal to improve its value; in a bailment no added value is given to the animal. (Panon 1952)

In a bailment the owner or keeper delivers the personal property to the bailee for a specific purpose; keeping and caring for an animal. A bailment is a contract, express or implied, to carry out the purpose of the bailment and give the goods back to the owner or keeper when the terms of the bailment are ended. A dog owner leaves the animal in a veterinary hospital while on vacation, returns, picks up the animal and pays the board bill. In a bailment the bailor agrees to compensate the bailee in some manner for the services provided.

Good Samaritan Rule

This rule covers the duties and responsibilities of the health professional who under emergency conditions gives treatment to an injured patient. A well-meaning professional may be held liable for negligence or abandonment of the case after giving emergency care by not providing for follow-up treatment. In some instances statutes have been enacted to define the professional's responsibilities. One says that a veterinarian, who on his own initiative or other than at the request of the owner, gives emergency treatment to a sick or injured animal at the scene of an accident shall not be held liable for damages to the owner in the absence of gross negligence. Even if the veterinarian performs euthanasia to an animal there is presumptive evidence that this was the humane act necessary to relieve the animal from pain and suffering.

Veterinarians are one of the protected class of professionals under Good Samaritan statutes. These statutes do not grant an unqualified immunity; an emergency or accident must exist, it must be a gratuitous act, performed in good faith and follow proper standards of professional services. (JAVMA 1997:210.130) In emergency situations, the veterinarian should give the care the injury requires, stay with the case until relieved by a responsible person, owner or police officer, take caution in predicting the outcome of the case, make a record as soon as possible of the facts; names of persons involved, circumstances of the accident, location, time, date and keep the record for 2 years. (Kelliber 1977, Public Act 1973)

In emergency treatment of animals it is wise to follow a few rules: 1. find out if the owner is present or can be contacted; 2 render only the treatment considered necessary in your professional opinion; 3 treat the animal until arrangements are made for its removal and future care or relieved by a responsible person; 4. make a record of services given and the sequence of events involving the accident; 5. do not predict the outcome or other aspects of the case. (Hannah 1995)

Recovery for Fees

In a lawsuit for negligence the malpractice insurer or an attorney will be responsible for handing the details of the case, including payment of fees to concerned parties. The small claims court is a method that can be used by veterinarians to recover fees for services without resorting to the services of a lawyer and going to court.

The veterinarian's fee is often of an amount to forego the trauma of a trial and the actions of a court. For small amounts of money with the hope of collecting a fee, the small claims court can be used advantageously to seek settlement of a bill. The jurisdiction of these courts is limited to monetary claims arising out of contract disputes and some types of tort actions. The amount of money that can be recovered varies, but today this may be from 1 to 5000 dollars.

When a case is filed in a small claims court the one filing loses the right to collect any amount above the limits of the court; if its limit is $2000 and a veterinarian's bill is $3000, only $2000 can be collected. The location in which a small claims action can be brought is the city or county in which the client (defendant) lives. The veterinarian files with the clerk of the city or county his name, address, and the address of the client and the amount of the charges. The information is recorded in the court records and the plaintiff (veterinarian) agrees that the information is correct, signs the record, is given a time, date and place for the hearing. (Southall 1971, Small Claims 1972, Hannah 1993)

Premises Liability

Premises liability is the responsibility of owners, or occupiers, of real property for injuries sustained by persons roaming onto the property. Liability for bodily injury may occur from a breach of duty owed to the injured person. This duty is the obligation to meet certain standards in maintaining the safety of business properties. These standards must be met for invitees, those coming on the property legitimately for business purposes, but not for trespassers or illegal ones (burglars). An invitee is anyone entering the property with the occupiers permission, or by invitation. The invitee come on the land with the assurance and understanding that reasonable care has been taken to maintain the premises and make it safe for the invitee. Pickup and delivery persons are regarded as invitees by the mutual benefit rule; they are invitees because their function is necessary to the occupier of the property.

Legally, clients are invitees entering the veterinarian's premises on business. The veterinarian has obligations to those coming on his property recognized by law; a safe place to enter and do business; a waiting room, examination area and possibly a parking lot, any place the client may enter for business reasons. This applies not only to clients but to delivery persons, sales persons, and any others on the premises for business. Broken steps, slippery floors, defects in the structure of the building or furnishings may make the veterinarian liable for injuries. Broken sidewalks or snow and ice in front of the veterinary hospital may or may not be the responsibility of the occupier of the property, depending on local ordinances.

Statute of Limitations

The legal system recognizes that individuals, or groups of persons, should not be liable for some types of wrongdoings forever. To take care of this the law in its evolution developed the concept of statutes of limitation. Under this doctrine liability for a wrong lasts for a specific period of time; 1 to 2 years for some misdemeanors, 5 to 10 years for more serious offenses and a lifetime for murder or treason. Most of the wrongs that occur against a veterinarian have a limitation period of less than 5 years.

The time the statute begins to run is when the client discovers, or should have discovered, an animal was injured. In most jurisdictions if a lawsuit is began the day before that statute is due to run out, the legal action may continue. The death of an animal does not preclude the right of the owner to recover for damages to the animal.

Statutory limitation periods are used to promote justice by preventing surprises to litigants by the revival of claims that have been allowed to lie dormant, with much of the evidence lost; concerned person's memories have faded and witnesses have disappeared.

An exception to the time periods given in statutes of limitation may be given where negligence occurs due to the action of a professional; sponges or instruments left in an animal following surgery. This represents gross negligence and the right to sue may be extended to allow recovery for damages. Discovery of this type of negligence may occur after the period of limitation has expired.

Statutes of limitation are sometimes placed in the category of statutes of repose. Statutes of limitation bar the right of legal action unless it is filed with the Curt within a specific period of time after the injury has occurred. Statutes of repose terminate the right of legal action after a specific period of time has elapsed, regardless of whether there has been an injury or not. (Blacks Law Dictionary, 1995)

CHAPTER FOUR
VETERINARY PRACTICE

General Considerations

What is a veterinarian and what does he do? This question may be asked by the public but in reality many veterinarians are not familiar with all of the various facets of the profession. A simple, straightforward answer is, "A veterinarian treats and care for animals." But veterinary medicine has become more than this, more complex and difficult to define. Like the professions of law and medicine, time and knowledge have diversified and fragmented the profession into many specialties and sub-specialties. The computer age, manipulation of genes, embryo transfers, genetic engineering are all part of the problem; an abundance of knowledge forces individuals to choose certain areas in which to place their expertise. The veterinarian used to be a horse doctor, today members of the profession are engaged in many fields; virology, biochemistry, genetics, microsurgery, radiology, microbiology, ecology and guardians of the environment.

Legally, the definition of the profession has been given as; A veterinary surgeon is a person lawfully practicing the art of treating and healing the injuries and diseases of domestic animals. Also, one who practices the art of treating diseases and injuries of domestic animals surgically or medically. Note that this legal definition names the veterinarian as one who legally practices the profession emphasizing valid licensure as a prerequisite to the definition, excluding the lay person or unlicensed veterinarian from the definition. (Corpus Juris 1929)

A veterinarian's allegiance and responsibility rests with the health and welfare of the animals he serves. However, animals are items of personal property and an owner of animals has the legal right to make the decision to treat or humanely destroy an animal. In instances where an animal disease may endanger the health and welfare of the public, owner's decisions might not apply. In such cases the government may require a veterinarian to perform specific acts; destroy, vaccinate or quarantine animals.

Previously, some procedures have been debatable as to whether or not they constitute the practice of veterinary medicine, these being veterinary dentistry, pregnancy examinations, and embryo transfers. Most state practice acts exclude the owners of animals from their provisions; leaving the owners of animals to treat their animals without guilt or illegality. Owners of animals or their agents may perform procedures on animals normally considered to fall under the description of the practice of veterinary medicine. An exception to this rule is when the condition of an animal(s) constitute a public health hazard to human beings and should be handled by a veterinarian and humanely treated or disposed of to protect the health of the public.

A few test questions to use to determine if a procedure falls under the definition of veterinary medicine are:

1.   Do persons performing the procedures on animals have necessary skill and training to do so?

2.   Will the animal's health and welfare be in danger due to this lack of skill and training?

3.   May contagious diseases be transmitted to animals and/or human beings due to the lack of skill and training?

4.   Is the possibility of cruel and inhumane handling or faulty treatment present?

5.   Is the health and welfare of the public involved? (Corpus Juris 1951, Hannah 1990, 1993)

Practice Acts

The purpose of veterinary practice acts are to protect the public from persons with inadequate training and knowledge from practicing the profession illegally and endangering the public by doing so. The legislatures of state governments are empowered by law to make and enforce laws governing the practice of veterinary medicine. Such laws or statutes are enacted by state legislatures and are enforced for the protection of the general public from unqualified persons and to protect the qualified ones who have spent years in study and preparation for a professional career, from unlicensed persons assuming to be professionally qualified.

These acts endeavor to reasonably and fairly test the training and proficiency of those meeting the qualifications to become certified to practice veterinary medicine. Requirements vary among the states but, in general, all require graduation from an accredited school of veterinary medicine and an examination on prescribed subjects covering the field of veterinary medicine. Usually, a fee is required to register for the examination and for licensure and annual renewal of the license. The license is used for 2 purposes; as a tax levied to support the costs of the licensing program and as a means of registering of all veterinarians in the state and regulating their activities. The latter purpose places all information on veterinarians in one central place; their numbers, location, type of practice.

Administration of the profession rests with a Board of Veterinary Medical Examiners who carry out the business of regulating the profession under the state's Practice Act. The Board is a semi or quasi-legal body empowered to examine prospective licensees to ensure competence of the applicants, to grant and revoke licenses, to investigate breaches of professional conduct, to hold hearings and function as a control on the profession as required by state law. Boards are not only a policing body only to be heard from in their annual report, but a group of individuals that should cooperate closely with the state veterinary medical association and individual veterinarians to help them maintain and elevate the standards of the profession within the state. Practitioners should contact their board with suggestions as well as grievances.

Qualifications to Practice

States allow an individual to practice veterinary medicine after proving he or she have the qualifications to do so. Individuals are permitted to practice as long as they abide by the rules in force; the business and professional codes or statutes governing veterinary medicine. Some states have reciprocity with other states and will recognize a license granted by another state. States that grant reciprocity with your state can be determined by contacting the state board.

The ability to practice veterinary medicine and the license granted to do so are items of personal property. As such the right to practice cannot be taken away from licensed persons without the due process of law. The license to practice veterinary medicine has a monetary value.

It represents the means to earn a living. For this reason it cannot taken away frivolously but must be done by the proceedings of a court of law or a board of veterinary examiners. Such actions only occur after the veterinarian, alleged to have committed a wrong, has had a chance to be heard and offer a defense to the proper authorities.

A license to engage in the practice of a profession is a valuable property right. Courts have said, with reference to physicians, "The right to follow the profession of medicine and surgery as a lawful occupation is one of the fundamental rights of citizenship. Further, it is a valuable property right in which, under the constitution and laws of states, one is entitled to be protected and secured. These decisions on the practice of medicine apply equally to the practice of veterinary medicine as well. (People v state 1917, 1921, Hewrn 1906)

Conversely, the right to practice one's profession cannot be protected to the extent that it endangers or compromises the rights of the public at large. The right to practice medicine must yield to the all-encompassing right of the government to protect the public health by any rational means. (Lawrence 1921)

The right of a citizen to practice medicine is subject to the powers of the state to impose such regulations, within the limitations of the constitution as may be required to protect the public from ignorance, incapacity, deception or fraud in the practice of that profession. The constitutionality of requiring licenses to practice a profession has been challenged many times. Invariably the power to grant licenses and regulate businesses and professions properly fall within the power of the state and this has been upheld. (People 1925, City of Rome 1875, State 1848, State 1831)

The regulation of veterinary medicine is within the scope of the permissive powers of state legislatures and their administrative rules applying to the profession. Such statutes and administrative rules have not always been upheld by the courts. In Bone for instance a statute allowing for the issuance of a veterinary license to a specified person was held invalid due to favoritism. An administrative regulation that allowed the issuance of a license to persons not graduates of a veterinary school recognized and accredited by the American Veterinary Medical Association and the United States Bureau of Animal Industry was held invalid. (Marmot 1887, Reid 1947)

There are several cases in the law records challenging the authority of the state to require examination and licensing for the professions. In no case has it been judged that the regulation of veterinary medicine is not within the authority of the state and statutes defining the qualifications for persons seeking to take an examination for licensure have been held reasonable, authorized and applicable. (Kramer 1952)

The authority of the state to regulate veterinary medicine was challenged in the following case; A company producing a product for animals alleged it was necessary to include directions on the bottle label to aid farmers in the use of the product. This was in violation of the veterinary practice act in the state where the product was sold. The company brought legal action against the state declaring the act unconstitutional, alleging that preventing a company from putting advice on their product label was an infringement of their citizen rights. The court held a state has a right to regulate business and professions as long as its acts are not contrary to the constitution or discriminatory; the constitutionality of the practice act was upheld. In some instances Federal law has usurped state laws in relation to the control of businesses. (Nebraska Law 1927, Nat'l Labor Rel Act 29 USCA, see 151 et seq.)

The prosecution of persons practicing veterinary medicine without a valid license or in violation of practice acts are conducted under state statutes giving power to state boards to enforce violations. Veterinary associations are not the proper bodies to carry out such proceedings, although they may bring violations of the practice acts to the attention of the state boards. (Peet 1929, Missouri 1950, Corpus Juris 1995)

Quotations from cases emphasize the powers of boards of examiners in veterinary medicine and illustrate such powers are accepted and upheld by the courts. A state statute provided for the licensing, without examination, of a veterinarian who had practiced veterinary medicine in the state for 2 years prior to a specified date. A practitioner of veterinary medicine was defined as one who habitually held himself out to the public as such, since the word practice implied a continuing occupation and did not denote a few isolated acts. The court held that this applicant for licensure had only occasionally treated animals during a 2 years period; therefore there was nothing to show arbitrary abuse of authority on the part of the state board in denying the license.

The power of a state board of veterinary examiners to revoke the license of a veterinarian includes the power to suspend him. A statute

making gross moral or professional misconduct on the part of a
veterinarian grounds for suspension or revocation of license is not void
for uncertainty. (West's 1991) In the State of Nebraska v Jeffrey (525
NW 2d 193, 1994) the state took injunctive action against a lay equine
dentist practitioner who practiced dentistry without a license and was not
a graduate veterinarian. The court found the licensing statute was not
overly broad and the issuance of an injunction was the appropriate
remedy to be applied.

　　A veterinarian's unprofessional alliance with a lay person, the use
of this person to treat sick animals, and the sharing of fees, justifies the
revocation of the veterinarian's license under the statute defining
professional misconduct. In this case a veterinarian opened a branch
office in a town separate from his main practice location. He advertised
the opening and stated a certain individual, not a veterinarian, would be
his manager in this town. A farmer called this branch office regarding
a sick horse. The lay person went out to the farm and examined the
horse, returned to the office and called the veterinarian who directed him
over the telephone as to the type of treatment to prescribe for the horse.
The diagnosis was spinal septicemia. The employee returned to the farm
and gave the animal oral treatment and a muscular injection. Later the
veterinarian and his employee came to the farm and examined the horse.
The horse recovered and the medical services were paid for with a check
made out to the veterinarian and his employee. The employee cashed the
check and apparently split the feel with the veterinarian. (Sanborn 1921)

　　This veterinarian maintained informers in 3 counties of the state
who advertised for him and called when they encountered someone who
needed his services, for which he paid them 25 cents a call. The court
found the veterinarian had a non-professional alliance with lay persons
and was guilty of unethical practices. The sentence revoking and
suspending his license was not contrary to the evidence presented to the
court. In this case the veterinarian was both careless and unethical in the
operation of his business and engaged in practices contrary to the statutes
regulating the practice of veterinary medicine. Such practices as
fee-splitting, commissions or rebates are not acceptable or ethical
practices by veterinarians and should be strictly avoided. Charging for
something other than direct services or being paid for services not
directly or personally involved in the treatment of animals is poor
practice policy. (Hannah JAVMA 1998;212;988)

A statute giving a board of veterinary medical examiners the right to determine the standing of the school from which an applicant received his diploma as an acceptable one was held not invalid as an improper act of discretion by the board.

Other reasons for the revocation or suspension of a veterinarian's license have been: allowing an unlicensed person to castrate goats, permitting a senior veterinary student to suture incisions of animals, allowing students to perform hysterectomies, allowing a lay person to use metal clips to close an incision, the hysterectomy of a cat which later gave birth to 5 kittens, certifying a health certificate without seeing the animal involved, keeping dirty and insanitary premises and improper euthanasia methods. (Walker 1941, Cooper 1934)

A veterinarian's license was revoked due to the conviction of a conspiracy to import marijuana in violation of the federal law and for mail fraud in an attempt to recover the insurance on property falsely reported to have been stolen. The smuggling of 12,000 pounds of marijuana into this country consists of a crime involving moral turpitude and the conviction of mail fraud showed dishonesty and was also a basis for revocation of license. Revocation upheld. (Thorpe v Board of Exam in Vet Med 8 ALR 4, 218, 1980)

In another case a veterinary board revoked a veterinarian's license due to conviction in a federal court for violation of the Internal Revenue Service Code. It was held the Board had no jurisdiction over the subject matter of a federal crime. (Rhodes v Oregon State Vet Exam Bd 223 P 2d 804, 1950)

Board of Veterinary Examiners

All states have provisions in their legislative structure for a board to administer their veterinary practice act and the affairs of the profession. These have veterinarians appointed to serve as members. Most states have one or more lay persons on their boards to counteract any accusations of favoritism or nepotism in their decisions.

Such boards are under the jurisdiction of a department of the state: education, registration, business and professions or agriculture. The number of members vary from 3 to 7, appointment is by the governor or a department head, often upon the recommendation of the state veterinary association. In general, veterinary members must be graduates of an acceptable veterinary school, have good professional standing, be residents of the state. have a minimum of 2 to 5 years of professional experience. The board members and staff may or may not receive compensation. State statutes and codes expressly define and describe procedures for board meetings and the powers and actions of the board.

The boards have the power to make rules and regulations necessary for their function, to subpoena and hear witnesses, issue, rescind and revoke licenses, levy fines and give examinations. Board proceedings and hearings may be reviewed by state legal authorities and, in some cases, by the public. Persons charged with violations of practice acts have the right to hearings, representation by a lawyer and the right to appeal decisions of the board.

Licenses granted for the practice of veterinary medicine are in some states required to be recorded with the appropriate authorities. This may be accomplished by the Board or by the licensee veterinarian, usually with a county recorder. Recording is a safeguard if a license is lost, challenged, date of issue questioned, proof of title doubted, etc.

Persons exempted from the provisions of veterinary practice acts may include members of the United States Uniformed Services, U.S. Department of Agriculture employees, persons who treat their own animals, licensed veterinarians from another state serving as consultants. Some states exempt spaying, castration and the dehorning of cattle from the provisions of their acts.

In an early decision, the courts said that a veterinary surgeon of 5 years standing who was not entitled to use the degree of Veterinary Surgeon must register within 8 months after the passage of the act (practice) or be guilty of a misdemeanor in using the professional title. (8 PA County Court Rep 451, 1880)

With regard to the degree of skill expected of a veterinarian a court said over 100 years ago, "A veterinary surgeon in the absence of a specific contract, engages to use such reasonable skill, diligence and attention as may ordinarily expected of persons in that profession. He does not undertake to use the highest degree of skill nor an extraordinary amount of diligence. (45 NW 894, 1890)

A common method of practice today is through the use of mobile veterinary clinics. Regarding the use of these, following some basic requirements has been recommended; information should be given to clients on the limitation of services available, a licensed veterinarian should be in charge who has practice and vehicle insurance and the mobile vehicle should have the necessary utilities, follow sanitary standards, and have drug security provisions (JAVMA 1998;213;824)

Example of a State's
Board Regulations

Board of examiners in veterinary medicine; creation, powers, membership: There is in the Department of (appropriate one) a Board of Examiners in Veterinary Medicine in which the administration of this chapter is vested. The board consists of (?) members, 2 of whom shall be public members.

Qualifications of members: Each member, except the public members, shall be a graduate of some veterinary college authorized by law to confer degrees, a bona fide resident of the state, for a period of at least 5 years immediately preceding his appointment, and shall have been actively engaged in the practice of his profession in this state during this period. The public members shall have been residents of this state for a period of at least 5 years past before their appointment and shall not be licentiates of the board or any other board under this division or of any board referred to in other sections. At no time shall there be 2 members on the board from the same congressional district. No person shall serve as a member of the board for more than 2 consecutive terms.

Tenure and appointment of board members: vacancies: The members of the board shall hold office for a term of 4 years. Each member shall serve until the appointment and qualifications of his successor or until one year shall have elapsed since the expiration of the term for which he was appointed, whichever occurs first. A member may be reappointed subject to the limitation contained in section x.

Vacancies occurring shall be filled by appointment for the unexpired term within 90 days after they occur: The Governor shall appoint the professional members, the Senate rules committee and the Speaker of the Assembly shall each appoint a public member.

Removal of a member: The Governor may, in his judgment, remove any member of the board for neglect of duty or other sufficient cause, after notice and hearing.

Officers of board; bonds, attorney general as counsel: The board shall elect a president, vice president, and such other officers as shall be necessary, from its membership. The board may require any or all officers of the board to give a bond to the State in such form and penalty as it deems proper. The Attorney General shall act as counsel for the board and the members thereof in their official or individual capacity for any act done under the color of official right.

Executive officer; power and duties: The board may appoint a person exempt from civil service who shall be designated as an executive officer and who shall exercise the powers and perform the duties delegated by the board and vested in him or her by this chapter.

Oaths; perjury: The executive officer of the board may administer oaths or affirmations upon matters pertaining to the business of the board. Any person willfully making any false oath or affirmation is guilty of perjury.

Compensation of members and secretary; expenses: Each member of the board shall receive a per diem and expenses as provided in section x. The secretary of the Board of Examiners in Veterinary Medicine shall receive expenses.

Rules and regulations; meetings; licensing power: The board may in accordance with the provisions of the Administrative Procedure Act, adopt, amend, or repeal such rules and regulations as are reasonably necessary to carry into effect the provisions of this chapter. The board may hold such meetings as are necessary for the transacting of business. It shall issue all licenses to practice veterinary medicine in this state.

Records; register of license applicants; register as evidence: The board shall keep an official record of its meetings, and shall also keep an official register of all applicants for licenses. The register shall be prima facie evidence of all matters contained therein.

Inspection of premises: The board may at any time inspect the premises in which veterinary medicine, veterinary dentistry, or veterinary surgery is being practiced.

Enforcement of cleanliness and sanitary requirements: The enforcement of sections x and y of this chapter is a function exclusively reserved to the Board of Examiners in Veterinary Medicine and the state has preempted and occupied this field of enforcing the cleanliness and sanitary requirements of this chapter.

Regular inspection program: The board shall establish a regular inspection program which will provide for random, unannounced inspections.

Practice Provisions

Any person practices veterinary medicine, surgery, and dentistry and various branches thereof, when he does any of the following:

(a)   Represents himself as engaged in the practice of veterinary medicine veterinary surgery, or veterinary dentistry in any of its branches.

(b)   Diagnoses or prescribes a drug, medicine, appliance or treatment of whatever nature for the prevention, cure of a wound, fracture, or bodily injury or disease of animals.

(c)   Administers a drug. medicine, appliance or treatment of whatever nature for the prevention, cure or relief of a wound, fracture, or bodily injury or disease of animals, except where such drug, medicine appliance or application or treatment is administered by an animal health technician or an unregistered assistant at the direction of and under the direct of supervision of a licensed veterinarian subject to the provisions of Article X commencing with section XY of this chapter. However, no person, other than a licensed veterinarian, may induce anesthesia unless authorized by regulation of the board.

(d)   performs a surgical or dental operation upon an animal.

(e)   Performs any manual procedure for the diagnosis of pregnancy, sterility, or infertility upon livestock.

(f)   Uses any words, letters or titles in such connection or under such circumstances as to induce the belief that the person using them is engaged in the practice of veterinary medicine, veterinary surgery, or veterinary dentistry.

Emergency treatment; immunity: A veterinarian who on his own initiative, at the request of an owner, or at the request of someone other than the owner, renders emergency treatment to a sick or injured animal at the scene of an accident shall not be liable in damages to the owner of such animal in the absence of gross negligence.

Excepted acts: Nothing in this chapter prohibits any person from:

(a)   Practicing veterinary medicine upon his own animals.

(b)   Being assisted in such practice by his employees when employed in the conduct of such person's business.

(c)   Being assisted in such practice by some other person gratuitously.

(d)   The lay testing of poultry by the whole agglutination test.

(e)   Making a determination as to the status of pregnancy, sterility, or infertility upon livestock at the time an animal is being inseminated, providing no direct charge is made for such determination.

(f)   Administering sodium pentobarbital for euthanasia of sick, injured, homeless, or unwanted domestic pets or animals, without the presence of a veterinarian when such person is an employee of a public pound or humane society and has received proper training in the administration of sodium pentobarbital for such purposes. (State Code 1991)

Funds for the functioning of boards of veterinary medicine are collected through fees for examination, annual license renewal charges, and fines levied by the board.

Grounds for the revocation of a license are: use of fraud in obtaining a license, conviction of a felony or a crime involving moral turpitude, chronic alcoholism, violation of the controlled substance act, the use of drugs, violations of the provisions of the practice act, conviction of malpractice, aiding and abetting an unlicensed veterinarian in an illegal act, conduct reflecting unfavorably on the veterinary profession.

Qualifications for those applying for examination for licensure are investigated and verified by the board, or the licensing body. Usually, these are: 21 years or older, graduation from a recognized and accredited veterinary college with a degree in veterinary medicine and good moral character. An acceptable veterinary school is one approved by the board, usually one that is accredited by the American Veterinary Medical Association. Violations of any of the provisions of a practice act constitute a misdemeanor and as such are punishable by a fine, jail sentence, or both. The amount of the fine and length of the jail sentence is under the control of the board.

Definitions of what constitutes the practice of veterinary medicine are important because this is usually the basis for prosecution. The definition should be clear and thorough because it represents the intent of the veterinary profession. Here is where violators will try to find loopholes and ways to practice without a license.

The law recognizes a degree of fluidity and the need for change in practice acts, illustrated in a decision related to the practice of human medicine. "The insertion of a needle beneath the skin to alleviate pain, infirmity or disease, commonly known as acupuncture, constitutes the practice of medicine." With the changing of the times and medical practice, the law changes to meet the needs of society. (Hannah 1977)

Restrictive Covenants

A veterinarian's employee veterinarian, on leaving the service of the employer, may agree to refrain from practicing within a specified area for an agreed upon amount of time. These are principal-agent agreements and are legal contracts if they do not embrace too great a geographical area or are made to last too long a time or put one or both parties under undue hardship. Conversely, a veterinarian buying a practice from another one may make a similar agreement with the seller not to practice nearby for a specified period of time. An example case involves a physician who agreed not to practice within 8 miles of his former practice, or to sell medicine, for 10 years. The arrangement was upheld by the courts. The enforceability of restrictive agreements is shown in a case where the seller of a veterinary hospital agreed not to open a practice in the vicinity of the one sold. A short time later he attempted to begin a practice within the restricted area. The court upheld the restrictive agreement and prevented the seller from starting a new practice in the area. (Wilkinson 1894, Griffin 1954) In a recent case a professional corporation of practicing veterinarians brought an action against a former veterinarian employee to enforce a non-competitive agreement. The court found for the veterinary corporation and said although the employee veterinarian's employment contract had been modified it had not been terminated and was in effect during employment and was valid. (Shelbina Vet Clin v Holthause 892 SW 2d 803, 1995)

Another restrictive agreement was not upheld by a court because a purchaser of a veterinary hospital allowed the seller, who had agreed not to re-open a practice in the general area to buy land receive a use permit from the city and begin to build another hospital before the purchaser of the veterinary hospital attempted to force the selling veterinarian to cease. The court said the purchaser had ample time to object to the seller's actions before he had invested thousands of dollars.

A contract under which the defendant agreed that upon termination of his employment as a veterinarian's employee he would not engage in the practice of veterinarian medicine within a 25 mile radius in the city and the restriction was unlimited as to time. The agreement was declared void as embracing too great an area and unlimited time and the restrictions were greater than necessary for the protection of the veterinarian attempting to enforce the agreement. (Breecher 1945)

Graduates in the health professions often seek employment in established practices to gain experience, further their careers, learn to deal with the public and to save money for starting their own practice. These graduate employees may be required to agree to an employment contract with a restrictive condition not to compete, open a practice, within a specified area for a given amount of time. Such agreements are common and enforceable under the conditions given above. (Hannah 1992,) With such agreements the courts examine if these place a burden on the professional employer and employee and the public. They cannot be unlimited as to time nor cover an area greater than necessary to protect the established practitioner. (Hannah 1978, Am Jur 1971)

Ethics

I am concerned and dismayed about the deterioration and loss of manners, courtesy, and ethics in our present business society and in our social life. Laws govern the ways in which we interact and deal with human beings and other animals. Manner, ethics and customs form the building blocks and the basis for our legal system and laws and these have been essential for the evolution of the legal principles upon which society depends for its continued operation.

Business and ethics in the United States is involved and entangled with the law. Morality and law share concerns over matters of basic social importance and often have in common certain principles, obligations and criteria of evidence. Law is the agency of the public for translating morality into guidelines and practices for developing punishments for offenses against society. The common law has established precedents that give us material for reflection on both legal and moral questions. In reality, the moral evaluation of a situation should be separated and distinguished from the legal one. There is an interaction between morals and the law, but a law-abiding person is not necessarily a moral one. Something may be legally acceptable but not morally so. The doctrine of employment-at-will allows employers to fire employees at will, without cause and this may be legally right but not morally so. (Beauchamp TL, Bowie NE, Ethical Theory and Business, 5th Ed. 1997, New Jersey, Prentice-Hall)

Ethics involves standards of right and wrong. Business decisions have social consequences and social responsibility is related to ethics. Businesses have an obligation to contribute to the good of society as well as to the good of their business. Social responsibility contrasts with legal responsibility which is forced responsibility to comply with laws and regulations.

1.   Ethical conflicts are inherent in business decision-making; do we
     use drugs still in the experimental stage, not proven to be safe or
     effective?

2.   Proper ethical behavior is on a level above the law. The law only
     requires the minimal or lowest acceptable degree of behavior;
     actions of the average person under similar circumstances — not
     the responses of an above-the average individual.

If a business is concerned with moral issues the staff will be also.
The moral tone of a business is set by its management. The key in
business and life is impartiality and the Golden Rule is the oldest
principle of life. In general it says: "Do as you would be done by; if you
want to be treated fairly, treat others fairly; if you want to be told the
truth, tell others the truth; if you want your privacy protected, respect
the privacy of others." (Business Ethics, 1995-1996, Brown and
Benchmark Publ., Guilford, CT.)

Whatever business has been in the past is now a much more
complex social phenomenon with consequent social as well as economic
consequences. Business is now interrelated with other social problems
and is also international. In addition to making money there is the social,
environmental and ethical role of business and businessmen must be
aware of this. Business should have social and ethical aims in addition
to financial ones. There is no point in knowing what is wrong if nothing
is done to fix it. (Valiance E, Business Ethics at Work. 1995, Cambridge
Univ Press.)

As professional people and members of society we often encounter
the words ethics and morals, often without a precise concept of the
significance of these words. The dictionary defines ethics as, "the science
of moral character or of ideal character. The discipline of dealing with
what is good or bad, with moral duty and obligation. A theory or system
of moral values. Of or in relation to principles of right and wrong in
behavior. Conforming to a standard of right behavior manner, custom or
habit characterized by excellence in what pertains to practice or conduct.
Dealing with or concerned with establishing principles of right and
wrong in behavior." Ethics is the study of standards of conduct and
moral judgment; moral philosophy. The system or code of morals of a
particular, religions, group, or profession." (Webster's Dictionary 1983)

Concepts of what is right or wrong are as old as society. As human beings settled into family and tribal living, unwritten rules related to daily contact with one another evolved. Rules against robbery, murder, stealing developed because experience of time showed that following basic rules allowed people in close association to live together peacefully. Codes of ethics grew and developed in the learned professions of law, medicine and religion. The essence of veterinary medical ethics was captured by the founder of the profession in America, Alexandre Liautard. He originated the motto of the U. S. veterinary profession, "Non nobis solum," (not for ourselves alone) a challenging ethical statement.

Liautard, a learned physician-veterinarian of French extraction, led the evolving American profession for the last 40 years of the 19th century. "Non nobis solum," was chosen as the motto because it represented the goal of American veterinarians. The profession in the United States was small, disorganized and originated with members from a number of foreign countries since there were no American veterinary colleges until later in the century. This struggling band of professionals were fighting for recognition and financial independence. Guarantees of cures, quack remedies, and widespread advertising were common within the profession. Even early veterinary colleges that were founded tended to advertise widely and to claim great advantages over their competitors in their promotional literature. (Hall 1931)

By the beginning of the 1900's a group of ethical American veterinarians had become professionalized and attention was being given to the merits of ethical behavior in professional publications and in the veterinary colleges. The first code of ethics for the profession appeared in the Journal of the American Veterinary Medical Association in 1931, written by Maurice Hall. He presented the profession with an admirable code to follow, with a scholarly apology for the inclusion of such a philosophical requirement in the veterinarian's moral obligations. Dr. Hall was a scientist in the Bureau of Animal Industry of the U.S. Department of Agriculture and is best known for his discovery of the anti-hookworm drug tetrachlorethylene, for man and animals. (Crawford 1976)

A modified version of the Hall Code of Ethics was adopted by the veterinary profession in 1940 and in 1952 the Association approved the title, "Principles of Veterinary Medical Ethics." Since this time the principles have been modified and modernized. (Merillat 1940, Joint Cong 1952)

The honor and dignity of our profession is in our obedience to a just and reasonable code of ethics set forth as a guide to members. The purpose of this code is more far reaching because exemplary professional conduct not only upholds honor and dignity, but also enlarges our sphere of usefulness, exalts our social standards, promotes the science we cultivate. Briefly stated, our code of ethics is the foundation of our individual and collective efforts. It is based on the Golden Rule. (JAVMA 1979)

The principal criticism of the original code was it seemed more of a handbook of etiquette than a working manual of professional ethics. The AVMA makes available a booklet containing the principles with annotations and appendix containing examples of the AVMA Judicial Council rulings. With these decisions the practicing veterinarian can review precedent cases and the veterinary student can develop an appreciation of the traditional and dynamic concept of veterinary medical ethics.

The veterinary profession is bound together in a common discipline which fosters a spirit of fraternity, scholarship and public service. The principle of caveat emptor (let the buyer beware) does not apply; the professed watchword of the profession is the Golden Rule. This is the antithesis of caveat emptor. Do unto others as you would have them do unto you bespeaks of a policy of a highly idealized business practice wherein the customer will be protected and held in high moral esteem. The term customer is a misnomer; the term client is preferred in order to differentiate the veterinarian advisor and client advisee relationship of mutual trust from the usual business-customer relationship of the merchant-customer trade.

The principles of veterinary medical ethics recognize the obligations of scholarship, specific duties to clientele and it emphasizes the essentials of interprofessional courtesy. In essence, the profession is devoted to serve the public. Financial security is a component, but not the primary one in the practice of veterinary medicine. The veterinarian is trained to offer service. For this the client must be prepared to surrender an appropriate payment for that service. In exchange for this the veterinarian is required to guarantee that throughout his professional career he will give acceptable veterinary medical service and temper the practice of his profession with humane treatment for the animals and fair treatment for the public.

Veterinary medicine is an ennobling profession. Two major factors enhance that ennoblement; the genuine compassion for animals which is a major reason for entering veterinary medicine, and the application of the principles of veterinary medical ethics in the practice of the profession.

Medical confidentiality is of ancient origin dating back to early civilizations The early priest-physicians wanted to keep a closed profession and protect their medical secrets from the common horde, consequently, types of treatments were secret and remedies were not discussed with patients. There is no legal basis for strict confidence between doctor and client. However, there are several reasons to observe the rule; essentially it is for the protection of the client, mentally, physically, to avoid embarrassment, gossip, or possible involvement in a lawsuit. (Hannah 1995, JAVMA 1991)

In the practice of veterinary medicine the consent, or agreement, of the client to perform a specific procedure is necessary and the only acceptable and ethical approach to the management of a practice. Proceeding without this can lead to a lawsuit for damages if something goes wrong. Informed consent has been covered elsewhere.

Ethical and moral areas exist regarding the publication of information gained from treating a clients animal or using a patient for research, in addition to treatment. Ethically, the veterinarian should inform the client that their animal's problem may warrant a publication or that the animal is being used for an investigative project. (Mason 1991)

In investigative research scientific misconduct has been frequent enough to cause the Congress in 1989 to establish within the National Institutes of Health an Office of Scientific Integrity Review to attempt to minimize scientific misconduct. Research misconduct is plagiarism, fabrication, or deliberate falsification of data, research procedures, or data analysis, or other deliberate misrepresentations in proposing, conducting, reporting or reviewing research. (JAMA 1993)

Advances in science and medicine have increased the number of situations where ethical guidelines may be stretched or breached. In medicine the Hippocratic Oath still serves as the ethical creed throughout the world. Recently, The World Health Organization of the UN issued the Declaration of Geneva as an addenda to the Hippocratic Oath. Its major obligations are:

1. Exercise the profession with conscience and dignity.

2. Treat the health of the patient as the principal concern.

3. Respect confidences

4. Abstain from discrimination when seeing patients.

5. Have respect for the patient's life.

6. Never use medial knowledge contrary to the laws of humanity. (Ziekinski 1994)

Resolution of Ethical Conflicts

This discourse should be prefaced with a question often asked by veterinary students in ethics and jurisprudence courses, "Ethical principles, like laws, are often breached, but what can be done about the practitioner who does not follow ethical principles?" This is a serious problem. As in any profession or trade there are people that cause trouble by practicing in a selfish professional style contrary to the best interests of the profession. Such behavior open results from ignorance of ethical principles or from traditional customs. One of the major purposes of organized veterinary medicine is to foster professional courtesy through educational programs and adjudication of intraprofessional disagreements.

Local, state and national veterinary medical associations have standing committees on ethics. Their areas of responsibility include infractions of professional demeanor not covered by statutory laws or veterinary board precedents. Examples of this are self-aggrandizing behavior, non-professional business practices such as discounting or splitting fees, guarantees, the demeaning of colleagues.

The uttering of derogatory remarks to colleagues or in front of clients creates a maximum amount of ill-will between veterinarians. It is tempting when a client replaces one veterinarian with another to imply that the first veterinarian has had previous troubles or is not up-to-date. Such remarks can make clients doubt the adequacy of the first veterinarian's treatment of the case and lead to lawsuits. The second veterinarian could be called in as an expert witness, further embarrassing himself. Most important the veterinarian "knocking" another one loses the respect and often friendship of the one knocked and fellow practitioners.

Aggrieved veterinarians should ideally first take their grievance to the fellow veterinarian involved. Lack of satisfaction between colleagues may cause presentation of the case before an ethics committee of the first level of the local, regional or state veterinary medical association. Lack of resolution at these levels allows the aggrieved veterinarian to proceed to the national level; The Judicial Council of the AVMA. The Judicial council hears cases, publishes their rulings and establishes a body of precedential actions which are routinely updated and serve as guides for state and local ethics committees

Most state veterinary practice acts have provisions for dealing with unethical practices of licensees. Practitioners who repeatedly disregard the warnings of local or state ethics committees should be referred to the state board of veterinary medicine.

Fees

Fees charged for veterinary services by veterinarians constitute a common complaint against veterinarians. There are no set or fixed rules regarding what amounts to a fair price for services rendered, but the subject is a matter of concern to the profession and a topic frequently discussed at professional meetings.

Veterinary boards are concerned with licensees who charge exorbitant prices for their work. There is no law that limits charges for professional services, but moral obligations do exist and professional associations do attempt to influence members in the rationale for charging reasonable fees. Professions have been accused of meeting and setting fees which could be in contradiction of free competition. (Wall Street Journal 1992) There is an ethical and moral obligation on the part of professionals to charge a fee consistent with material costs and the reasonable value of the use of professional ability and services

A few ethical questions to consider are:

1.   The use of expensive drugs when cheaper one would give the same results.

2.   The use of expensive procedures, radiation or chemotherapy, when there is no hope for a cure.

3.   The use of surgical techniques where no benefits from these have been shown to be effective.

4.   Thoughtless and wasteful use of medical resources, employing unnecessary treatment.

5.   Failure to refer a case to a specialist when this is indicated (Ellos 1990).

Environmental Protection
Agency [EPA]

In the 1960s and 70s citizens of the United States and the world became alarmed at the increasing deterioration of the environment, destruction of animal habitats and the decreasing numbers of wildlife. The Environmental Protection Agency (EPA) was created by Congress in 1975 to institute a coordinated and effective governmental action on behalf of the environment (CFR 40, pt 1, 1993). The agency endeavors to control pollution by integrating several functions under government control; research on pollution, monitoring for the presence of pollutants, or potential ones, monitoring of minimal standards for pollutants, and applying preventive and restrictive actions when standards are violated.

The EPA is designed to serve as the public watchdog and advocate for the development and maintenance of a liveable, acceptable environment. Its mission is to protect and enhance the environment to the fullest extent possible under the law. This includes the abatement of the pollution of the air and water, the emission of solid wastes, the production of excessive noise, release of toxic substances into the atmosphere and the dangerous emission of radioactive particles. The mission is accomplished by several subdivisions of the EPA; Offices of

Air and Radiation, Pesticides, Toxic Substances, Water, and the Office of Prevention

Veterinary hospitals and animal facilities are subject to EPA regulation and the operators of such premises may receive periodic inspection visits of their premises and equipment. X-ray machines may be monitored for malfunction and dangerous radiation emissions; pollution of air, water or soil can be checked and abatement measures recommended if acceptable standards are violated.

Veterinarians may face charges of malpractice, negligence or creating a nuisance if they violate EPA regulations. Using X-ray equipment that releases radiations above the acceptable standards could constitute negligence if persons or animals are injured; if not, EPA may impose fines and orders to desist. Pollution of water supplies with infectious agents or putrefactive material or the creation of excessive noise from a veterinary hospital or kennel all could come under EPA jurisdiction and regulation.

Veterinarians, veterinary hospitals and their surrounding premises are subject to EPA control and if the operation of a veterinary practice affects the environment in an objectionable manner, damages it or infringes on the rights of citizens to peaceful, quiet, healthy, and pleasant enjoyment of the environment, the veterinarian may be liable.

In the enforcement of the EPA the government has stated, "The world environment means something more than rocks, trees and streams, or the amount of air pollution; it encompasses all the factors that affect the quality of life: crowding, squalor and other adverse environmental factors. (390 F Supp 198) Aesthetic and environmental wellbeing, like economic well-being, are important ingredients of our life ". (42 USCA 1985) Protection of the quality of life for city residents must consider noise, traffic, stench and the control of harmful drugs. (42 USCA 1985)

Veterinarians are subject to EPA regulations and there are several areas where they could forseeably violate these; incineration of waste material or animals, violation of the Clean Water Acts, discharge of objectionable waste into sewers, methods of disposal of manure, placing hazardous waste in containers when the refuse could be hazardous to waste disposal personnel. (Hannah 1995)

Occupational Safety
and Health Act [OSHA]

The Occupational Safety and Health Act was enacted by Congress in 1970 to protect citizens from dangers present in the natural or artificial environment; air, water, buildings, machines, equipment, chemicals, gases, sanitation and to provide services for injuries to the public; fire control, medical support, warning systems, danger signs and protective equipment.

States are required to submit to OSHA plans for their implementation of OSHA requirements. For a state's plans to be approved they must demonstrate:

1.   They meet OSHA criteria and requirements.

2.   Name a state agency responsible for administration of the Act.

3.   Have developed their own acceptable standards.

4.   Have enforcement capabilities.

5.   Have the compliance of employers.

6.   Have the ability to obtain the legal right of entry and inspection of business properties.

7.   Have sufficient trained personnel to carry out their mission.

OSHA Standards include:

1.   Access to employer medical and hazardous exposure records.

2.   Standards for the minimal safety of floors, stairs, ladders, scaffolds, doors, buildings.

3.   Existence of adequate fire control systems and the control of excessive noise.

4.   Adequate ventilation and a sanitary environment.

5.   Control of radiation emissions to a harmless level, and harmless amounts of hazardous chemicals, safe equipment including all electrical equipment.

6.   Provisions for personnel protection; safety equipment, gloves, eye protection, masks, boots, etc.

Veterinary hospitals and animal facilities are subject to OSHA requirements and inspections by the Agencies personnel. To protect employees and clients veterinarians should be aware of OSHA regulations and requirements and understand they must adhere to these in the operation of their business. (29 CFR 1990)

Agency

Agency is defined as a relationship where one person, the principal, authorizes another person, the agent, to act for him on his behalf with discretionary powers in business dealings with other individuals, called third persons.

Whenever one person acts for another, with his permission, he becomes in law that person's representative or agent. The law of agency includes part of the relationship known in old English common law as the law of master and servant. Today, this arrangement is usually called employer-employee law.. A difference between the two is that an agent has greater discretionary powers than the servant. (3 AJ 2d 498, 1989)

A principal, or employer, is responsible for the acts, and the wrongs, committed by an agent or employee when the act is done and the agent or employee is acting within the scope of employment. For example, if a veterinarian's technician, due to poor restraint, injures an animal when working for the veterinarian, the veterinarian is responsible for the damages.

In a personal injury action against a veterinarian by the owner of a car struck by the veterinarian's employee when the employee's car ran into the plaintiff's car, the employee was driving his car after normal working hours, going to a friend's house to look at a sick dog on behalf of the veterinarian, supposedly acting as his agent. The veterinarian was not liable since the employee was acting on his own, after working hours and had no duty to transport animals to and from the veterinary hospital. (Vangerosky v Moogan 513 NYS 2d 199, 1987)

In Acherman v Robertson (3 NW 2d 723, 1942) A veterinarian's son delivered to a farmer client Iysol solution instead of mange oil for the skin, resulting in the death of 89 hogs. The son was found to be the agent of the veterinarian and he was responsible for the son's negligent act as his agent.

An employer or principal is bound by and responsible for the agreements made with other persons by his or her employees if these are made while the employee (agent) is working and acting for the benefit and with the knowledge of the employer. If a veterinarians employee places a large order for drugs, and often does this, the veterinarian is liable for the bill even though he did not expressly authorize this order. The law assumes an employee is functioning under the orders of the employer. Without the law of agency, business and trade persons would have to deal only with the boss for every minor business act — the buying of paper or soap for the veterinary hospital. Businesses could not function efficiently without the law of agency. If the operator of any business, a veterinarian, does not wish to have agents (employees) represent him he must notify, in writing is best, to all business associates of this fact to be free of liability for the acts of his employees.

A veterinarian employer asks an employee to drive to a nearby pharmacy to pick up some drugs. In carrying out this assignment the employee strikes and injures a pedestrian. The veterinarian, as the principal, may be liable for damages and costs since the employee was acting for and under the direction of the veterinarian. The principal is also responsible for any negligent acts employees may commit during the course of his business, as shown in the case above. (3 AJ 2d 498, 1989)

The relationship between principal and agent is a contractual one, often an oral agreement between the parties laying out the employees duties and specifying the wages to be paid for the work performed. An agent may be employed for a single task or piece of work; a real estate agent to find and aid in the purchase of a site for a veterinary hospital or a contractor to build an addition to one; once the acts are performed to the satisfaction of the parties involved, the contract is terminated.

The employer-employee relationship is part of the law of principal and agent and the law assumes a valid contract exists between a veterinarian and employee who works for him. An animal technician is employed to perform specific tasks for an agreed-upon salary; this is a contractual agreement subject to contract law.   Written agreements of employment can be made listing all duties and salary, but this is an exception, especially with non-professional employees. A veterinarian who represents that a person is his agent, or implies that this is so, causing third parties to rely on the actions of the agent, is liable to such third parties for any harm caused by the lack of care and skill of the agent or employee . The dispensing of drugs or medicines by unlicensed veterinarians, receptionists, technicians, kennelman, or unpaid help without the direction of the veterinarian is illegal (Ackerman 1941, Mod Vet Pract)

Another example of employer responsibility for employees acts is the case where a client brought several puppies to a veterinary hospital for worming. The attending veterinarian left the treatment to an assistant who gave the puppies 10 times the manufacturer's recommended dose of the vermifuge. All of the puppies died - the veterinarian was liable for the loss. (JAMA 1974)

Employer Responsibility
for Injuries to Employees

Since the veterinarian is often responsible for the acts of employees as well as their injuries on-the-job, work-related injuries are included here. A significant number of work-related injuries and disease cost employers a lot of money and lost labor time. The United Nations places work-related accidents on the-job at 180,000 a day, or 50 million per year. In the United States injury rates have increased 14 percent in the past 30 years, with 400,000 occupational injuries annually with 10,000 fatalities. (Morganstern 1982)

In veterinary clinics workers are exposed to several toxic substances as well as detergents and disinfectants. The U. S Bureau of Labor Statistics reported that skin diseases accounted for 37% of all work-related injuries in 1983. One-fourth of work associated skin diseases resulted in an average of 12 days lost from work, and the Bureau estimates it only receives reports on 10% of all skin disease cases. These dermatological cases cost medical insurance companies one billion dollars for the years 1972-1978, or $200,000 a year. (Robinson 1986, President's rep 1978)

In animal facilities employees use toxic compounds which can produce a dermatitis. Exposure to these products can also cause a cough, itching, sinus congestion, dizziness and respiratory distress. Hospital and laboratory personnel exhibit such symptoms twice as frequently as the general population. (Georgetown Law J 1984, Stout-Weigand 1988, Yale Law J 1981)

In veterinary facilities products dangerous to human beings include soaps, organophosphates, pesticides and disinfectants. Cases that emphasize potential dangers to employees are: On a farm 17 persons became ill, with one fatality, after using an organophosphate spray. Patients experienced abdominal pain. nausea, impaired vision, vomiting, sweating and excessive salivation. In another instance, 10 employees of a restaurant had similar symptoms after using an insecticide in the premises. In California in 1984 over 1,000 farm workers exposed to organophosphates became ill with visual disturbances, dizziness, headache, nausea, and irritation of the eyes. In an animal hospital a technician, after using fenthion, developed generalized pains, muscular weakness, and numbness of the hands and feet. Veterinarians should realize their employees may be exposed to several toxic compounds and use protective measures to prevent injuries and damage, such as gloves, masks, eye glasses, boots, protective clothing and have their employees have laboratory monitoring of blood samples for the detection of the presence of chronic toxicity. (MMWR 1977, 1985, Simmons 1982)

Allergies to animal material are common in animal facilities with the symptoms ranging from a mild to severe dermatitis. Sources of animal antigens can be dandruff from animal epithelial cells and aerosols from fecal material and urine. Inhalation of these may produce a dermatitis and respiratory illness. Allergies to chemical aerosols may result in allergic rhinitis, conjunctivitis, bronchial asthma, atopic dermatitis, and anaphylactic shock.

Animal bites, especially dog and cat ones, are a constant employee hazard in veterinary hospital facilities. The U. S. Public Health Service reports over 2 million dog bites a year. These can result in cellulitis, lymphangitis, osteomyelitis, meningitis, brain absesses, bacteremia, and at times death (MMWR 1977, Vesley 1988.)

Employer, master or principal and employee relations have been defined. Under the law minors may be employees and the employer is responsible for their work injuries in many instances. Employers may not be responsible for the injuries to casual employees whose work is of short duration and of a temporary nature (Hood 1984)

An employer faces responsibilities and duties under the common law and, more recently, under statutory laws of the United States; These responsibilities include:

1.   Provide a safe place to work.

2.   Provide safe appliances, tools and equipment.

3.   Give warnings of dangers employees might not be aware of or suspect in their work.

4.   Provide fit, trained and suitable fellow workers to perform the assigned task.

5.   Establish and enforce rules governing employee conduct that contribute to a safe place to work.

6.   Identify hazardous substances and explain safe handling procedures for these.

7.   Disclose to all parties at risk the possible hazards they might encounter at work.

8.   Provide accessory equipment when necessary — gowns, mask, gloves, goggles, shoe covers, boots, etc.

9.   Monitor possible damaging exposure to hazardous substances through laboratory tests.

10.   Provide medical care and supervision appropriate for the work hazards. A significant duty because employers commonly fail to warn employees of dangerous work conditions, (Baram 1984)

The employer is usually responsible for employee injuries. At times the manufacturer of equipment or supplies may be liable if their products do not meet safety requirements before, while and after the buyer (employer) uses them. Manufacturers must demonstrate to courts their products are:

1.   Designed and constructed as safely as possible.

2.   Adequately tested for safety.

3.   Not marketed until proved to be safe.

4.   Sold with adequate directions for use.

5.   Marked with understandable labels for use and with warnings of toxic and hazardous contents of the products. (Stapleton 1986)

When the owner of an animal entrusts its custody to someone else, a member of the family or an employee, master and servant or principal and agent, they are generally charged with having the same knowledge of the animal as the owner. If someone's animal is known to be dangerous then anyone who keeps or harbors that animal is liable if he or she has that same knowledge.

Defendant owns and operates a dairy farm where the plaintiff, a herdsman for 15 years and the defendant's employee for 3, was kicked and injured by one of the defendant's cows as he was trying to attach an electrically operated milking apparatus to the cow. Plaintiff sued contending that the owner kept a vicious, dangerous animal and was negligent in his operation of the dairy. Defendant counters saying that the plaintiff assumed the risks attached to his employment. Finding was for the defendant the court saying that the herdsman with 15 years experience assumed the ordinary risks attached to his employment. (Hatched v Field 120 SE 2d 401, 1961)

Plaintiff and son went to a stable to rent horses to ride. An attendant saddled up horses and helped the plaintiff to mount. As plaintiff mounted the stirrup slipped and as the attendant was adjusting this a dog came out and charged the horse, barking and snapping at his legs. The horse shied and bolted, throwing the plaintiff to the ground and dragging him bout 20 feet. Plaintiff, for his son's sake, remounted and road a while. Later, on going to a hospital, plaintiff found he had fractured a vertebrae. Finding was for the plaintiff, the attendant of the riding stable, as an employee of the owner and his agent. had prior knowledge that the dog had previously frightened the horse and this knowledge was attached to the owner also. (Herbert v Ziegler 139 A 2d 699, 1958)

A veterinarian and former university employee, brought suit against the university for wrongful discharge. The supreme court of the state held the employee could mount an action for wrongful discharge where he conceded he was a contractual employee as a licensed veterinarian with the assignment of assuring university compliance with the Animal Welfare Act. The veterinarian held he was wrongfully discharged for reporting abuses of the Act to his superiors and perhaps to others outside the university. (Luethaus v Washington University, 894 SW 2d 189, 1995)

A former employee brought charges against a veterinarian for violation of state and federal wage payment and employment discrimination laws, charging tortious discharge, fraudulent misrepresentation and slander. The employee veterinarian presented evidence that the employer veterinarian retaliated against the employee when she filed a claim for unemployment compensation.

The employee veterinarian failed to show she performed the same duties as two other male veterinary employees and failed to establish a violation of the equal pay provisions of the Act. The employers inquiries of co-workers of the plaintiff (veterinarian) as to whether or not she had drug or alcohol problems amounted to slander. Slander per se is actionable without proof of harm. Employee veterinarian was awarded monetary damages and attorney's fees. (Lara v Thomas 512 NW Ed 777, 1994)

In Brandon v Molesworth, 855 A 2d 1292, 1995, a former veterinarian employee brought an action against the employer for wrongful common law discharge. Brandon when a veterinary medical student was employed by Molesworth and when she graduated she came to work full time for routine care of horses. There were complaints which she attributed to being a female. Molesworth contended there were many complaints regarding her work as being of poor quality, with an inflexible attitude. Witnesses from the race track supported the complaint of poor work and inflexibility, she contends she was fired because of gender. The judge informed the court that if they found the hirer and firer was the same person and the employment period was short the jury could infer the discharge was not due to discrimination. The case was recommended for a new trial.

A woman veterinary employee of a humane society hospital brought an action against her former employers alleging discrimination on the basis of gender. After several years at the hospital she was paid less than male employees, she stated, and was fired without notice or warning and asked to leave in 15 minutes. Finding was for the woman veterinarian. (McMillan v SPCA 880 F Supp 900, 1995)

An employer veterinarian attempted to prevent employee veterinarian from appearing for jury duty. She sued for harassment and for being fired due to her actions. Finding was for the employee veterinarian and employer paid costs and fine. (Levy-Wegrzyn v Ediger and Kinredge Animal Hospital 899 P 2d 230, 1994)

Worker's Responsibilities

Workers have a duty to their employers to take reasonable care for their safety on the job and to consider the safety of fellow workers they come into contact with in their employment duties. An employer is not liable for injuries due to an employee's negligence, such as failure to follow orders, intoxication on the job, use of drugs or unacceptable behavior such as fooling around or misinforming or misleading fellow workers. Employees must behave reasonably and with responsibility. Employees performing personal business while on a work-related errand may relieve the employer of responsibility for injury. (Morganstern 1982)

Right to Know

Both common and statutory law give employees the right to know the health risks of their job. By 1985 most states in the United States had enacted right-to-know laws. The rationale behind such laws being that if employees know the dangers associated with their work they can make their own decisions regarding the risk-acceptability of the job. (NLRA 1976)

The Occupational Safety and Health Act (OSHA) of 1970 prohibits an employer from discriminating against an employee who exercises a right provided for by the Act. An employee has the right to choose not to perform an assigned task because of a reasonable fear of danger or injury. In most instances an employer can meet the right-to-know requirements of the Act by having safety programs informing employees of possible hazards connected with employment. (Areen 1984, OSHA 1970)

Health monitoring and screening of employees can also aid employers meet their responsibilities for worker protection. For example, monitoring workers for total body radiation can decrease employer liability. (ORB 1988) Employees have questioned medical screening programs as being a violation of personal rights and, in some instances, as an unwarranted exercise of power by an employer. Even so, if medical monitoring is a reasonable precaution for disease and injury prevention of employees, it should be used. (Ann Inst Med 1987, Field 1988, Mine 1986)

Worker's Compensation

A review of collective bargaining agreements showed 62 percent contained OSHA provisions. Most of these met minimal federal, state and local requirements. Under minimal requirements an employee may recover on a no-fault basis if an injury or disease is work-related. No fault means the employee did not contribute to his or her injury and it was due to the employer's failure to perform his required duties. However, in reality, only a small fraction of work-associated injuries receive compensation for these. (Raines 1988, Atherly 1988, Boyer 1988, Haluska)

Problems with employee compensation programs are:

1.   Employers have little incentive to spend time and money to prevent occupational diseases and injuries.

2.   Many workers cannot detect when they have a work-related illness. Length of incubation period, obscure symptoms, and the difficulty of connecting an illness with work make recovery for work-related illness difficult.

3.   It is difficult for employees to prove an illness is work-related or
      to demonstrate the no-fault requirement.

4   Because of the difficulty of proof in work-related disease and
      injuries employees seldom bring compensation cases to court.

5.   Workers may have to pay the fees for attorneys and court costs.

8.   Statutes of limitation often pass before an employee associates an
      illness with the workplace.

7.   Filing a compensation suit may jeopardize an employee's job
      security and future promotion. (Georgetown Law J 1984)

       Management and employers must realize their legal and moral
responsibilities to protect employee health and safety and institute
satisfactory occupational health programs. In the final analysis these
protect both the employer and the employee. Healthy employees with
little sick leave are an asset and save employers money. Medical
insurance, sick-leave and malingering are expensive and if these can be
reduced it is to employers advantage. (Off Tech Assess 1983, Miller
1984)
       State worker's compensation law is a humane law whose
fundamental purpose is to provide employees and their dependents
prompt and definite compensation, with a quick and effective remedy for
injury or death suffered in the course of employment. (ALR Dig 1995)
       Usually, the test for compensation for an injury is whether the
employee, at the time of the injury, was engaged in work which
reasonably would have been expected of him and which he should have
been expected to do under the terms of his employment. (West's Calif.
Dig 2d, 1982)
       Employees of animal hospitals are at risk for exposure to animal
intestinal parasites, enteric bacteria, viruses, pathogenic organisms,
animal bites and scratches. In addition to the exposure to animals other
dangers for employees include the mechanical equipment, toxic chemicals
and contact with drugs.
       Employers of veterinarians, technicians, and temporary help should
know their legal responsibilities and requirements to protect their

workers and prevent lawsuits for work-associated injuries or disease. Employers are responsible for their workers and, at times, for casual workers, volunteers and visitors on their premises for business matters. Coverage by worker's compensation laws at one time excluded non-profit and charitable organizations. Now, the law considers non-profit entities, such as universities, responsible for work-related injuries. (Stapleton 1988)

Managing Time and People

If you are engaged in an enterprise to make money you are in business; this is true of professionals, doctors, lawyers, veterinarians, dentists, as well as the bank president. To be successful you must find ways to save money, cut down on waste, determine the best way to spend your time most productively and effectively, and how to get the greatest effort from employees without alienating them.

Thousands of studies have been made on the subject of people management; how best to do it, what is the most successful approach. Graduate Schools of Business devote much of their time to the issue and publish numerous papers and books on how-to-do-it. There is no single solution for the conscientious manager to follow that will run his business for him with the least possible trauma. Different people handle similar problems differently, yet achieve laudable results. However, the experience of experts on time and people management offer ideas to business persons that can help them to effectively and successfully accomplish their missions.

Often quoted is the statement that good managers and executives are born, not trained. There may be inherent traits in some individuals that make them good managers, but people can be trained to apply the types of leadership that best fits their personality for the operation of their business. It is often a matter of knowing or realizing what you can or cannot do. What are your limitations and what are your strong points? Items to be considered are:

1.   Record and find out where the time goes, eliminate unnecessary time-wasters. Your administrator or secretary are essential for this job.

2.   Focus on contributions; what is your job in the total picture and that of your employees.

3.   Determine your strong points, emphasize these and make them productive. The problem here is that people often think that their weak points are the strong ones.

4.   Productive executives have a serious purpose toward what they produce. They have determination and dedication.

5.   Determine what needs to be done and in what sequence.

6.   Develop good work habits, unlearn bad ones.

7.   In the final analysis, being an effective manager is simply doing ones's job.

8.   The good manager raises the level of performance of the entire organization by his or her actions — doing the job, not goofing off. (Drucker 1987)

How much money do, or should one, make an hour? Can people who depend on me afford to have me waste my time? You should know what your time is worth and how you can get the most out of it. The more responsibility one has the more valuable their time becomes. How many people are depending on you for their house payment, grocery money? The more responsibility one has the more difficult it becomes to spend time more effectively; more help means more people asking for solutions, what to do, how to do it.

The value of a managers time is significant. If fringe benefits are figured at 40% of a salary, a manager getting paid $50,000 a year has an hourly wage of 34 dollars, at $60,000 this becomes 40 dollars, at $75,000 it is 50 dollars and at $100,000 annual income this is 67 dollars an hour.

The concept of time management was in use long before the industrial age. Twelve hundred years ago Charlemagne (742-814 A.D.) king of the Franks used candles having horizontal stripes painted around them. As the candle burned it showed the time persons spent on official duties, or taking up the king's time. When the candle burned down to the next stripe, the appointment was over. (Dorney 1988)

Directors and managers of large veterinary clinics are responsible for the operation of a significant business for its physical and financial success. Such a business may have 12 to 15 persons as employees with a gross budget of over one million dollars; not General Motors, but not bad for a small professional operation.

As a manager organizes, coordinates, plans and controls the activities of his unit many of the bosses activities last less than 30 minutes, only about 10% an hour or more. Working uninterrupted on one problem for an hour or more is rare. (Mineberg 1980)

Some ideas for managing your time:

1.   Select the maximum activities you should engage in, how you should spend your time and why.

2.   Delegate; this is a managers greatest need and the privilege of being a boss, but also the most difficult for some to do — to let go of some of their functions. Can someone else do the job as well as you can and thereby free you for more important activities?

3.   Do not spend too much time away from business. Being away from the job decreases your effectiveness and, more important, allows employees to shirk their duties.

4.   Try to minimize interruptions and control the demands on your time; do not become unapproachable to achieve this. There is nothing worse than giving clients the feeling of being brushed off.

5.   Use blocks of time for important activities that must be done; budgets, reports, reading business journals, employee evaluation, etc.

A quote from Parkinson says, "Work expands so as to fill the time for its completion." The more time one has to do a job, the longer it will take. (Perkins 1973)

The most efficient operations have six attributes in common to achieve excellence:

1.   A bias for action, getting on with it.

2.   Stay close to the customer; know what the people you serve want
      and what they need.

3.   Give your employees some freedom of expression.

4.   The more you respect your employees and their needs, the more
      productive they will be.

5.   Hands On, walk the floors, know what is going on in your
      operation.

6.   Stay with what you know, do not try to run something you know
      little or nothing about. People can tell when you are bluffing. You
      can usually hire someone to do things you cannot do.

The more a manager expects from his subordinates the better they perform. A managers expectations must be real, workers will not try to reach a high level of performance if they feel it is unrealistic or an impossible goal. Conversely, little or no motivation occurs when a goal is set that is seen by employees as being too easy or conversely, impossible to achieve.

Fortunately, in the work place workers do what they think is expected of them; if they are treated by the boss as the best they will try to live up to this image

Effective managers have self-confidence in their ability to achieve high productivity from their people. They don't give up.

The communication of a boss's expectations have a psychological influence on the help. For example, if a doctor exudes confidence that a patient will recover, chances for his recovery are greater than when the doctor is indifferent or has a defeatist attitude. Similarly, employees who are treated as if they have no chance of doing a better job are poor or low producers.

A severe way to influence employees is referred to as the KITA method, a kick-in-the ass, or fear method. This may work but it has disadvantages; it has a short time effect, it is in poor taste, it is contrary to the benevolence of management and you might get kicked back! Better motivating factors are being well-organized, set goals for employees to achieve, let employees know why they are doing what they are doing and how their work affects the whole picture. (Parkinson 1980, Peters 1982, Livingston 1988, Rosenthal 1988) The bottom line is:

> If you have employees on a job, use them.

> If you can't use them, get rid of them.

> If you can't use them and can't get rid of them, you have a work motivation problem.(Berlew 1966, Herzberg 1987, Lorsch 1987)

In hiring employees it is good policy to request references from former employers regarding the previous performance of a prospective employee. In giving references for a former employee a veterinarian should be fair and accurate. A former employee may sue the veterinarian if false or misleading statements are made in evaluating an employee. (Hadley 1977)

The employer should treat every employee fairly and consistently; set realistic goals to achieve and keep morale high by being interested in the employee as a person, one who is necessary in the operation. Work expectations and policies should be clearly and directly stated, employee performance noted and discussed with employees and they should be helped to improve their work habits, output and efficiency. Employees like to know what is expected of them and if they are doing a good job. They like to be treated like fellow workers, human beings, not slaves. (Krames Commun 1988)

Partnerships

A partnership contains many elements of agency since one partner is considered, in business dealings, as being the agent for the other partner(s). The business of one binds all of the remaining partners liable to the extent of all of their business holdings and their personal fortunes. This is the reason groups of professionals forming a practice together open incorporate. Under usual circumstances members of a corporation are only liable to the extent of the corporate assets, not for their personal belongings.

When physicians and surgeons, and veterinarians, are in a partnership all are liable in damages for the professional negligence of one of the partners. The act of one, dealing within the scope of partnership business, is the act of each and all of the partners as if each one were present and participating in all that has been done. (Haase 1908, Hyrne 1898)

Most of the states of the U. S. have adopted the Uniform Partnership Act. The Act controls the relationship between partners and the business dealings of the partnership with third parties, that is other people. The purpose of the Act is to develop national unity and to standardize interstate rules on partnerships. The pertinent sections of the Act are:

Partners defined: A partnership is an association of two or more people to carry on as co-owners of a business for profit. Receipt by a partner of a share of the profits of the business is evidence that he is indeed a partner in that business. A partnership may be formed by businesses which include every trade, occupation, or profession.

Property: All property originally brought into the partnership, or subsequently acquired by purchase or otherwise, is partnership property, including all property purchased or acquired with partnership funds. If it is the intent of the partnership, the share of property of a deceased partner may pass to the surviving partners. This is usually included in the partnership agreement

Agency: Every partner is an agent for the partnership and the act of each and every partner in carrying on the business in the usual manner for the partnership binds all of the other partners.

Relationship of partners: In general, partners are paid for their contribution to the partnership. They should be insured (indemnified) to protect each other from losses and liabilities. They have equal rights in the management of the business, access to records and accounts relating to the partnership. Partnerships do not have to be divided equally, provisions may be made for partners to have a one quarter or one third interest in the business.

Dissolution and winding up: Dissolution of a partnership is a change in partnership relations where a partner(s) cease to be associated with the partnership. The partnership is terminated by dissolution. Causes of dissolution may be: the termination of one of the partner's term, through agreement of the partners, expulsion of a partner by the others, bankruptcy of one or all partners, or death of a partner. The court may dissolve a partnership when one partner is declared of unsound mind, one is incapable of carrying on the business, physically or for other reasons, a breach of the partnership agreements, financial loss or ruin, and at the end of a specified previously agreed upon time for the existence of the partnership

A partnership may be wound-up, or cease to exist, upon the mutual agreement of the partners, providing no illegal or criminal acts are involved, all necessary accounting and financial requirements are met, records are available for inspection by the courts if necessary, property and monies are divided as required legally, debts and liabilities are satisfied, unfinished business is completed or provisions are made for its satisfactory conclusions.

Corporate Practice

Professional corporations are of relatively recent origin. Previously, courts ruled that a corporation could not practice a profession. The relationship between a professional and client was considered too personal and intimate to be carried on by a corporate entity, created by law and not a real person. Today, for professionals to incorporate, all members of the corporation must be licensed to practice their profession. In veterinary medicine a veterinarian-client-patient relationship must exist. (See Chapter 5, Protection of Animals, FDA) Reasons for professional corporations are to relieve individuals from personal liability as exists in partnerships, and to gain some federal, and sometimes state, tax benefits extended to business corporations.

In addition, a corporation protects its members from malpractice claims or lawsuits through insurance, buys and owns property, employs personnel to manage the business, keeps accounts and records, does the purchasing, and performs all the functions a real person can perform. (Hannah 1989, 81 AJ 2d 1978)

The Revised Model Business Corporation Act covers all of the requirements of corporations; creation, functions, duties, etc. Incorporation requires legal assistance to insure the completion and filing of the appropriate documents with the state office involved, to be certain all of the articles of incorporation are correct, adequately covered and included. Often the services of an accountant are needed to manage financial affairs, establish fringe benefits, retirement and medical care programs.

In human medical practice over 80% of physicians favor incorporation. Advantages include pension funds, profit-sharing, fixed annual salary, withholding of federal and state taxes, family medical and dental plans, retirement benefits which are often much more than are those for individual practitioners. For veterinarians incorporation depends on several factors; location of the practice, size of geographical area covered, growth potential, the need for specialists in the locality, and the number of veterinary practitioners in the general area. Veterinarians should seek legal and financial advice to decide if incorporation applies to their practice. (Model Bus Corp Act 1993, Garlick 1982)

In spite of the advantage of limited liability of members of a corporation there are times when the courts may override this protection given by corporations and pierce the corporate veil. The major reasons for courts to do this are:

1.   When several corporations are formed with inadequate control over each one. This is called the alter ego or instrumentality doctrine.

2.   Inadequate capitalization.

3.   Fraud — when the corporation exists for fraudulent reasons.

4.   Criminal acts.

5.   Corporate violation of the Environmental Protection Act. (Seligmen 1995)

Associations

There are no legal requirements that require a person to be a member of a professional association as a prerequisite to practicing his or her profession. A licensed practitioner does not have to be a member of the local, state or national professional association of his or her specialty. There are several advantages to belonging to a professional association, aside from fellowship, one receives continuing education, insurance possibilities, opportunities for investment, and as a group to protect the professional interests through political influence.

Non-profit associations are groups of natural persons organized for religious, scientific, social, literary, recreational, benevolent or other reasons not monetary. When an individual joins an unincorporated association there is an implied obligation to pay dues, if these are a part of the rules for members, and to abide by the principles of the organization. An unincorporated association is not a legal entity and cannot enter into contracts, sue or be sued, or bind all of the members to contractual agreements. Courts have found it difficult to identify the legal position of unincorporated groups and often apply the law of agency to them.

Under the law of agency an individual member of an unincorporated association may be personally liable for the acts of an officer or another member if the act was authorized by the membership. A non-profit society differs from a partnership in the view of some courts that feel only those members are liable for an action of the organization who expressly, or by implication, approved the act. If the members of an unincorporated association agree to purchase an award, and the secretary does so, the membership is liable for the reasonable cost of the award. This is predicated on the assumption that the purchaser of the award is a member and has acted as an agent for the entire group.

When a valid committee of an association enters into a contract, all members are personally liable, even though they had no knowledge the contract was being consummated. The committee has served as the agent for all of the members. (Lapp 1911)

When members of an unincorporated society have authorized a specific act and the cost, or damages, that result are greater than the amount of money in the treasury the entire membership is responsible for the debt. Officers of an association performing an act that damages other nonmember persons makes all members liable and they may be sued jointly or separately. Each member is liable for the debts of an association incurred during membership which are considered necessary and contracted for the purpose of carrying out the objectives of the association. (McDonald 1925) To improve the situation some state legislatures have modified the legal requirements of non-profit organizations, saying that no presumption or inference exists that a member of a not-for-profit association has consented or agreed to the incurring of any obligation by the association from the act of joining or becoming a member of an organization or by the act of signing its by-laws. Further, members of a non-profit association are not individually or personally liable for debts or liabilities incurred by the association in the acquisition of land or the purchase, lease, designing, planning, architectural supervision, construction, repair or furnishings of buildings or other structures to be used for the purposes of the association. (Smyth 1948)

When creditors have a claim against an unincorporated association, theoretically a suit must be entered against each member; all being joined together as the defendants. To simplify these legal actions, where numerous persons are all joined together in a single lawsuit, courts often allow one, or a few persons, to be named as representatives of the entire group. To include 2000 or 5000 members as plaintiffs or defendants in a lawsuit becomes unmanageable.

The American Veterinary
Medical Association
[AVMA]

The AVMA is an incorporated nonprofit association and is governed by corporate law as applied to non-profit organizations. The AVMA enjoys a large percent of the eligible veterinarians in the United States as members. Such strength makes the organization a strong arbiter of the professional and ethical conduct of the membership.

The association is governed by an executive board which acts as its administrative body. Members of the board are elected from 11 districts of the U.S., each for 6 year terms. The House of Delegates is the legislative body and consists of delegates and their alternates from the states and affiliated associations. The Executive Board and the House are elected by the membership, the officers by the House. Officers are: president, president-elect, vice president, treasurer, and executive vice president who is not elected but employed by the executive board. The Board of Governors (president, president-elect, and the chairman of the executive board) act for the executive board between its regular meetings

The AVMA has 7 councils: judicial, education, research, veterinary service, biologic and therapeutic agents, public health and regulatory veterinary medicine, and government relations. Members of the councils are elected by the House of Delegates.

The Judicial Council consists of 5 members elected for staggered 5 year terms. This council handles disciplinary actions including dismissal of members. Disciplinary options are censure, suspension, expulsion, or probation. Infraction categories are: (1) violation of the constitution or by-laws of the AVMA, (2) violation of the principles of veterinary medical ethics, (3) conviction of a felony or a crime involving moral turpitude, (4) guilt or other behavior detrimental to the profession. The judicial council may elect to hear individual cases upon complaint by a person or a constituent association. Procedures for notice and hearing of the accused are in "Rules of Disciplinary Procedures of the Judicial Council of the AVMA."

The council also has jurisdiction over all questions of ethics and the interpretation of the constitution, by-laws and the rules of the AVMA. The Judicial Council is empowered by the AVMA by-laws to investigate general professional conditions and all matters pertaining to the relations of veterinarians to one another or to the public, and to make recommendations to the House of Delegates or constituent associations as it deems necessary.

For effective day-to-day operation of the association appointees or employees run and manage daily operational functions. The president, executive secretary and full time employees have the powers to carry on all the functions required for effective performance and the mission of the organization. It is not feasible to poll the membership each time a check must be written or a new employee be hired. In contrast, the formation of policy and major operational functions are decided by the general membership, indirectly through the Executive Board and the House of Delegates. The names of the other councils indicate their function.

The Sherman Antitrust Act

By the late 1890's in the United States a vast amount of wealth and power was under the control of a relatively few individuals and large corporations. Such an imbalance in money and influence created fear and apprehension in the general public that these combinations of wealth and power would result in the control of commerce by large monopolies with the interests of the public becoming secondary and of little importance.

In 1890 to prevent such an occurrence Congress passed the Sherman Antitrust Act. Its aim was to preserve competition, prevent or suppress devices or practices which create monopolies or restrain trade or commerce by eliminating competition and otherwise obstruct the course of trade. Congress further deemed illegal and unenforceable contracts that suspended competition and any agreements to fix prices, divide marketing territories, apportion customers, restrict production,, and any like practices which result in higher prices or otherwise take away from buyers or customers the advantages which accrue to them from the existence of free competition in the market place. (March 1890)

Since the passage of the Sherman Antitrust Act professional organizations and their members have considered themselves outside of the terms of the Act. The argument for their exemption was based on three premises:

1.   The Act prohibits the restraint of trade; a profession is not a trade.

2.   The Act applies to the conduct of private business, it does not prohibit the government's conduct of business. Most state and national professional associations derive from the government their authority to exercise control and supervision over their profession and members, hence they should be exempt from the powers of the Act.

3.   Antitrust laws deal with the conduct and business arrangements that are commercially motivated and are not applicable to the actions and structure of organizations whose basic motivating forces are not economic but to serve the public.

The legal case which placed the professions within the meaning of the Sherman Act was a case of price-fixing by an association. The association held the practice of law was a learned profession and not within the meaning of a trade or commerce under the language of the Act. The court said, "The exchange of a service for money is commerce. It is no disparagement to the practice of a profession to acknowledge that it has a business aspect. Price-fixing is in violation of paragraph one of the Act.

Since this decision the United States Department of Justice has attempted to expand the application of the Act to include bans on professional advertising, distinctions between open and closed practices, price-fixing, dividing by professionals of practice areas, limiting membership in professional organizations to certain individuals, boycotts of professionals for insufficient reasons, and restricting hospital use to specific persons. A judge said, "One can search in vain for a connection between professional ethics and price-fixing and one cannot find that price-fixing is ethical. The setting of a fee raises a conflict of interest between the profession and the client he is providing services for. (Bender 1942, Smyth 1949)

Portions of the Sherman Antitrust Act that apply to the veterinary profession are:

1.   Limited restrictive covenants are legal.

2.   Advertising by veterinarians is permissible.

3.   Price-fixing is illegal.

4.   Actions that result in preventing competition are illegal.

5.   Attempts to limit the number of veterinarians in a specific area may be illegal

6.   Accreditation of hospitals or individuals if unreasonable is illegal.

7.   Unreasonable licensing requirements are illegal.

Advertising

The right of practitioners of the healing arts to advertise their experience and abilities was prohibited for years as being unworthy of the learned professions and unethical. Recent court decisions have changed the ban on publicizing professional services. The case legally permitting professional advertising was decided in 1977. The court decided a ban on promoting one's services, orally or in writing, was contrary to the First Amendment of the U.S. Constitution; freedom of speech. Some restrictions on advertising continue to be in force, these being: advertising cannot be false or misleading, fees and discounts or endorsements of products are prohibited. Indications that secret remedies are used, or unknown ones, and the publication of case reports of successful treatments are not allowed. Fixed fee advertising for specific treatments and a notice that credit cards are accepted, notice of membership in a specialty board, lists of services available, dispensing cards, calendars, and the use of personal or hospital names on a vehicle are all allowed.

In 1980 the American Medical Association was ordered by the Federal Trade Commission to cease and desist from promulgating and enforcing restrictions on advertising by their members. Permission for members of the medical profession to advertise was upheld. (AMA v FTC 638 F 2d 443,1980)

Records

The maintenance of complete and accurate records is an important factor in safeguarding against lawsuits and in protecting oneself in the event of litigation. Courts give significant weight to records written at the time an animal is treated or during or immediately following a transaction. Records should include name, address of client, description of animal(s), diagnosis, treatment, drugs used, date, diagnostic procedures; x-rays or laboratory tests, subsequent visits, discharge dates, outcome of the case. Financial information may be kept separately. In a case against a veterinarian, the client was assured that x-rays had been taken of their animal. An examination of the medical records showed no evidence or notation that x-rays had been taken; poor record-keeping or the client was misled.

Protection against lawsuits is not the primary reason for the keeping of adequate records. These are essential for recording medical histories, to assemble scientific knowledge, as a learning process, and for regular clients, to follow their animals and know their medical history and what treatments have been previously used. Also, notes regarding euthanasia and disposal of an animal are important inclusions. A request to destroy an animal from a minor child should be verified before proceeding. It is safest to hold the animal until the owner, or an adult representative, can sign a form for disposal of an animal. Requirement for a release form for euthanasia can save a veterinarian grief at a later date (Laridasn 1951, Trial Law Guide 1988, Hawaii Law Rev 1982)

Surgery or treatment of an animal, like euthanasia, by a minor should be approached with caution. Does the minor really know what the owner intended with respect to treatment? It is best to speak to the owner of an animal before proceeding. (New York Law Rev 1988)

Some states of the U.S. have legal requirements governing what constitutes satisfactory and acceptable medical records. These should be investigated since some of the information will apply to veterinary hospitals and can give an indication of the type and extent of records to be maintained. Records are the property of the hospital or proprietor of the practice preparing them. The surrender of records depends on the veterinarian. In lawsuits records may be demanded by the court and must be made available. (Wl Bar Bull 1984)

Keeping medical records is time-consuming, tedious and unrewarding, but necessary. Evidence for lawsuits is a very minor reason for good records, however, when these arise, it is advantageous to have good records. These are given a lot of credence by courts because they, ostensibly, were made at or near the time of treatment, are presumed to be accurate, and serve as evidence of what was done. After the death of a veterinarian records from the practice should be kept for a time specified by state or local statutes. The estates of deceased veterinarians have been held accountable even though the wrong-doing veterinarian is dead. (DeVincenzi 1959)

Acceptable records as court evidence are written memorandums, case records, log books, health and vaccination certificate copies made at the time the service was performed. These can be shown to the court or jury and serve as an indication of the intent of the parties and what medical service was performed. It is important to keep certificates of vaccinations, dates of visits, records of charges, medicines given or dispensed. All such information is good evidence in the event of a lawsuit. Local, state and the national organization may provide guidelines for acceptable records.

A veterinarian presented oral evidence that he had treated some hogs for sale and made certificates of this act. The oral statement was held by the court to be inadmissible because the actual certificates should have been produced for the court to examine. (43 FFDCA 1988)

In an action for the death of a horse, recovery for fees for the veterinarian's services were held unauthorized where there was no evidence of the charges made or of the value of the services rendered. (Colorado Lawyer 1990)

Nuisance

The courts have been struggling with this word for centuries. It is a word with many definitions; obnoxious, annoying, offensive. It also has several interpretations and shades of meanings. Legal scholars have said there is no greater impenetrable jungle in law than the word nuisance and its interpretations by the courts. A nuisance is a type of wrong or tort, which infringes on the right of peaceful and quiet enjoyment of life. As such, nuisances can be abated by law. A public nuisance is an act or omission which interferes with the interests of the community, or comfort and convenience of the general public, including interference with the public health. Public nuisances usually affect a whole community, neighborhood, or a large number of persons. It may constitute a danger or an irritation to the public. A private nuisance is an actionable interference with a private person's use and enjoyment of his land.

Nuisance is the use of property in such a way that it interferes with the use by others of their property; noise, odors, filth, vermin, insects, interference with water supply, drainage, or waste disposal. Even if a nuisance statute is not in force, if the behavior of a person or persons adversely affects other persons in their peaceful enjoyment of their property, such behavior may be deemed a nuisance by the courts and the guilty one forced to desist. (Bruister 1958)

Nuisance may be, or can become, an important factor in the operation of a veterinary practice or an animal hospital. This is not uncommon with so many hospitals located in a city, often on the boundary of a residential district. Barking dogs, unpleasant odors, unsanitary refuse or effluence of possible infectious or toxic materials can be annoying and dangerous to the health of the surrounding public. At common law, if a business, a veterinary hospital, was in existence before the residential community expanded into the area it is not considered to be a nuisance, per se. It becomes one if it is operated in a negligent, careless or inconsiderate manner. The fact that the animal hospital was there first does not make it immune from becoming a nuisance. Veterinary hospitals have been excluded from being built in business districts prohibiting the maintenance of a nuisance because of the potential of this type of business to create a nuisance. (ALR 3d 1987)

A retired person sought an injunction against a veterinarian because the dogs in his kennel created a nuisance due to their disturbing barking at night. An injunction was granted against the veterinarian. (ALR 4th 1987)

A veterinarian maintained a hospital in a residential part of a city, keeping sick animals and barking dogs. The public walked by in front of the hospital, exposed to diseased and noisy animals. The court held the veterinarian was creating a public nuisance and ordered abatement. (Hannah 1993)

A veterinary hospital, located on 3 acres of land, was subsequently incorporated into the city. The practice grew and eventually included an animal cemetery. A citizen claimed the business was a nuisance and should be abated. The veterinarian defended by saying he was there before the objecting party and should not be interfered with. The court held differently, stating conditions had changed and the hospitals activities amounted to a nuisance. (NW 2d 1978)

The mere suspicion that the operation of a veterinary hospital may become a nuisance is not sufficient to interfere with the business. The operation of a dog and cat hospital is not a nuisance per se and its operation cannot be prevented unless it does become a nuisance. (Calif App 3 rd. 1984)

A plaintiff files a suit to enjoin the construction of a broiler house in a residential area, stating it would constitute a nuisance and also be a sanitary hazard. The plaintiff was granted injunctive relief as the court agreed the operation of the plant would produce the ill effects claimed by the plaintiff. (Griffin v Newman 123 SE 2d 723, 1982)

The defendant company owns a building where poultry are fattened, slaughtered and prepared for market. The plant is in an industrial complex which contains a coal yard, creamery, ice house, etc. Nearby is a small residential area, the residents of which charge they are subjected to foul and offensive odors, offal is hauled away in an open truck, and the crowing of roosters at night is bothersome. The court found for the defendant plant and refused an injunction, but instructed the plant to employ measures to reduce offensive odors and practices. The plant employs a large number of employees, has a substantial payroll and the residential area is small. (Higgins v Decorah Prod Co 242 NW 109,1932)

A city ordinance prohibited the raising, keeping, maintenance or handling of pigeons, chickens, geese, ducks, turkeys, guinea hens, rabbits, mice, rats, pigs, sheep, goats, cows, horses or any birds, fowl or rodents, or animals detrimental to the public health and general welfare, on any parcel, lot, or sublot within the village limits which parcel has less than 8000 square feet of area. The plaintiff maintains pigeons in a loft of a garage with no odors, vermin, rodents, etc and the loft is maintained in a sanitary manner. The court said a city council is presumed to have good reasons for passing the ordinance and the court is not authorized to substitute its judgment for the city council so long as the ordinance is passed under a valid exercise of the powers granted to it. In this case, due to the sanitary condition of the pigeon loft and the care spent in its maintenance, the court found the ordinance unreasonable and arbitrary. (Hahn v City of Brooklyn 153 NE 2d 359, 1958)

The state filed a complaint to enjoin the operation of a training track for greyhound dogs as a public nuisance. Live rabbits are released into an enclosure from which they cannot escape and greyhounds let into the enclosure to chase rabbits, catch them and chew them up. In the second part of the operation live rabbits are attached to a mechanical device and propelled around a track with the dogs chasing them, often catching them and chewing them to pieces. The court held this certainly may be a violation of a statute on cruelty to animals, but is not necessarily a public nuisance. (Kiper v State of FL 310 So 2d 42, 1975)

Plaintiff shared her residence with 50 dogs, was charged with keeping a public nuisance, ordered to get rid of all but a few of the dogs and placed on probation for one year. Probation was violated and finally the dogs were picked up by the humane society and eventually killed when plaintiff failed to find homes for the animals or make other arrangements. Plaintiff sues for destruction of property and mental suffering. Decision for the county def. (Romero v Santa Clara Co. 3 Cal App 3d 700, 1970)

Consider this as a potential nuisance; A 1000 pound horse produces about 20,000 pounds of manure a year. What does the horse owner do with this and what about odors, filth, flies and the unpleasantness

Many states have statutes with the intent to protect farmers from nuisance suits who have been in operation for a long time before the surrounding, complaining parties. So long as the farmer is not negligent or careless in the operation of his business, such statutes have been considered necessary to protect the farm industry because suburbs have spread into what was once prime agricultural areas. (NE 2d 1978)

Remedies Against Nuisance

The remedies against a nuisance are a suit at law for damages, a suit in equity to enjoin or abate the nuisance, a summary abatement by the government and the imposition of a penalty or revocation of a license for violation of a statute or ordinance against some nuisances. The last remedy is important because a veterinarian, creating a nuisance and refusing to desist, could lose the license to practice. A veterinary hospital may become a nuisance but is not considered to be so just because it is an animal hospital. (Stat Law Rev 1992)

In a case where the defendant proposed to erect a veterinary hospital on his land the findings of the court were that his building would not be a nuisance and the business, if properly conducted, would be acceptable to the community and therefore no reason existed to prevent construction of the hospital. (Blair 1951)

Noise is not the only factor that may constitute a nuisance; odors, garbage, and objectionable sights may also be offenders. Any situation that annoys the public and is an infringement upon their right to peace and quiet enjoyment of their property and neighborhood amounts to an annoyance or nuisance.Courts have invariably ruled that citizens have the right to enjoy the confines of their homes or property without disturbance.

Zoning

The freedom to use one's property as one sees fit is conditioned by legislation, including local ordinances, statutes and contractual restrictions between persons. Veterinarians may be affected, in some cases completely restricted, by city and county zoning laws. If a veterinary hospital is established before a zoning law is put into effect, the practice may be continued as a non-conforming use even though the area now prohibits the operation of a veterinary practice; the business may continue to legally function in spite of the change in zoning.

Zoning ordinances of cities are very important to veterinarians desiring to engage in the practice of veterinary medicine. Most cities have specific requirements related to the type of businesses or residences that may exist and operate in prescribed areas of the city as defined by the city government. Following is an example of a city's zoning ordinance:

Designation of Districts: The several districts into which the city is divided are designated as follows: Single Family residential districts, hereby referred to as R-2 districts; Restricted Two family residential districts, hereinafter referred to as R-2A districts; Multiple Family residential districts, hereinafter referred to as R-4 districts; Limited Central Commercial districts, hereinafter referred to as C-1 districts; Central Commercial districts hereinafter referred to as C-2 districts; General Commercial Districts, hereinafter referred to as C-3 districts; Industrial or Manufacturing districts, hereinafter referred to as M districts.

The following regulations shall apply to all C-1 districts: (Note: C-1 districts are the first non-residential zone permitting the operation of a veterinary hospital.)

a.   All the uses that are permitted in any R district, without the necessity of securing a use permit.

b.   This paragraph allows for the inclusion of a small business in a C-1 district.

c.   This paragraph allows for the inclusion of a small animal veterinary hospital in a C-1 district

Public Hearings: A public hearing shall be held before a use permit is issued for an animal hospital in a C-1 districts.

The architect or contractor employed to plan or build a veterinary hospital should be conversant with the zoning ordinances of the locality and be responsible for securing all of the necessary permits for the planned building. A knowledge of zoning ordinances or regulations are important to the veterinarian who purchases a lot with the intent of building an animal hospital in the future. Before purchasing a site for a planned business it is advantageous to investigate existing restrictions on the types of businesses that can be operated in the area.

The owner of a veterinary clinic claimed the change in direction in a road passing his clinic damaged his business and amounted to the taking of his property without due process of law. The court ruled, "The change of a travel route does not itself result in legal impairment of the rights of the complainant." (Thiele 1957)

A city zoning ordinance contained a "B" residence zone permitting some business and professional buildings, including hospitals and sanitariums. A veterinarian received a permit to build a veterinary hospital in the B zone. The neighbors complained, but he was allowed to continue construction of the hospital as having a vested interest in it since he began construction before the complaints of the neighbors (State 1939)

In another zoning case, the court held it was not an abuse of discretion on the part of the zoning commission permitting the operation of a small animal hospital in a residential neighborhood where the animals, for the most part, would be confined indoors and no change would be made to existing buildings. Further, the court said, if the operation of the hospital developed into a nuisance, relief could be granted. (City of Birmingham 1938)

An owner of a veterinary clinic challenged the validity of a re-zoning ordinance permitting other animal hospitals to operate in the re-zoned area. Other veterinarians claimed the re-zoning was valid and they could build or operate veterinary hospitals in the area. The court held that the re-zoning of the locality was invalid as attempting to fragment an already zoned area. With zoning ordinances in some localities veterinarians have been allowed to use a part of their home or garage as an office for a clinic for seeing patients, but not for overnight hospitalization. (Daffy 1960, Ruona 1958, State 1948, Perkins 1958)

A County Commission on zoning filed a suit to stop a resident with 5 dogs from the operation of a commercial kennel in a single family residence district as being in violation of the zoning ordinance. The court did not find the ordinance vague and the resident was restricted from keeping more than 3 dogs on the residence. (Bell v Bennett 243 SE 2d 40, 1978)

In an action challenging the granting of a permit to operate a veterinary clinic in a re-zoned area of a city the court refused to accept the re-zoning saying there was no evidence the character of the neighborhood had changed and the city does not have the authority to arbitrarily make a zoning change without a need which is for the public good. (Lauritzen v City of New Orleans 503 So 2d, 1987)

In the application of Cottrell (614 A 2d 381, 1992) for a use permit to operate a veterinary clinic in the Town Center Commercial District of the city was refused the review Board saying the zoning amendment authorizing a veterinary clinic was invalid and not to the best interests of the City.

An application was made for a use permit to the city Board to use a building as a veterinary clinic. The permit was denied and this was appealed by the veterinarian. The building involved was already in use as a veterinary clinic and had been moved 150 feet with improvements made on the inside of the building. The court found the move and improvement in the building did not amount to a structural alteration of the building as the zoning statute required and the use of the building as a veterinary clinic could continue. (Zoning Board v Laurence 309 SW 2d 883, 1958)

A veterinarian appealed to the Township for an interpretation of an ordinance which allowed the construction of a shelter by a Humane Society on land zoned as light industrial. The Board found for the Humane Society and allowed construction of the shelter. (Sziuna v Township of Avon 340 NW 2d 105, 1983)

Expert Witnesses,
Evidence and Testimony

Over one hundred years ago, with respect to expert witnesses, English courts said. If you have a firm opinion, be firm about it; if there is room for argument admit it freely; be as concise as possible; use non-technical language if possible; if you have to give ground do so honestly with good grace." (Ramadge v Ryan 9 Bing 333, 1832, Alcock v Royal Exchange Co. 13 QB 292, 1849)

Testimony and evidence are the means by which a court or jury are able to collect facts relative to a case being tried or heard by a judge. This material must be carefully analyzed for its relevance to the case in question, and for honesty and accuracy. Some types of evidence are admissible, others are not. In general, evidence must have a direct relationship to the case, must not be hearsay, and must be from personal experience dealing with the issues before the court or jury.

Ordinarily, what a person has heard is considered hearsay and is not admissible in court. This is also true of opinion evidence; a matter of opinion is not factual material. However, a qualified expert witness may give an opinion relative to a case by answering direct questions of an attorney regarding example questions. In answering a hypothetical question from an attorney the expert witness has an opportunity to present and support his or her technical or scientific opinion on the question. (Laude 1936)

A veterinarian called by a court as an expert witness should be familiar with the subject matter, study its content and merit, be cooperative and courteous, keep calm, not deviate from the truth or facts, use understandable language, admit being paid if true, not try to match wits with attorneys as this is usually a losing battle. If a statement is read for the witness to interpret its significance, ask to see the source of the statement as it is possible only a portion has been read. (Rumbaugh 1978)

Before persons may testify as an expert, they must qualify to the satisfaction of the court as being one. They must be an expert in the field for which an opinion is being sought. A veterinarian called upon to give an expert opinion as to a disease causing death in a herd of cattle would be asked about education, time spent in practice, specialty training and other pertinent factors to support eligibility as an expert in the field in question. (Richardson 1974)

Expert witnesses are called upon when it is necessary for the court to prove or establish a specific point in a case which can only be done by an individual trained in the field in question. To establish that Brucellosis probably existed in a herd of dairy cattle would require the testimony of an expert who could present epidemiology, clinical disease, pathology and laboratory tests available; such information that would be acceptable only from a trained and qualified person familiar with Brucellosis

For an example, an expert witness is asked, "If you saw a group of dead cattle in a field, lying on their sides, bodies swollen, legs sticking out rigid, what disease in your opinion might have been the cause of death of the cattle?" Such a hypothetical question could be used to show the court that a qualified veterinarian could recognize the characteristics of a specific disease.

Veterinarians called as expert witnesses should answer only the questions directed to them, stay strictly within the areas of their technical knowledge. Expressing opinions outside of the expert's field are not admissible evidence. (Richardson 1974)

Some examples of the use of veterinarians as expert witnesses: The expert testimony of a veterinarian of long experience in observing tuberculous cattle, condition of the carcasses, and estimating the length of time the cattle were affected with tuberculosis were held to be admissible statements by the veterinarian, even though made without absolute certainty. A witness is permitted to state a fact known, or observed, even though the statement involves an amount of inference or supposition. (Hausman 1934)

A veterinarian was held to be a competent witness in testifying about cattle he had treated were affected with arsenic poisoning. In another case a veterinarian's testimony regarding the illness of cattle as being due to cotton seed oil was admissible. In a case against the seller of corn for cattle feed, an insecticide had been applied to the corn by the defendant and the court held a veterinarian's expert testimony as to the effect of the insecticide on the cattle was admissible.

An awkward situation may arise when a veterinarian is called upon to give expert testimony or evidence against another veterinarian in court on malpractice charges. It rests with the witness veterinarian to forego malice and personal prejudice and give honest, straightforward evidence. Professionals may have to appear in court to defend themselves and an honest, respected colleague as a witness would be appreciated. Consider this if you are ever an expert witness.

In an action against a veterinarian damages were sought by the plaintiff for the loss of his dogs. The dogs died soon anger being dipped by the defendant veterinarian in a lye solution as a treatment for mange. A veterinarian testified the lye solution used was too strong and could have caused the death of the dogs. Other witnesses testified the dogs were in good health a few days before treatment.

The existence of malpractice is usually proved through the use of expert testimony. A person familiar with the veterinary profession, often a veterinarian, is considered to be the most qualified person to present what constitutes malpractice and negligence.

Expert testimony in malpractice actions is necessary to show a poor result was caused by an alleged unskillful or negligent act. (Judd 1933)

A horse owner brought a malpractice suit against a veterinarian alleging negligence in performing surgery and providing aftercare for the horse. A verdict was given for the veterinarian because it was held by the court that expert testimony was necessary to establish the application of the standard of care necessary in this case. The veterinarian was called to examine a colt and found it was a cryptorchid and took the animal to his clinic for castration. The surgery was performed and the colt returned to the stallion farm. The veterinarian was again called to treat the colt for a respiratory infection. The horse was treated daily for over one week with antibiotics and it seemed to be improving. To facilitate healing of the incision made for castration, Dermago was applied to the site. An abscess appeared at the surgical site and the animal was again taken to the clinic, the abscess drained and antibiotics given. Later, the colt died and on autopsy a large abscess was found in the spleen from which Streptococcus epidemicus was isolated. Expert testimony was not provided which was necessary for the plaintiff to prove professional negligence. In medicine an expert witness is necessary to prove malpractice and this applies to dentists, attorneys, pharmaceutical manufacturers, and should include veterinarians. There can be no findings of negligence in the absence of expert testimony to support it. (Zimmerman v Robertson 854 P 2d 338, 1993)

A carrier company, introduced a veterinarian as an expert witness, who held that the death of a mule the company was transporting was due to gastroenteritis, satisfied the burden of proving a defense for the company that the mule's death resulted from a cause that was exempted in the transportation contract.

In an action for shrinkage in weight and injuries to hogs while in transit, a question addressed to a veterinarian as to whether or not 24 hours in transit was a long enough time to fatigue and wear the hogs out, judged an improper question, was held admissible due to the veterinarian's expert witness answer. (Bradley 1934, Swift 1956, Doake 1959)

A witness summoned to court has the privilege against self-incrimination protected by the 5th amendment of the Constitution. Some courts also grant the privilege of selfdegradation; if an answer to a question by a witness would degrade or disgrace the witness refusal to answer is allowed, especially if the question is not pertinent to the case's resolution.

In summary, veterinarians qualify as expert witnesses by demonstrating expertise in the areas covered by the case. A veterinarian who has treated animals that are the subjects of a lawsuit may be called upon to testify by either party; plaintiff or defense. They may be called upon to give expert information on the action of drugs and their safety, as well as animal health and disease. (Hannah 1992)

Questions which may be asked by a court of an expert witness are:

1.   Please state your name.

2.   Where do you reside?

3.   What is your profession?

4.   What has been your general education?

5.   What veterinary school or schools have you attended and did you graduate?

6.   Have you had any post-graduate training?

7.   How long have you practiced veterinary medicine and where?

8.   What has been the nature of your practice?

9.   Are you certified by a specialty board?

10. Have you had experience in this kind of case and what has it been?

11. Do you belong to veterinary medical professional societies and what are they?

12. What professional journals do you subscribe to and/or read?

The expert witness should prepare thoroughly for his or her appearance in court. One does not wish to be a poor example for the profession. Areas to cover are:

1.   Adequate preparation, review the literature.

2.   Have a thorough knowledge of all of the parameters of the case in question.

3.   Show that you keep good and reliable records of your work

A good witness has the following qualities:

1.   Honesty
2.   Dignity
3.   Good personal appearance.
4.   Uses understandable language, defines medical terms.
5.   Is not overbearing or superior, uses careful diction.
6.   Shows a degree of modesty.
7.   Keeps control of the temper. (Curran 1985)

CHAPTER FIVE
PROTECTION OF ANIMALS

In 1978 the United Nations (UN) Assembly adopted a Universal declaration of the rights of animals, "All animals are born with an equal claim on life and the same rights to existence." The UN declaration was emblematic of the maturation of the world humane movement. The progress of that movement has been predicated on sensitizing human practices and laws to the needs of animals. The transformation of sentiment to one of concern for the rights of animals has provided an intellectual basis for man's relationship with the animal kingdom that promises to revolutionize that relationship.

Historical Antecedents

Perhaps the dominant dictum that has governed man's relationship with the animal kingdom came from the book of Genesis, "And God said, let us make man in our image, after our likeness: and let them have dominion over the fish of the sea, and over the cattle, and over all the earth, and over every creeping thing that creepeth upon the earth." The precise meaning of dominion in this context has been argued for centuries Clearly, dominion denotes supreme authority and perhaps implies stewardship. Whether there was inferred beneficence is arguable. (Gen 1:26) Some of the excesses of the industrial revolution resulted in a callous, impersonal attitude toward animals. Pet animals were mass-produced and food-producing animals were indifferently processed. Upton Sinclair's epochal book, *The Jungle*, aroused concern of the world by passages such as the following: "It was all very businesslike that one watched it fascinated. It was pork-making by applied mathematics. And yet somehow the most matter-of-fact person could not help thinking of the hogs; they were so innocuous, they came so very trustingly, and they were so very human in their protests — and so perfectly within their rights. They had done nothing to deserve it, and it was adding insult to injury, as the thing was done here, swinging them up in this cold-blooded, impersonal way, without a pretence of apology, without the homage of a tear. Now and then a visitor wept, to be sure, but this slaughtering machine ran on, visitors or no visitors. It was like some horrible crime committed in a dungeon, all unseen and unheeded, buried out of sight and memory." (Sinclair 1906)

The German philosopher, Arthur Schopenhauer (1788-1860) had presaged the animal rights movement, "The assumption that animals are without rights and the illusion that our treatment of them has no moral significance is a positively outrageous example of Western crudity and barbarity."

Animal Rights

The present movement for animal rights owes much of its impetus to the activism of Michael Fox and Peter Singer. The concept that animals have innate rights to life and freedom from suffering has been the subject of discussion by humanists, animal welfarists, veterinarians, animal scientists, livestock producers and others. The movement has spawned legislation and reform actions. (Morris 1977, Singer 1976)

In the United States questions of animal rights, animal welfare, and biomedical experimentation have been debated for over 100 years. The groups involved in this debate may be divided into four categories:

1.   Animal rightists who wish o abolish all exploitation of animals and give them legal rights.

2.   Animal liberationists who support physical confrontation against all who would exploit animals, to the extent of breaking into areas where animals are maintained and liberating them.

3.   Animal welfarists who promote and support good, reasonable and humane care of animals under all circumstances.

4.   Animal users, scientists, industrialists,commercial interests who, in the opinion of the rightists are exploiting and taking unacceptable advantage of animals.

Animal rightists and welfarists do not have the same goals and aims; the rightists goal is the abolition of all activities using animals for man's benefit and to give animals legal and moral rights, the same as human beings. The welfarists are not against human beings using animals for their benefit, providing the animals are treated humanely and are free from pain and discomfort

The views of Animal Rightists:

1.   Animals have the right to live.

2.   Animal interests must be considered.

3.   Animals do not differ from human beings. The rationale for this being that animals and human beings share the following common qualities:

a.   Ability to perceive pain and suffering.
b.   An interest in living.
c.   A self-awareness
d.   Beliefs and desires.
e.   A purposeness.
f.   A kinship awareness.
g.   A sense of past and future.
h.   A concern for others and an ability to relate to others.
i.   Ability to communicate.
j.   A sense of curiosity.

4.   Research on animals; rightists say to perform research on animals is to approve the violation of their rights. The rightists seek the total elimination of the use of animals for research or any other exploitation of animals. Animals, like human beings, are conscious and sentient creatures and have moral rights to respectful treatment. (Singer 1976)

Factors Against Animal Rights,
Legal View

Man is always a living being, but he is the highest representative of the whole series of living beings. He is distinct from other animals by having a perception of good and evil, justice and injustice (Aristotle 384-322 B C.)

Brute beasts, not having understanding and
therefore not being persons, cannot have
rights. We have no duties to them; not of
justice, not of religion, not of fidelity, for they
are incapable of accepting a promise. (Rickaby
1899)

Only beings which possess things can have rights, only those who
have interests can have rights. To have a right is to have a claim to
something or against other persons. Neither dogs nor trees can make or
insist upon or petition the courts on behalf of their claims or rights. The
criteria for rights are the possession of a rational mind, a language for
communication, the ability to make choices, to exercise a free will, a
recognition and ability to discharge moral obligations, the possession of
a culture, an acceptance and participation in social and communal
relations and the possession of interests.

Animal rightists emphasize the possession of sentience as being a
condition which gives animals the ability to have rights. Sentience means
to perceive by the senses, or, having a capability of feeling, or
perception, consciousness, as a man is a sentient being.

Sentience is not a sufficient condition for the bearing of rights. It
does not cover all of the attributes of human beings that give them rights
in the eyes of the law. Animals do not possess an interest in the future,
whereas the premature death of a person destroys their future. At present
the legal system does not provide for rights to be held by animals but
they are, under the law, entitled to protection from cruelty and given
humane treatment. The painless sacrifice of animals, when necessary, is
not considered to be cruel by the law.

In the past 25 years many books and articles have been written
promoting animal rights or representing the opposite position that animals
cannot have rights as we interpret human rights. Excerpts from a few of
these positions follow:

The fundamental properties of living systems are the conversion
of energy for living and the exchange of information. All organisms
receive signs from their environment. Human beings have the added
faculty of a complex language. Being human suggests civilization, a
capacity for culture. Human beings are endowed with intentions and
purposes, they are motivated by social values and moral consciousness;

animals are not responsible for what they do. The concept that animals may be regarded as self-conscious subjects with thoughts and feelings of their own is still questionable in ethological and psychological fields. An ever-present question is do animals engage in conscious thinking? Are animals endowed with the faculty of language? Language is considered to be an instrument of cognition. A device to construct the future, formulate plans of actions or alternative ones, to interpret the results of actions. Animal communication may consist of instructions, not propositions; in essence, they do not converse.

Sentience means a living thing has interests and moral standing. Domestic animals are human creations, living artifacts, bred to docility, tractability, stupidity and dependency, dependent on human beings, becoming slaves or symbionts. Domestic animals and human beings have a mutual interest. But no interpretation of contractualism will accord moral status to animals.

Human beings should treat animals humanely, but animals cannot have rights. To have rights means accepting the rules of a society. Animals have no sense of morality nor do they consider the rights of others. Animals can have neither rights or obligations under the law, but as sentient creatures they require protection against abuse by owners or keepers.

The *animal rights theory* recognizes that animals have an inherent value that cannot be sacrificed to achieve benefit for human beings. Animal welfare tenants rest on the concept that animals are property and that every animal interest can be sacrificed for the benefit of human beings. Under law, animals are property and, as such, may be used exclusively as a means to the ends of their human owners. (see animal rights references)

Federal Laws Protecting Animals

The Animal Welfare Act (7 USCA 21 et seq) was passed by Congress in 1966 with three original purposes: (1) to protect dog and cat owners from theft of their pets, (2) to prevent the use of stolen pets for research and experimentation, and (3) to establish humane standards for the treatment of dogs and cats, and some other species of animals, by medical research facilities and animal dealers.

The Act was amended in 1970, 1976 and 1985. the essence of these changes are found in section 13: The Secretary (of the U. S. Dept. of Agriculture) shall promulgate standards to govern the humane handling, care, treatment, transportation of animals by dealers, research facilities and exhibitors. Such standards shall include minimum requirements with respects to handling, housing, feeding, watering, sanitation, ventilation, shelter from extremes of weather and temperatures, adequate veterinary care, including the appropriate use of anesthetic, analgesic and tranquilizing drugs when such use would be proper in the opinion of the attending veterinarian of such research facilities, and separation by species when the Secretary finds such separation necessary for the humane handling, care and treatment of animals

The Act has been enforced by the Animal Plant Health Inspection Service of the U. S. Dept. of Agriculture (USDA) for over 30 years and has had a positive effect on the welfare of experimental animals. Enforcement of the Act has improved research involving animals by enhancing veterinary medical care, overall laboratory animal health, and improved record keeping.

The body of the Act states: The Congress finds that animals and activities which are regulated under this chapter are either in interstate commerce or foreign commerce or substantially affect such commerce, of the free flow thereof and that regulation of animals and activities as provided in this chapter is necessary to prevent and eliminate burdens upon such commerce and to effectively regulate such commerce in order to:

1.   Insure that animals intended for use in research or for exhibition purposes or for use as pets are provided humane care and treatment.

2.   To insure humane treatment of animals during transportation in commerce, and

3.   Protect the owners of animals from the theft of their animals which have been stolen for experimental use.

Requirements of the Act are:

1. Licensing of animal dealers and exhibitors.

2. A period of five business days before dealers of dogs and cats may dispose of an animal.

3. The registration of research facilities with the USDA.

4. The purchase of dogs and cats by research facilities only from licensed dealers.

5. Record-keeping by research facilities of the purchase, transportation, identification, sale or disposal of animals.

6. The marking and/or identification of animals.

7. Humane handing, care, and treatment of animals, including adequate housing, feeding, watering, ventilation, sanitation. shelter, separation of animals by species where necessary or feasible, and adequate veterinary care.

8. Sufficient space for dogs and nonhuman primates, exercise of dogs and a physical environment to promote psychological well-being in primates.

9. The appropriate use of anesthetics, analgesics, or tranquilizers, or euthanasia and veterinary care where indicated. Any procedure on animals causing pain must include the use of the above drugs.

10. Research facilities must have an animal care and use committee which shall include, but is not limited to, at least one veterinarian, one member not connected with the research facility and others as deemed necessary. Functions of the committee; inspection of all premises involving animals at least twice a year, a review of research protocols using animals, maintenance of records and minutes of meetings, the training of scientists, animal technicians and caretakers in the handling, care and maintenance of animals.

USDA personnel are required to make inspections of research animal facilities periodically, but at least annually, to examine records, protocols, and tour facilities. In total, personnel make about 15,000 inspections per year to 1500 animal research facilities, 5,000 animal dealers, 1500 animal exhibitors and 150 animal carriers or intermediate handlers of animals registered with the USDA. These inspections discover about 100 cases of violations of the Act and result in almost 500 warning letters regarding these violations sent to registered facilities, dealers or exhibitors; culminating in 60 suspensions, cease and desist orders or revocation of licenses annually.

Some examples of violations have been: A holder of exotic animals was fined $10,000 for operating without a license and for failure to keep animals in secure quarters; an animal dealer was fined $4,000 with a 5 month suspension of license for the improper storage of animal feed and improper record keeping; a dog dealer was given a 10 year suspension of his license for improper care of animals and multiple record keeping failures; an exotic cat exhibitor was fined $3,000 for animal care violation; a supplier of animals for laboratory dissection was fined $21,000 for multiple violations of animal care.

The major violations of the Act involve poor, late or faulty reports to the USDA, inadequate veterinary care, substandard housing, poor care, incomplete reports on the experimental use of animals. (USDA Animal Welfare Enforcement, 1994)

Few cases of violations of the Animal Welfare Act end up in court because most of these are resolved before they reach the need for court action. Following is a summary of some of the cases that have been abjudicated in the courts:

1.   An animal rights group petitioned a court for a review of a professor's grant proposal to study the auditory system of barn owls. Members of the animal rights group were allowed to attend the animal care committee proposal review meeting, but could not participate in the discussion. The judge found the Animal Welfare Act requirement to file assurances with the federal government that they comply with federal policy on the care and use of vertebrates in research as a condition for federal funding were met by the committee's minutes of the meeting which included a review of the research protocol and, in addition, the animal rights

group did not have standing in the issue; i.e., was not involved to the point of being affected. (Peta v IACUC 1990)

2.   In several instances animal rights groups were found guilty of breaking and entering into research facilities with the theft of animals. At the University of Oregon in 1983 they entered and raided the animal facilities, releasing over 200 animals and causing $50,000 damage to property and equipment. At Loma Linda University 5 puppies to be used for heart research and 2 dogs and 2 goats were stolen from the animal facilities. In 1987 an animal interest organization started a fire in a research building under construction, causing 3 5 million dollars in damage. (Animal Agenda 1987, 1988)

3.   In 1991 an animal rights group (PETA) caused the National institutes of Health to investigate an alleged abuse of cats at one of their institutes. Forty-eight cats were blinded and implanted with electrodes. Many were sick and without medical care for at least one month. Remedial measures were taken, but no legal action. (Animal Agenda 1992)

Horse, Wild Horses
& Burro Protection Acts

The Horse Protection Act was passed by Congress as Public Law 91-540 in 1970 and amended in 1976 as P L 91-360. As a consequence of the Act, Regulations were published in the Federal Register on May 17, 1979, 9 CFR part 11. The law is administered by the USDA's APHI Service.

The Horse Protection Act was passed in an effort to correct some inhumane practices by horsemen. Specifically, the law deals with the use of methods or devices that cause pain and distress and are used to make horses perform better and more consistently, i.e., the exaggerated extension of the forelimb of the Tennessee Walking Horse was frequently the result of an inhumane and purposeful induction of soreness in the front feet of the animals

The law expressly covers three groups involved with the Walking Horses: (1) sponsors, administrators and managers of horse shows, sales and auctions; (2) owners, trainers and riders who show their horses or enter them for competition or consign them for public sale or auction; (3) persons who ship horses to shows, sales, or auctions. Enforcement activities are centered on horse shows. Horse races, rodeos or parades are not usually visited by enforcement personnel.

The law prohibits the use of beads, bangles or other trotting devices affixed to the feet, but it does allow for the use of boots and collar-like devices of any weight, hardwood rollers, aluminum or stainless steel rollers weighing less than 14 ounces and single chain bracelets weighing less than 10 ounces. Foot pads are required to be no thicker than 1 inch at the heel, and the length of the toe must be at least 1 inch longer than the height of the heel Additionally, horses are considered misused if scars or granulation tissue can be found on the pasterns or coronary areas of both front legs. Violations of these conditions are a criminal offense.

For legal purposes horses are pronounced sore on the testimony of expert witnesses. Bilateral inflammation or abnormal sensitivity in both front or hind feet has been legally adopted as valid evidence for prosecution. Heat sensitive devices which electronically record the heat output of affected limbs are evidence that is legally admissible.

Violations of the Act represent criminal offense and may be punished with a fine of $3,000 or more and up to one year in prison for a first offense. Repeat violators may be disqualified from showing or selling horses or managing or judging events. The Horse Protection Act also provides for penalties for persons that falsify records for the purposes of avoiding prosecution and for persons that physically attempt to prevent inspection of premises or horses by qualified officials of the USDA.

Wild Horses and Burros

In 1971 Congress found that free-roaming horses and burros are living symbols of the historical and pioneering spirit of the west; they are fast-disappearing from the American scene and they shall be protected from capture, branding, harassment or death. Where they are found they are an integral part of the national system of the public lands. The Secretary of the Interior was given the authority to protect the animals on public lands. The Act's criminal provisions prohibit, unless authorized by the Secretary the following:

1.   The willful removal of horses and burros from public lands.

2.   The conversion of an animal to private use

3.   The malicious killing or harassment of horses or burros

4.   The processing of the animals into commercial pet food.

The constitutionality of the Act was challenged in Kleppe v New Mexico (426 US 529, 1976) where the Livestock Board of New Mexico brought an action against the U.S. claiming it was illegal for the U.S. to claim authority to control animals on public lands formerly under state control. The court found that under the complete power that Congress has over public lands it includes the power to regulate and protect wildlife living there. The Secretary is directed to manage free roaming horses and burros in a manner that is designed to achieve and maintain a thriving natural ecological balance of the animals on the public lands.

A 1978 Amendment allowed a person to obtain no more than 4 animals per year, assuring the Secretary that the individual is capable of providing humane care and transportation for the animals. Prior to this amendment, an individual adopted 109 wild horses and then sold them for $25,000 to meat processors. He was convicted for conversion of U. S. government property. (Amer Horse Prot Assoc v Frizzell, 403 F Supp 1206, 1975)

In an action brought by a horse owner and trainer against the Secretary of Agriculture for the reversal of an order imposing sanctions on the horse owner for violation of the Horse Protection Act when a horse had a sore leg and was entered in a show against the advice of a veterinarian, the owner was found guilty. (Lewis v Secretary of Agriculture 73 F ad 312, 1996)

Eagle Protection Act

By 1940 Congress recognized that our national symbol, the bald eagle, was threatened with extinction. The original Bald Eagle Protection

Act was passed in 1940 making it illegal to take, possess, sell, or purchase any bald eagle, alive or dead or any part thereof. Later the golden eagle was included and the penalty for violation made a $5000 fine and up to one year in jail. The Act makes provisions, under certain circumstances, for Native Americans to kill, capture, obtain and keep eagles or their parts for religious or ceremonial purposes. (16 U.S.C. 668)

Migratory Bird Treaty Act

In 1916 the U. S Congress signed a migratory bird treaty with Great Britain for the protection of birds that migrate between the U.S. and Canada. In 1918 the Congress passed the Migratory Bird Treaty Act which was upheld by the Supreme Court as being a constitutional exercise of federal authority. The Court rejected claims of states that through the 10th Amendment power and authority to control wildlife was reserved to the states. (MO v Holland 252 US 416, 1920, US v Richards 583 F 2d 491, 1978) Later, treaties were signed with Mexico and Japan.

The Act makes it unlawful to hunt capture or kill or possess any protected bird except as permitted by regulation of the Secretary of the Interior. (16 USC 701 et seq) Although the original intent of the act was to control hunting its protective powers have been extended to include many areas. In US v FMC Corp, (572 F 2d 902, 1978) the government obtained a conviction where defendant discharged toxic chemicals into an open pond used by migratory birds and, as a result, up to 70 birds were killed in a 3 month period. Defendant knew it was discharging toxic materials but had no intent to harm the birds. The court held when one engages in a dangerous activity he will be liable for the foreseeable results. (16 U.S.C. 708 et seq)

Humane Slaughter Act

This Act (Public Law 85-765) was passed by Congress in 1953. It was the declared policy of the U.S that the slaughtering of livestock and the handling of livestock in connection with slaughter shall be carried out only by humane methods.

The Act provided for two methods of slaughtering considered to be humane:

1.   In the case of cattle, calves, horses, mules, sheep, swine and other livestock, all animals are rendered insensible to pain by a single blow or gunshot or electrical or chemical or by other means that are rapid and effective before being shackled, hoisted, thrown, cast or cut.

2.   By slaughtering in accordance with the ritual requirements of the Jewish faith or any other religious faith that prescribes a method of slaughter whereby the animals suffer loss of consciousness by anemia of the brain caused by the simultaneous and instantaneous severance of the carotid arteries with a sharp instrument. (7 USCA 1901-6)

The Act was weak because it was only a declaration of policy but it was important because all federal agencies required humane slaughter in connection with procurement and price support programs and operations. The Act also provided for research to develop humane methods of slaughter and handling of animals in its provisions. Poultry and minor food animals, such as rabbits, were not included in the Act.

In 1978 the Humane Methods of Slaughter Act (Public Law 92-445) was passed. The 1978 law amended the Federal Meat Inspection Act (PL 59-242) and required that meat inspected and approved for human consumption be produced only from livestock slaughtered in accordance with humane methods. The Secretary of the USDA was empowered to refuse to provide inspection at any slaughtering establishment not in compliance with the Humane Slaughter Act. Such refusal would result in the inability of the establishment to sell meat in interstate commerce. The Act also forbids the importation of meat from countries not slaughtering and handling livestock in accordance with the Humane Slaughter Act.

Endangered Species Act

The Endangered Species Acts of 1966 and 1969 were replaced in 1973 by Congress. (16 USC 1500, 12 Int'l Leg Mats 1085, 1973) This remains the foundation of the Act with several amendments. The Act states, "The Congress finds and declares that:

1. Various species of fish, wildlife and plants in the United States have been rendered extinct as a consequence of economic growth and development intemperate by adequate concern and conservation.

2. Other species of fish, wildlife and plants have been so depleted in numbers that they are in danger or threatened with extinction.

3. These species of fish wildlife and plants are one of aesthetic, ecological, educational, historical, recreational and scientific value to the nation and its people.

4. The United States has pledged itself as a sovereign state in the international community to conserve, to the extent practical, the various species of fish, wildlife and plants facing extinction.

5. Encouraging the states and other interested parties, through federal financial assistance or incentives, to develop and maintain conservation programs.

The government intends to realize the survival and increase of endangered species by:

1. Protective regulations against hunting, killing, destruction of eggs, young, or plants, or the habitats of endangered species.

2. Monitoring the numbers of fish, wildlife, or plants.

3. Acquisition of land.

4. Cooperative programs with states.

5. Making federal funds available to the states.

6. Establishing civil and criminal penalties for offenders. (34 ALR Fed 332)

The United States Endangered Species Act, Section 1538, Prohibited acts:

(a) Generally

1. Except as provided in sections 1535 (9)(2) and 1539 of this title, with respect to any endangered species of fish, wildlife listed pursuant to section 1533 of this title it is unlawful for any person subject to the jurisdiction of the United States to:

    (A) Import any such species (as listed in the Act) into, or export any such species from the United States

    (B) Take any such species within the United States or the territorial sea of the United States.

    (C) Take any such species on the high seas.

    (D) Possess, sell, deliver, carry, transport, or ship, by any means whatsoever, any such species taken in violation of subparagraphs (B) and (C).

    (E) Deliver, receive, carry, transport, or ship in interstate or foreign commerce, by any means whatsoever and in the course of a commercial activity, any such species.

    (F) Sell or offer for sale in interstate or foreign commerce any such species, or

    (G) Violate any regulation pertaining to such species or to any threatened species of fish, wildlife listed pursuant to section 1533 of this title and promulgated by the Secretary pursuant to authority provided in this chapter. (16 USCA 1538)

The power of the Act is illustrated in the Snail Darter case. The TVA wished to complete a dam on the Little Tennessee river but a small fish, the Snail Darter, was found where the water would be backed up by the dam which would destroy the habitat of the fish. The Supreme Court held that since the habitat would be destroyed the construction of the dam could not continue. If the infringement on the endangered species would not have threatened the continued existence of the species, the building of the dam could have continued. (TVA v Hill 437 US 153, 1978)

Marine Mammal Protection
Act (MMPA)

The Marine Mammal Protection Act (MMPA) represents a compromise among several groups interested in marine mammals, from free capture and killing to complete prohibition of taking of marine mammals. The Act imposes a complete moratorium on the taking or importation of marine mammals or their products. It then grants some specific exceptions where permits may be granted; scientific purposes and for public display. Another one is when marine mammals are incidentally killed in the course of commercial fishing. The Secretary of the Interior has the responsibility for polar bears, sea otters, walruses, while the Secretary of Commerce for seals, porpoises and whales. (16 USC 1316 et seq) The Act states:

1.   No person subject to the jurisdiction of the United States may take any marine mammal on the high seas. Nor may any person take any marine mammal in water or land under the jurisdiction of the United States.

2.   It is illegal for any person to use any port, harbor, or other place, under the jurisdiction of the United States for any activity concerned with the taking (capture) or the importation of marine mammals or marine mammal products.

3.   It is illegal to possess said mammals or any product of the mammal.

4. It is illegal for any person to transport, purchase, sell or offer to purchase or sell any marine mammal or marine mammal products. (16 USC 1361)

A defendant was convicted of taking marine mammals in violation of the MMPA. The defendant fired rifle shots into the water behind porpoises to divert them from eating tuna caught on his fishing lines. On appeal the judgment was reversed, the court saying the MMPA was not intended to interfere with reasonably practiced commercial fishing and the firing of shots, without hitting any of the porpoises, was not unreasonable to protect the fisherman's catch. (USA v Hayashi, 1993)

In another case the court said, "Congress's primary purpose in the passage of the MMPA was to provide marine mammals, especially porpoises, with the necessary and extended protection against man's activities. The Act is not an attempt to balance the existence of marine mammals and the activities of the tuna industry." (Humane Legislation Inc v Richardson 1986)

A defendant was charged with the unauthorized taking of dolphins within the 3 mile limit of the Commonwealth of the Bahamas. the court found the MMPA did not extend on the high seas beyond the extra-territorial limits of the United States. (U.S. v Mitchell, 1977)

A section of the Act prohibits the importation of a mammal if it was:

1. Pregnant at the time of taking.

2. Nursing at the time of taking or is less is than 8 months old.

3. Taken from a depleted stock.

4. Taken in a manner deemed inhumane.

Globe Fur Dyeing Corp. contested the constitutionality of the Act. (612 F 2d 586, 1980) The court found that the provisions of the Act did not violate the equal protection or the due process clauses of the U. S. Constitution. Alaskan Indians are exempted from the act for subsistence and the making of artifacts, as long as the method of taking of the animals is not wasteful.

Cruelty to Animals

Beginning in the 19th century society's attitude toward animals began to change. In the first half of the 1800's lawmakers recognized animal's potential for pain and suffering and for the necessity for their protection from the abuses of human beings. In the last half of the 1800;s anti-cruelty laws were in force in every state of the United States.

In 1867 the New York State anti-cruelty law included penalties for: (1) overcrowding or cruelly treating animals, (2) use of poultry, bulls, or dogs, for fighting, (3) keeping animals without sufficient food and water, (4) transporting animals in a cruel or inappropriate manner, and (5) abandoning animals, well or infirm, in a public place. When these laws are challenged, the courts say the control of animals and the prevention of cruelty come under the police powers of the state. (Public Law 94-279)

All fifty states have anti-cruelty laws for the protection of animals. Most make it an offense to cruelly beat, kick, ill treat, override, overburden, overload, torture, infuriate or terrify an animal. It is also an offense for a person to cause or allow such treatment by others. The laws, in general, provide for the complete care of animals.

Usually, acts exempted from anti-cruelty statutes are dehorning of cattle, docking of the tails of horses and sheep, cropping of dog's ears (some states prohibit this last one). Other activities that are sometimes exempted are the destruction of some species of birds, the destruction of venomous reptiles, killing of any animal known as dangerous to life, killing of animals used for food, and the sacrifice of animals used for scientific experiments in universities and medical colleges, and the killing of an animal in self defense.

Questions to be asked in an analysis of anti-cruelty statutes:

1.   Is the animal in question included in the statute?

2.   Is the human being and his action within the scope of the statute?

3.   Is the act performed covered by the statute?

4.   Does the statute require any particular level of knowledge or intent by the person?

5. Is the particular act specifically exempted from the statute?

6. Are any statutory defenses provided for in the statute or related ones?

An example of a state's cruelty law:

(a) Except as provided for in subdivision (c), every person who maliciously, intentionally maims, mutilates, tortures, or wounds a living animal which is the property of the person or which is the property of another, or maliciously and intentionally kills an animal which is the property of the person or which is the property of another, is guilty of an offense punishable by imprisonment in the state prison or by a fine of not more than twenty thousand dollars (20,000), or both the fine and the imprisonment, or, alternatively, by imprisonment in the county jail for not more than one year, or by a fine of not more than twenty thousand dollars (20,000), or both by fine and imprisonment.

(b) Except as provided in subdivision (a) or (c), every person who overdrives, overloads, drives when overloaded, overworks, tortures, torments, deprives of necessary sustenance, drink or shelter, cruelly beats, mutilates, or cruelly kills any animal, or causes or procures any animal to be so over driven, overloaded, driven when overloaded, overworked, tortured, tormented, deprived of necessary sustenance, drink, shelter, or to be cruelly beaten, mutilated, or cruelly killed; and whoever, having the charge or custody of any animal, either as owner or otherwise, subjects any animal to needless suffering or inflicts unnecessary cruelty upon the animal, or in any manner abuses any animal, or fails to provide the animal with proper food, drink, or shelter or protection from the weather, or who drives, rides or otherwise uses the animal when unfit for labor, is, for every such offense guilty of a misdemeanor.

(c) Every person who maliciously and intentionally maims, mutilates, or tortures any mammal, bird, reptile, amphibian, or fish as described in subdivision (d), is guilty of an offense punishable by imprisonment in the state prison, or by a fine of not more than twenty thousand dollars (20,000), or by both the fine and imprisonment, or, alternatively, by imprisonment in the county jail for not more than one year, by a fine of not more than 20,000 dollars (20,000), or by both fine and imprisonment.

(d)   Subdivision (c) applies to any mammal, bird, reptile or fish, which is a creature described as follows:

    (1)   Endangered or threatened species as described in Chapter 1 5 (section 2050) of division 3 of the Fish and Game Code.

    (2)   Fully protected birds as described in section 3511 of the Fish and Game Code.

    (3)   Fully protected mammals as described in Chapter 8 (Section 4700 of Part 3 of Division 4) of the Fish and Game Code.

    (4)   Fully protected reptiles and amphibians described in Chapter 2 (Section 5050) of Division 5 of the Fish and Game Code.

    (5)   Fully protected fish as described in Section 5515 of the Fish and Game Code. This subdivision does not supersede or affect any provisions of law relating to taking of the described species, including, but not limited to, Section 12008 of the Fish and Game Code.

(e)   For the purposes of subdivision (c) each act of malicious and intentional maiming, mutilating, or torturing a separate specimen of a creature described in subdivision (d) is a separate offense. If any person is charged with a violation of subdivision (c), the proceedings be subject to Section 12157 of the Fish and Game Code. Upon conviction of a person charged with a violation of this section by causing or permitting an act of cruelty, as defined in Section 599b, all animals lawfully seized and impounded with respect to the violation by a peace officer, officer of a humane society, or officer of a pound or animal regulation department of a public agency shall be adjudged by the court to be forfeited and shall thereupon be awarded to the impounding officer for proper disposition. A person convicted of a violation of this section by causing or perpetrating an act of cruelty, as defined in Section 599b, shall be liable to the impounding officer for all costs of impoundment from the time of seizure to the time of proper disposition.

Mandatory seizure or impoundment shall not apply to animals in properly conducted scientific experiments or investigation performed under the authority of a regularly incorporated medical college or university of this state. (Calif. Penal Code pg. 401, par. 597)

Court cases involving cruelty to animals:

A cafeteria worker placed a cat in a microwave oven, turned it on and left the kitchen. Another worker saw the cat in the oven, turned it off and rescued the cat. It was still alive, but died a short time later. The accused admitted putting the cat in the oven, turning it on and leaving the cafeteria. His only concern was not for the cat but if he had jeopardized his job. (State v Tweedie, 1982)

A juvenile was found guilty of burning a dog to the extent the animal had to be destroyed. The act was deemed to constitute torture, torment and extreme cruelty. The male dog, belonging to the juvenile, attempted to mount a female dog belonging to a neighbor of the juvenile. The efforts of the male dog were repulsed by the female and the boy kicked the female dog and threatened to kill her. Later, he poured turpentine on the female dog and set her coat on fire with a match. A police officer was called and found the dog turning in circles and in obvious pain; the animal was destroyed. (William G., 1982)

The owner of a horse, licensed by the state horse racing commission, had his owner's license suspended for 45 days, racing license suspended for one year and was ejected from the state's racing tracks. After the owner's horse had run the first race at the track, it fell to the ground, apparently from heat exhaustion and possibly shock. The owner used 2 plastic buckets to water down the horse, the horse got to its feet and stumbled toward the owner who hit the horse on the nose with one of the buckets. A veterinarian testified that the owners attempt to move the horse in its condition was contrary to the accepted method for the treatment of heat exhaustion. (Martinez v Commonwealth of PA, 1984)

A person, while in his house, heard the cries of a dog which sounded distressful. He went outside and saw the defendant holding a puppy up in the air by a rope and beating it with his loose hand. The neighbor asked him to quit and he replied, "Get off my back." A humane officer was called and he found the pup tied in the back yard of the accused who admitted owning the pup but said the obvious injuries on its head were the result of a car accident a week ago. The pup was tied with a rope in such a way it could not freely move. In attempting to untie the pup the owner again hit the dog in the presence of the humane officer.. A decision of cruelty to animals was rendered. (Regaldo v U.S. 1990)

Five Great Danes belonging to one Biggerstaff were seized by humane officers and placed in the humane society shelter. The dogs when taken into custody were extremely thin, had poor coats, bad teeth, diarrheic mucoid stools, hookworms and evidence of malnutrition. Biggerstaff was convicted of cruelty to animals, appealed and sought a court order to prohibit the humane society from placing the dogs in homes or euthanizing them. Conviction was upheld. (Biggerstaff v Vanderburgh Humane Society, 1983)

A police officer responded to a call regarding cruelty to animals on a day when the temperature was 103 degrees Fahrenheit. In a pet shop he observed several animals in a closed, unventilated display window, apparently suffering from the heat. A rabbit was lying sprawled out in a semi-conscious condition, panting and covered with its saliva. The officer entered the store and removed the rabbit without first obtaining a warrant. The court's decision was that under such dire and serious conditions the needs of law enforcement were so compelling that the seizure of the rabbit without a warrant was a reasonable action. (Tuch v U.S. 1984)

A court held that a statute prohibiting the depriving an animal of sufficient food, water, air and exercise when measured by common and reasonable practice was not unconstitutional as being overly vague. (State v Wilson 1985)

The defendant acquired two wild mares which had been captured by the Bureau of Land Management during a roundup of wild horses. He put the mares in a small enclosure with two mules and a donkey. The enclosure was covered with grass which was quickly eaten up by the animals. The condition of the animals deteriorated and when seen by humane officers they impounded one mare and destroyed the other one. The defendant had a reputation of providing poor care for his animals and the evidence in this case was sufficient to sustain a conviction of cruelty to animals. (State v Flynn, 1984)

An individual was convicted of cruelty to animals and appealed the case. Evidence was presented to the court that his dogs were in bad shape, suffering from several disease problems including mange, blindness, parasites, pneumonia, and distemper. On the recommendations of a veterinarian, the animals were destroyed and on autopsy found to be suffering from the conditions mentioned. The conviction of cruelty to animals was upheld. (LaRue v State 1985) A plaintiff sought to obtain the legal right, a license, to stage Portuguese-style bullfights. The court found that saving animals from harassment and ill treatment was a valid exercise of the statute's police power. The Statute was valid in prohibiting cruelty to animals, and encounters between man and any animal are prohibited, including bulls. (C E. America Inc. v Antinori, 1968)

A local sheriff, with a search warrant, seized 41 dogs, items of personal property, $5581 in cash, fire arms, dog cages and equipment used for dog fights. The court held that the statute against dog fighting was not unconstitutional due to vagueness nor overly broad and did not violate equal protection under the law nor constitute cruel or unusual punishment. (State v Gaines 1990)

A police officer to execute a search warrant went to the defendant's home on a matter unrelated to the findings uncovered by the visit. In the basement of the home he hound 23 roosters in cages groomed is a manner consistent with cockfighting; fluffy appendages on the heads and necks, (the combs and wattles were cut), the feathers on the chest and legs were closely shaved. He also found equipment used for cock-fighting, medicines, hormones, and a trophy inscribed with the writing, "Number one Bird." and a newspaper clipping to the effect that cockfighting was a felony in the state. The owner of the house and roosters was convicted of cruelty (Commonwealth v Gonzalez, 1991)

Horse Racing Legislation

States where the racing of horses is legal have laws governing this activity to protect the horses and the public. Doping horses, i.e., giving them drugs, is a common practice at racetracks. Even in states that forbid drugs to be given to animals for a specified time prior to a race, it is still a problem The reasons animals are given drugs are to either improve or decrease performance, to deaden pain in the legs with local anesthetics, or at times for acceptable therapeutic reasons; this type of medication not being illegal. Legitimate race enthusiasts say racehorses should only receive hay, oats and water; if they need medication they should not be racing.

Horse racing legislation is aimed at protecting the integrity of the sport, to insure the safety of the horses, and to protect the interests of the public. By law at most race tracks, blood samples are taken from the race horses at specified times. If the presence of a prohibited drug is found in the sample the horse is disqualified from future races, any prize money received is forfeited, and the owner, trainer or other persons involved may be fined, their licenses suspended and a jail sentence imposed. (Bartlett 1990)

Sacrifice of Animals

A local ordinance forbidding the sacrifice of animals for religious purposes was challenged recently as being in violation of the first amendment of the U.S. Constitution granting religious freedom. For over 100 years the Supreme Court of the U.S. has recognized that this amendment involves two concepts; freedom to believe and freedom to act. The first being absolute and inviolate but the second, freedom to act, may have some restrictions applied to it. Consequently, a state or city may enforce legislation preventing animal sacrifice for religious reasons, but not the belief itself.

With some religious groups with branches in the United States the sacrifice of animals is an integral part of their religious ritual. These groups having immigrated to this country wish to continue their practice of worship. Notwithstanding, in the United States the sacrifice of animals for religious purposes is illegal. (Fliegal 1993)

Most states have laws controlling or prohibiting the following: cruel methods of transporting animals; use of animals for fighting; keeping animals without adequate food and water; polling a horse; illegal dog, cock, bull fighting; illegal docking of horses; illegal abandonment of animals; decompression chambers for killing dogs and cats. (Calif Penal Code, sec. 597,1988)

Alternatives to the Use
of Animals for Research

The United States government has attempted to encourage investigation into available or new alternatives to the use of animals for biomedical research for the past 30 years. Federal support and encouragement for such work is available and significant progress has been made in this field. In some instances laboratories using animals in their work have reported a reduction of from 40 to 60 percent in the use of animals due to the employment of alternative test systems; single cell cultures, the use of bacterial cultures, tissue culture systems, computer and mathematical simulation programs. In spite of this progress, one quote says, "Nothing but research on animals will provide us with the knowledge that will make it possible for us one day to dispense with the use of them altogether. (Parsons 1986)

Advocates of alternatives to the use of animals cite the duplication of similar and related experiments in a multitude of laboratories as being wasteful and an unnecessary use of animals. Conversely, it is difficult to establish a scientific truth unequivocally, unless this has been tested and duplicated in several reliable laboratories; this being the rationale for the repetition of experiments (Rose 1985)

Research in compliance with federal regulations for the demonstration of drug safety will continue, for the present, to use animals as the final and ultimate proof of acceptability for the marketing of drugs. Alternative techniques can, and are, useful supplements and can reduce the numbers of animals needed for safety tests. (Miller 1986) The importance of the search for alternatives to the use of animals for testing and research is emphasized by the medical reference resource Index Medicus adding the subject heading Animal Testing Alternatives to its listings in 1985.

Cost is a major factor influencing the reduction of experimental animal use in the laboratory. In the years 1972-1978 the costs for the purchase and maintenance of animals for research increased over 500% compared to the inflation rate in the U.S. for the same period of less than 100%. The financial impact of animal laws and regulations are significant. Requirements of the Animal Welfare Act for dogs and nonhuman primates have added an estimated $50,000 for each grant using these species of animals. Since 1986 the costs for random source dogs has averaged about $300 each. (Glantz 1989)

Compared with some of the current complicated and involved scientific techniques using molecular biology, biochemistry of cells and manipulation of genes, animal experimentation provides results that are open crude and only approximations of the true situation. When the use of animals can be confidently replaced by other methods, it will be done. (Soave 1982) The demands for increased and more thorough testing of products to protect the public means more dollars and laboratory space and personnel. If increasing reliance on alternative methods to animal use becomes a reality, the expenses for insuring public health safety and the continual evolution of scientific experimentation can be tolerable.

CHAPTER SIX
PROTECTION OF THE PUBLIC

Police Power

In early times with the beginnings of the English common law the question of when the government could be held liable for its actions was easily resolved. The King can do no wrong, was the original interpretation of the law. There was no redress against the government for its wrongdoings. Times and the law have changed; the government does enjoy some degree of immunity from liability, but this is no longer absolute. When the government performs a service which could be provided by a private corporation this function is considered proprietary with the possibility of producing revenue, making the government liable for its actions

The protection of the health and welfare of citizens of a state is a duty and essential function of that state. Control of epidemics of disease, intrastate movement of animals, the inspection of meat and milk for safety all come under the powers of the state. No other single agency is better equipped or has the authority to supervise and perform these functions. The Police Powers of the government have been challenged an immeasurable number of times, but if enforced reasonably and not abused these powers have been overwhelmingly upheld. Police power is not limited to merely guarding the physical or material interests of the citizens. His moral and spiritual needs must also be considered. The eagle is preserved not for its use but for its beauty. (Barret v State 116 NW 99, 1917)

Laws pertaining to animals and their control come under the category of legislation which are placed within the police powers of a state and its subdivisions. Police power is the inherent force in government used for the protection of the state and its citizens. To prevent the powers of a state to be unduly restricted the limits of police powers are not rigidly defined by the law, but the intent of this power is to control excessive liberties that might be taken by individuals or groups of individuals which might result in, or cause harm, to other citizens of the state.

The states have been granted this power by the 9th and 10th amendments of the United States Constitution. Such powers are extremely broad and most legal actions taken by a state can, or will be, interpreted as being executed for the protection of the public. The federal government, states and municipalities have laws and regulations which apply to the transportation of animals, control of animals by owners, and the licensing of some species of animals. The purposes of such laws are to control animal diseases, prevent animals from damaging persons or property, protect individuals from harm due to contact with animals, to preserve the rights of citizens and to protect the animals. A state may require a fish to be a certain size before it may be taken from the water and kept. The state, as owner of wild game and fish may restrict the capture of wild game and fish on terms and conditions aimed at protection of the animals. (People v Zimberg 33 NW 2d 104, 1948) Federal and State control over animals on the Endangered Species List precludes private individuals from possession of these subjecting them to criminal sanctions. (Favre DS, Animal Law, London 1983, Quorum Books, 16 USC1538)

Statutes enacted to control or eradicate animal diseases dangerous to the health and welfare of the public come under the police powers of the state. The courts have made every effort to uphold the validity of such statutes as necessary for the protection of the public, for example, considering diseased animals public nuisances and a hazard to citizens.

With the vast numbers of animals owned and kept by citizens and the amount of money involved in their care and maintenance, it is inevitable that citizens will be injured or their property damaged by the actions of animals and the government will become involved legally as the defender or challenger of lawsuits involving animals. The laws concerning animals have three purposes; protection of persons and their property, protection of the animals, and protection of the health and welfare of the public.

A few cases involving animals and the exercise of police power emphasize the need and legality of this power.

Assuming that dogs are property in the fullest sense of the word, they are still subject to the police power of the state and may be destroyed or otherwise dealt with as, in the judgment of the legislature, is necessary for the protection of citizens. Decisions upholding the validity of statutes and ordinances providing for the destruction of dogs have invariably viewed enactments of this kind as proper exercise of police power. (Haller v Sheridan 1867, Morey v Brown 1861)

A court held valid a statute authorizing a specially appointed police officer to destroy unlicensed and uncontrolled dogs whenever and wherever found within the jurisdiction. The legislature, in the exercise of its police power, may provide that some kinds of property may be seized and confiscated, upon legal notice and hearing of the parties involved and may also, when deemed necessary to insure the public safety, authorize the destruction of specific property without previous notice to the owner. There is no kind or type of property where the exercise of police power is more frequent or necessary than with dogs (Blair v Forehand 1868)

A law requiring dog owners to pay a fee, register their dogs with the proper authorities and place tags on their animals has been deemed legal and within the police power of the state. (Sentell v R R. Co 1897)

Where an individual allowed their cat to run at large in violation of a county ordinance the court said the county has the express power to dispose of stray animals and to control and regulate the movements of dogs, cats and other animals. (County of Peoria v Capitelli 494 NE 2d 155, 1986)

The defendant was charged with disorderly conduct in allowing two cats to run at large on the premises of the plaintiff in violation of a city ordinance providing no person shall cause, suffer or allow any animal or fowls to run at large or be at large within the village. The finding was for the defendant since this was not a general wandering as only on two occasions had the cats appeared on the plaintiff's lawn. (NY v Christo 225 NE 2d 558, 1967)

When there is a violation of a city ordinance prohibiting dogs to run-at-large, the city must prove the dog owner intentionally or negligently allowed the dog to run at large and took no steps to prevent such an occurrence. No person shall suffer or permit their dog to disturb the peace and quiet of the neighborhood by barking or running through or across public or private property other than that of the owner. (City of Champaign v Auer, 442 NE 2d 330, 1982)

A city ordinance prohibiting the keeping of swine in certain locations within the city was held a valid exercise of police powers. A city has the right through state statutes to determine what constitutes a nuisance. The keeping of a stallion for service within one-half mile of the city public square was determined to be a nuisance. The prohibition of keeping swine within one mile of the county court house was held valid.

Since 1900 New York City, under their Sanitary Code, has had an ordinance preventing the keeping of chickens or other fowl in the built up portions of the city. (Hahn c City of Brooklyn 153 NE2d 359, 1958, Hoop v Village of Ipana 97 Mass 221, 1897, People v Davis 79 NYS 747, 1900)

A defendant was convicted of violating an ordinance requiring the removal and sanitary disposal of dog excrement from the city street and sidewalks. The court said the ordinance was a valid one. A neighbor saw the defendant with his great Dane on the street in front of his house. The dog defecated and the owner walked away without removing the feces. The neighbor called and told the dog owner he was violating a city ordinance, the dog owner replied, "What are worried about its not on your lawn." Found guilty. (Town of Nutley v Forny 283 A 2d 142, 1971)

In a case against a state the plaintiff sought to destroy beavers on his property who were knocking down trees and destroying valuable property. Plaintiff reasoned that the state set free animals with a natural propensity to destroy trees and were therefore liable for the damage. The law states that no person shall molest or disturb any wild beaver or the dams, houses, homes or abiding places of same. Findings were for the defendant state the court saying that the state has a general right to protect wild animals, their preservation being a matter of public interest. The police power is not limited to guarding merely the physical interests of the citizens but also extends to his moral, intellectual and spiritual needs, as in the preservation of wild animals. (Barred v State of New York 220 NY 423, 1917)

A state and the federal government disagreed on the rights of the Department of the Interior to kill deer for research purposes in the state without authority from the state. The decision was for the Secretary of the Interior, the court reasoning that the authority granted to the Secretary for the management of national parks authorizes the killing of deer for an ecology study without first obtaining state permission, even though the United States does not have exclusive jurisdiction over lands within its national parks. (NM Game Comm v Udall 410 F 2d 1197, 1969)

Related to police power are some statutes governing driving under the influence (DUI). Does horseback riding or operating a horse-drawn vehicle come under DUI statutes? This depends on whether the law says motor vehicle or just vehicle. If just vehicle is used, which is defined as a device in, upon or by which any person or property can be transported or drawn upon a street or highway, then horses and horse-drawn vehicles come under the DUI statutes. Several states accept this definition. (State v Williams 449 So 2d 744, 1984, State v Dellinger 327 SE 2d 609, 1985)

In a case where the use of police power may prove to be expensive is where a jury awarded a dog owner $255,000 for the shooting of his dog by two police officers. The officers, with guns drawn, were looking for a car thief . As they passed the dog owner's yard one policeman said the dog growled, barked and rushed at him, so he shot the dog. The owner said the dog was old, arthritic, and friendly. The jury said the officers had seized the dog owner's property in violation of the ban on unreasonable seizures. (Palo Alto Daily News, 12/31/98)

United States Department
of Agriculture [USDA]

The association of veterinary medicine with federal and state governments has been long and productive. The accomplishments of veterinarians in the U. S. Department of Agriculture (USDA) have been of benefit to the government and the profession. It was the resolute honesty and professionalism of a USDA veterinarian, Dr. W. K. Jaques, that led to the passage of the Pure Food and Drug Act and the Beef Inspection Act. Veterinarians continue to perform vital and important roles in several departments of the government.

Federal, state and local governments have for over 100 years seen the necessity for protecting animals from abuse and the public from harm from animals or their products. By the late 1800's anti-cruelty laws, protecting animals from mistreatment by human beings, were enacted by all of the states. In 1906 the Food and Drug Act was passed by the U. S. Congress to protect the public from unsanitary or dangerous practices carried on by the food and drug industries. Since this time protection of the public and animals has resulted in passage of the Humane Slaughter Act, Marine Mammal Protection Act, Animal Welfare Act, and others previously described.

Dr. Jaques, head of meat inspection at the Chicago Stockyards, was fired because he insisted on the condemnation of diseased meat. His testimony was instrumental in the passage of federal acts to improve the quality of foods for consumption by the public. He was largely responsible for the publication of The Jungle by Upton Sinclair.

The two divisions of the USDA most concerned with veterinary medicine are the Animal and Plant Health inspection Service (APHIS) and the Food Safety Inspection Service (FSIS). APHIS controls the reportable and eradicable disease programs, interstate animal health certificates and the Animal Welfare Act as major activities. Private veterinarians may participate in some of these programs if they become USDA accredited. This involves being licensed by a state and applying to the USDA for accreditation. USDA accredited veterinarians participate in disease control programs, disease reporting and activities where federal veterinarians are not available or lack the necessary expertise. FSIS is responsible for pre and post slaughter inspection of food animals in accordance with federal laws and regulations. FSIS cooperates with the FDA on drug residues in food animal tissues and reporting to this agency when levels above the allowable amount occur.

The Science Education Administration (SEA) of the USDA manages the research grant and contract programs of the USDA. SEA funds are managed for agricultural grants in the same manner as the National Institutes of Health manages biomedical research grants.

Meat, Poultry, Milk
Inspection

The protection of the public, consumers, and the maintenance of their confidence in the meat, poultry and milk supply is a major priority of the USDA, FDA, state and local health authorities. In the future the USDA is projecting an increased of shared responsibility with the entire food industry to insure safe products for the public with greater dependability on voluntary compliance and regulations by the industry. (43 FFDCA p 369, 379, 1986)

With respect to meat inspection the U. S. Code says, 'For the purpose of preventing the use in commerce of meat and meat food products which are adulterated, the Secretary (of Agriculture) shall cause to be made by inspectors, appointed for that purpose, an examination and inspection of all cattle, sheep, swine, goats, horses, mules and other equines, before they shall be allowed to enter a slaughter establishment.

Provisions for post-mortem examination of all carcasses, their condemnation, disposal and other actions shall be provided for. Similar provisions are contained in the code for the regulation of poultry processing, antemortem, postmortem inspection, condemnation, sanitation of facilities, labelling and packaging of poultry products." (21 USC 451, ch 10, 21 USC, ch 11 2)

The FDA administers a Federal-State Milk Sanitation Program that provides the public with a safe and wholesome supply of fresh milk and cream. The FDA, in cooperation with the states, has developed a model Pasteurized Milk Ordinance which is the basis for milk sanitation laws and regulations throughout the United States.

Food and Drug
Administration [FDA]

The Food and Drug Act was passed in 1906 because of scandals involving the purity and safety of foods and drugs. Initially, the FDA was part of the USDA, becoming separated in 1941, and more recently becoming a unit of the Department of Health and Human Services (HHS).

Laws enforced by the FDA include the Federal Food Drug and Cosmetic Act (FFDCA, 21 USC 301-392), the Fair Packaging and Labeling Act (21 USC 1 4511 461), which apply to foods and drugs for man and animals, cosmetics and medical devices; sections of the Public Health Service Act relating to biological products for human use, (42 USC 262-263), and the control of communicable diseases, (42 USC 264); The Radiation Control Health and Safety Act relating to electronic products which emit radiation, such as x-rays, lasers, micro wave ovens and TV sets, (42 USC 263b-263n); and Animal Drugs Feeds and Related Products (21 USC 500-599)

The FDA is organized into 6 centers; Biologics, Drugs, Foods, Veterinary Medicine, Radiological Health and Medical Devices. The Center for Veterinary Medicine's mission is to protect the population of the United States by insuring that food additives and food products derived from animals treated with drugs are safe for human consumption, and by regulating animal drugs and feed for safety and effectiveness. These goals are accomplished by:

1.   Developing and recommending veterinary medical policy to the
      FDA Commissioner.

2.   Evaluating proposed and marketed animal drugs, feed additives,
      and veterinary devices for safety and efficacy.

3.   Coordinating veterinary medical parts of FDA's inspection and
      investigation programs and providing veterinary medical support
      for FDA hearings on drugs in court cases.

4.   Planning, directing and evaluating the FDA's surveillance and
      compliance programs related to animal drugs, feeds, and other
      pertinent veterinary medical matters.

5.   Providing policy development and direction to the FDA and other
      governmental agencies for the environmental impact caused by
      toxic substances. (FDA Org. Delegat Manual 1967)

The Durham-Humphrey
Amendment to the FFDCA of 1951

Under previous law a drug manufacturer decided whether a given
drug would be available by prescription or sold over-the-counter (OTC).
This resulted in a lack of conformity and confusion regarding hazardous
drugs. This amendment was aimed at resolving the status of drugs the
FDA believed should be dispensed only by prescription. The result was
that prescription drugs could now only be dispensed by or on the order
of a licensed practitioner - physician, dentist, or veterinarian. In general,
a drug is restricted to the prescription class if it is not safe for use except
under professional supervision. Originally, the law was vague regarding
the veterinarian and prescription drugs, even though the courts implied
that the law applied to veterinarians. The problem was further clarified
in the Generic Animal Drug and Patent Term Restoration Act of 1988,
which made prescriptions legal for veterinarians for the first time. Under
this law veterinary prescription drugs can only be dispensed by, or upon
the written or oral order of a licensed veterinarian in the course of his or
her professional practice. The law also provides for the approval (by the
FDA) of generic drugs without the submission by the manufacturer of

safety and effectiveness data provided they show the drug to be equivalent to an approved brand name drug in all respects. The Act also extended the patent protection term to credit manufacturer's time spent in the research and development of new drugs. (FDA Vet 1989;4;11)

In the United States v JJC et al., the United States alleged that veterinarians had sold drugs directly to farmers without a prescription and this was in violation of FDA regulations. The court said the defendant veterinarians erred in their interpretation of the FFDCA, the defendant's interpretation would either allow unrestricted over-the-counter sale of all veterinary drugs or withdrawal by the FDA of useful drugs from the market the FDA considers to be dangerous unless sold only by prescription. The intent of the FDA for years had been to restrict the use of certain veterinary drugs to the prescription status in order to prevent indiscriminate use of them. (FFDCA 21 USCA 352)

In United States v IBA inc. (1982), The government sought to prevent IBA from shipping misbranded drugs because they were veterinary prescription drugs which had been sold directly to dairymen without a valid prescription from a veterinarian. The judge stated United States regulations require a prescription for drugs so ordered by the FDA. Without the protection given by federal regulations, the health of animals would be put to risk because of misuse of drugs by laymen who are not properly trained in the diagnosis and treatment of diseases for which such drugs are labeled.

A veterinarian who dispenses or sells prescription drugs over-the-counter, without a valid prescription, is considered by the FDA to be guilty of misbranding these products since he or she is stating a prescription is not needed when it actually is. The FFDCA requires all drugs to be labeled with adequate directions for use by lay persons. If such directions cannot be written then the drugs must be dispensed by prescription only. Under the Criminal Endorsement Act (Public Law 98-596, 1984) a veterinarian dispensing drugs without a prescription where one is required may be fined up to $250,000; and such an act is a misdemeanor and can be a felony where damage results in severe injury. Dispensing of drugs outside of a valid veterinarian-client patient relationship is not considered to be satisfactory professional conduct by the FDA, or the veterinary profession. (CFR, Title 21, Food and Drugs)

Extra Label Use of Drugs

Extra label use of drugs refers to any use of a drug, which has been approved by the FDA, not in accordance with the directions on the drug's label, e.g., using a drug for a species of animal not recommended on the label; the label on the drug says for use in horses only, and a veterinarian uses it to treat hogs or, using a drug for a condition or disease for which it was not intended to be used, for example, using an anthelminthic compound as an antibacterial agent. The FDA considers such unapproved use of drugs to be an adulterabon of it because it has been misused. The FDA in the case of extra label use of drugs, may take regulatory or legal action to prevent such misuse or adulteration of drugs.

Extra label use of drugs by veterinarians has been a continuing problem for the FDA. In recent years the law covering this misuse has been more strictly enforced to attempt to curb such use. (Reg. of Animal Drugs, 99th Congress, 1st session, no. 263, 1985) Upon challenge of this regulation courts have ruled that this control of drugs by the FDA does not undermine the practice of medicine or the treatment decisions of veterinarians. (U. S. v Algon Chem. Inc. 1989)

The demonstration and finding of tissue residues of drugs used in food-producing animals has contributed to more rigid controls on extra label drug use. Congress, the public and the FDA have become sensitized to the presence of tissue residues of drugs in food animals because the finding of these occurs frequently. The FDA may allow the extra label use of drugs in food-producing animals when the health on the animals is threatened and suffering or death could result from the failure to treat affected animals. In such cases the following criteria should be met:

1. The attending veterinarian makes a careful medical diagnosis within the scope of a valid veterinarian-client- patient relationship.

2. A determination is made that there in no marketed drug labeled to treat the condition diagnosed, or a drug treatment at the dosage recommended has been found clinically ineffective in treatment.

3.   Records are kept to insure that the identities of the animals treated are known and maintained.

4.   Sufficient time is allowed for the drug's withdrawal or disappearance from tissues before the marketing of meat, milk or eggs to insure that illegal amounts of drug residues do not remain the food products.

A valid veterinarian-client-patient relationship consists of:

1.   The veterinarian has assumed the responsibility for making the medical judgments regarding the health of the animals and the need for medical treatment, and the client has agreed to follow the instructions of the veterinarian.

2.   The veterinarian has sufficient knowledge of the animals condition to arrive at a diagnosis of their medical problems. This means the veterinarian has personally acquainted himself or herself with the keeping and care of the animals through examination and by recent visits to the premises where the animals are kept.

3.   The attending veterinarian is readily available for follow-up visits in the case of adverse drug reactions or failure of the treatment program. (Fed Reg 1986, JAVMA 1987, 190;32)

Bulk Drugs

Bulk drugs, usually in powder form and sold in large containers or tubs, are used for mass treatment of food-producing animals, incorporated into their feed or water. Few, if any, bulk drugs have FDA approval nor do they have the FDA required New Animal Drug Applications. Consequently, these drugs are misbranded and their use is illegal. (JAVMA 1985:189:878)

As in the case of extra-label use of drugs by veterinarians, the FDA has been attempting to curb the illegal use of bulk drugs. In a case where the government sought condemnation of bulk drugs as being misbranded and adulterated, the court held that these drugs were subject to seizure and forfeiture because the chemicals used to produce these drugs had no New Animal Drug Application filed with the FDA and were therefore illegal drugs. (U.S. v KG Containers, 1988)

Because bulk drugs do not have a new animal drug application filed with the FDA they are treated as adulterated and misbranded products. In addition, the FFDCA requires all animal drugs to be correctly labeled as to source, type and nature of the chemicals, and appropriate use of the compound; most bulk drugs are not so labeled.

A licensed veterinarian, after purchasing bulk gentamicin, was charged with the use of an adulterated and misbranded drug and with the conspiracy to commit a crime through their use. The veterinarian failed to use appropriate labels, as required by law, on the gentamicin which he had purchased and illegally used. (U S. v Thomas 1993)

Food Additives
Amendment of 1958

This amendment to the FFDCA established a licensing plan for substances used as ingredients in formulated foods. It includes drugs, or other chemicals added to animal's food or water, such as antibiotics and growth hormone. Such additives must be shown to be safe for human beings and animals. If not, the food containing the additive is considered by the FDA to be adulterated and its use is illegal. The Delaney clause, as a part of this amendment, states; No additive shall be deemed to be safe if it is found to induce cancer when ingested by man or animal, or if it is found, after tests which are appropriate for the evaluation of the safety of food additives, to induce cancer in man or animal, except that this proviso shall not apply with respect to the use of a substance as an ingredient of feed for animals which are raised for food production if the Secretary finds (1) that, under the conditions of use and feeding specified in the proposed labeling and reasonably certain to be followed in practice, such an additive will not adversely affect the animals for which such feed is intended, and (2) that no residue of the additive will be found by methods of examination prescribed or approved by the Secretary by regulation, which regulations shall not be subject to subsection (f) and (9) in any edible portion of such animal after slaughter or in any yielded by or derived from the living animal. (FFDCA, sec. 409(c)(3))

The Delaney clause of the FFDCA has presented problems for the livestock industry, veterinarians, the FDA and the Environmental Protection Agency (EPA). It requires testing of tissues of animals that have been given drugs in their feed or water to insure that no residues are present in food intended for human consumption. This requirement has caused the FDA to specify periods of time for withholding the administration of drugs to food animals before slaughter or before their products can be used as food. The withholding times may be several days to weeks depending on the drugs involved, until no residues are detectable. These requirements must be followed by law and involve agriculturists, industry and veterinarians; this is often difficult to do and to arrive at an acceptable time before the food from treated animals can be used for public use.

A drug used in dairy cows to increase milk production, growth hormone or bovine somatotropin, has been of concern to scientists and the public. Its use may increase milk yield of dairy cows by 40% along with a significant increase in productive efficiency - meaning the milk yield per unit of feed consumed. In 1993 the FDA approved a recombinant DNA bovine somatotropin (rbst) for increasing milk production in dairy cable. This was the first genetically engineered drug approved for use in animals. Opponents to its use claim that the use of such a compound is against the laws of nature since it is not a natural phenomenon but a man-made thing and will increase animal suffering, promote growth of commercialism, contribute to mass farming, will defeat the small farmer and place human beings in the role of the creator. Notwithstanding, genetically engineered growth hormone has FDA approval and must meet FDA safety standards, approved withdrawal periods, and not appear in human food. (Bauman DE, 1993, CVM Update, Oct. 12,1995)

The 1962 Amendments
to the FFDC Act

These amendments to the FFDCA made the approval of drugs more complicated but more important, approval represented a more thorough and effective evaluation of chemical compounds and drugs. Prior to this amendment the approval of drugs under the existing law was granted on the basis of their safety alone; they did not have to work.

After approval of the amendment drugs had to be shown to be effective for their stated purpose, as well as being safe. For instance, now experimental and clinical evidence had to be presented to the FDA that an antibiotic, submitted to the FDA for approval, controlled or was lethal for the bacteria for which it is intended as well as being safe and not toxic to human beings or animals. This rendered the law more demanding and required an increase in laboratory testing by the drug industry, resulting in higher costs in the production of drugs. Now new drugs had to be shown to be generally recognized as safe (GRAS) and generally recognized as effective (GRAE). In reality, this is a logical requirement. To approve of drugs only if they are safe and ignore their effectiveness is ludicrous.

Good Laboratory Practices
[GLP's]

The FDA became concerned about the current laboratory toxicology testing of compounds in 1975 when the random inspection of several testing facilities at pharmaceutical companies and other laboratories showed major deficiencies. Instances of inaccurate results and the inability to substantiate previous findings were uncovered. The FDA took immediate action to insure that drug research and development would be accurate, valid and reproducible. The agency developed the Toxicology Laboratory Monitoring Program, designed to insure the quality and integrity of manufacturer's product safety data submitted to the FDA in support for approval of products regulated by the FDA. Human and animal drugs, food additives, biological and radiation emitting products and human medical devices are all included in the program. This toxicology effectiveness program became known as Good Laboratory Practices (GLP's) in 1979. The GLP,s are only applicable to nonclinical laboratory studies submitted to the FDA, or conducted for submission to the FDA, in support of a research or marketing permits for a product regulated by the FDA, and to nonclinical laboratory studies that involve animals, plants, and microorganisms or their parts. The GLP's are concerned with the acquisition of raw or preliminary data. The regulation requires; (1) only authorized persons may record data entries; (2) data entries may not be deleted, changes can only be made in the form of amendments to the data; (3) the data base must be as tamper-proof as possible; (4) standard operating procedures (SOP's) must be developed for each study to insure the validity of the data; (5) data must be maintained in an approved manner.

Independent of the research and laboratory functions of product development is the Quality Assurance Unit. This unit of the FDA must inspect all phases of a study; necropsy procedures, animal diet preparation, in vivo measurements and laboratory animal handling. These all come under the control of the Quality Assurance Unit.

Ownership of Animals

The dictionary defines an animal as any living creature capable of self-movement. Legally, they are said to be creatures other than man. A creature is a living being, an animal or a human being. In law animals are classified a being domitae — tame, or mansuetae — wild. (Corp Jur 1995)

The ownership of animals is accompanied with responsibilities. The law requires animal owners to keep and maintain their animals in such a manner that they do not harm, injure nor interfere with other persons or with public or private property. If they do owners must answer in the courts for their negligence or carelessness in keeping their animals. Responsibility for the actions of animals is legally rational. On the other hand, animals are considered in law to be items of personal property, like an automobile, and therefore owners are protected by the law if their property is damaged, injured, stolen or killed.

In early English common law dogs were considered to be inferior creatures and given no legal protection. In the minds of the early jurors three things made dogs inferior to other domestic animals; they did not serve as a source of food hence contribute to the economy, they were originally wild and potentially dangerous, were used for protection and hunting and therefore likely to cause injury to human beings and property. Cats in these times were given no legal status whatsoever.

In the United States, and most Western countries, dogs, cats and other domestic animals are considered to be personnel property (chattels personal) and they are governed by the laws and statutory regulations that apply to personal property.

Some early decisions on animals as property have been: a tame canary is the subject of property; peafowls are property in this state; a turkey is a domestic animal which may be the subject of ownership; a mockingbird which has been tamed is the subject of ownership. (47 Am Rep 764, GA 1883; 74 Mass 497,1657; State v Turner 66 NC 618, 1872; Hayward v State 41 Ark 479, 18)

Animals are regarded as property in the system of law of almost every country of the world. For animals to assume legal rights is difficult, if not impossible, where they are items of personal property. Animals are placed in the property category because of their inferiority to human beings and the law does not provide a level of protection for animals above that accorded to inanimate property objects. (Francione GL, Animals, property and the law. Phila 1995, Temple Univ Press)

Domestic animals are treated by law as any other form of moveable property and may be the subject of complete and absolute ownership. The owner has at his command all the protection the law provides in respect to absolute ownership; he may as easily bring a legal action due to injuries to any of his domestic animals as for damage to his person or his carriage. He may sue for their recovery against anyone in wrongful possession of them and they remain his property even when lost or straying. (Pun v Roster 2 Mod Rep 318, 1662; Binstead v Buck 2 Wm. Bl. 1117,1776)

Dogs have a special legal status, being the most regulated of all nonhuman species. Universally, dogs are regarded by the courts as in a class by themselves; unique from other domestic animals such as horses and cows, because of their ability to break through all discipline and act according to their original savage nature. (Fowler v Helck 128 SW Ed 564, 1939)

They have no intrinsic value which we place as being common to all dogs. Unlike other domestic animals they are useful neither as beasts of burden for draft nor for food. They are peculiar in the fact that they differ among themselves more widely than other classes of animals and can hardly be said to have a characteristic common to the entire race. While the larger breeds rank among the noblest representatives of the animal kingdom and are justly esteemed for their intelligence, sagacity, fidelity, watchfulness, affection and above all for their natural companionship with man, others are afflicted with such infirmities as temper as to be little better than a public nuisance. Attacks by dogs on human beings can be most serious in consequence. (Fowler v Helk 128

SW Ed 564, 1939; Boosman v Moudy 463 SW 2d 917, 1972; Williams v Pohiman 257 NE 2d 329, 1970)

Since animals are items of personal property, a legal question is who owns or has the title to offspring when the male (father) and female (mother) belong to different persons? Legally, the increase (litters or young) of tame domestic animals belong to the owner of the dam (female) unless other arrangements have been agreed upon or contracted for. Arrangements can be made that are valid and the owners of domestic animals can agree upon any distribution of the offspring they desire. In one case an agreement for the mating of a French poodle was to be the delivery of a female dog from the expected litter to the owner of the male, the plaintiff. When the owner of the female attempted to break the agreement the court said a female puppy of the litter was the one bargained for and since no other replacement was available, the owner of the male (plaintiff) was entitled to a female from the litter. Where there is a possibility of a breach of contract and the subject of the contract is unique, such as a female puppy from a purebred French poodle, the court can order the surrender of the desired puppy. (Dinken v Weinberger 1957)

Chattels are any tangible, moveable thing; real property - land or a building. Chattels personal are automobiles. clothing, jewelry, furniture, and include domestic animals. Court decisions in the United States have held that dogs and cats are items of personal property. The first decision given in this country recognizing a property right in dogs was given in 1871. It is accepted that dogs and cats come under the definition of domestic animals and come within the meaning of the word chattels, the same as any other livestock. (Niday 1955)

Trespass by Animals

In its simplest interpretation trespass is an entry onto someone else's property without lawful authority or special justification. Domestic animals, if not controlled, have a tendency to stray. If an animal wanders off an owner's property this does not affect the ownership of the animal. The rule of law is that the wandering of animals does not cause the loss of the property right in them held by the owner. By straying onto another's property they do not become the property of the non-owner . In the maintenance of livestock an owner must exercise reasonable care to confine his stock and take proper precautions to prevent their wandering onto another's property. Animal owners can be strictly liable for the acts of their wandering animals, but in most cases an owner has to be negligent before being held liable for damages caused by trespassing livestock. (Oakley 1946, Brownbach 1987)

The law has changed on the question of trespass. Formerly, the owner of property or an animal or an inanimate thing, was held strictly liable for the harm the animal caused. The owner was totally identified with his property for damages. Where my beasts without my will and knowledge enter onto another's property, I shall be punished for I am the trespasser with my beasts. This concept of absolute liability is no longer applied to the trespass of animals and the degree of liability may differ according to the circumstances of each case.

When livestock trespass upon the land of another person the occupant of the land may take possession of the wandering animals and keep them until paid for damages if any and receive a fee for the care and feeding of the animals while on his property. If a lawsuit occurs, legal fees may also be awarded.

Largely in the Western United States it was, and still is in some areas, the custom and accepted rule to allow livestock to range freely over the open land. Property owners fenced animals out, not in. Trespass on another's land was a common occurrence and suits for trespass were not allowed unless damage to a neighbor's property was proved.

Plaintiff owned a thoroughbred Holstein-Friesian heifer which he intended to breed to his prize bull, also a Holstein-Friesian purebred animal. Defendant's lowly born bull, with no prize connections, trespassed onto the plaintiff's land and finding the female Holstein in a receptive mood, proceeded to service her. A calf and a lawsuit were born from this alliance. Findings were for the plaintiff, the court ruled the defendant was negligent in allowing his bull to trespass and was fined the difference in value between the mixed breed calf that was born and that of a thoroughbred animal (Kopplin c Quade 145 Wisc 454, 1911)

Plaintiff's horses at night roamed on about 40 acres of unfenced land next to the plaintiffs. One night the horses strayed even farther, invading the land of the defendant, trampling and eating carefully planted flowers and shrubs. Defendant heard the animals, got his gun and shot, striking one horse in the hip, one in the neck and the other in the rump. Defendant claims the horses were trespassing and destroying his beautiful landscaped area. The court ruled the defendant had a right to drive the horses off but not to shoot them. (Steward v Oberholtzer 258 P 2d 369, 1953)

Plaintiff and defendant owned adjoining farms, separated by a fence, part of which had been built by the plaintiff and part by the defendant. It was the duty of each to maintain their section of the fence. Plaintiff had planted a corn crop on his land but the defendant's hogs got in and ate up the crop. Both claimed the other's portion of the fence was in disrepair. Finding was for the plaintiff as evidence showed the broken part of the fence was on the defendant's land and was broken and falling down due to the defendant's negligence. (Eichel v Dudley 179 NE 2d 812, 1961)

Plaintiff owned a valuable Russian wolfhound with an impressive pedigree. When the hound and some other dogs invaded defendant's property and attacked his chickens he drove the animals away. The wolfhound and another dog returned and again went after the chickens. Defendant shot and killed the wolfhound. Findings were for the defendant, the court saying regardless of the hound's pedigree the animal was trespassing and the defendant had the right to protect his poultry from attack, and even if the hound was worth more than the chickens, it was at fault in trespassing. (Sabin v Smith 147 P 1180, 1915)

Plaintiff had a 20 acre tract of land planted in alfalfa, enclosed by a barbed wire fence. Defendant's 800 sheep trespassed onto the land and demolished the crop, even though defendant removed them within 25 minutes. The plaintiff's fence did not satisfy the legal requirements of the state. Finding for the defendant who was not shown to have willfully turned the sheep loose and did attempt to promptly regain the sheep after they were loose. (Woofter v Lincoln et aux. 309 P 2d 622, 1957)

A newspaper boy come onto defendant's yard where the owner had a miniature poodle. The owner cried out "Keep away from the dog." The boy attempted to pet the dog and was bitten. The defendant dog owner claims the boy was either committing a trespass or was teasing, tormenting or abusing the dog. The court found for the plaintiff saying the boy was not trespassing but in the yard to deliver a newspaper and in petting the dog was not teasing or abusing the animal. (Doerfler v Redding 205 A 2d 502, 1964)

A five year-old boy and his sister entered defendant's fenced-in back yard and the boy was severely bitten by the defendant's dog. The plaintiff's attorney (for the boy) attempted to show the dog was a known vicious and dangerous animal and the child could not be guilty of contributory negligence. Findings were for the defendant. The dog's record as to viciousness was clean the boy was indeed trespassing. (Dykes v Alexander 411 SW 2d 47, 1967)

Plaintiff's had mining claims in an area of the state and had built roads and cabins. Defendant brought sheep onto the land to graze, resulting in damage to the roads and pollution of a stream used for water, and causing a stench around the area. Plaintiff's sue and were awarded damages since the boundaries of the mining claims were clearly marked and the sheep committed a trespass and interfered with the mining operations. (Ward v Chevallier Ranch (354 P 2d 1031, 1960)

A twelve-year old boy took a short cut home and was assaulted by a dog attached to a 15 foot chain connected to a building which contained a sign "beware of dog." Findings were for the dog owner, the court stating that even if the dog did have vicious propensities the dog owner acted in a reasonable prudent manner by posting warnings and chaining the animal within his own property. (Weber v Bob and Jim Inc. 296 NYS 2d, 1969)

The courts do not impose strict liability for the trespasses of pet animals such as dogs and cats, providing the owners are not negligent in allowing them to roam. Confining dogs and cats is difficult and their wanderings usually do not result in property damage, as with cows, horses or sheep. However, if a dog owner knew his animal was an invader of garbage cans or ruined flower beds, he could be liable for trespass. (Bender 1942)

A property owner brought suit for trespass and to recover damages to his property due to pollution. The plaintiff had 155 acres of land and raised cattle, some crops and had a pecan orchard. A lead company began operation next to plaintiff's property and the smelting process emissions of lead particles and sulfoxide gasses damaged the animals and crops. The plaintiff is allowed to recover damages if his losses are proximately caused by the lead company;s trespass (Borland v Saunder Lead Co 2 ALR 4, 1042, 1979.

Brands and Fences

Due to the wanderings of range animals where fences are rare animals were, and still are, branded for the purposes of identification of the roamers. Animal brands are considered to be legal evidence of ownership provided the sign or symbol used has been recorded with the proper authorities. The right to use a specific livestock brand is a property right in states that have statutes which include branding statutes. The brand belongs to its owner and it may be transferred or sold as long as this transaction is duly recorded. (Weaver 1985)

Requirements for renewal of registering brands vary for from 2 to 10 years. Animals that can be branded are cattle, horses, hogs, sheep, and mules. Some states include poultry, mules and asses. Branding is usually accomplished by means of the use of a branding iron (heat), the use of acids or caustic chemicals, or freeze branding. At least 30 states have branding laws today; the State of New Mexico has 30,000 registered brands. Brands must be unique, identifiable, recorded, and are required in most states where animals are allowed to roam free. (Meyer 1990)

Aside from range country, owners of domestic animals are responsible for damage their animals cause to another's land through trespass. If cattle break through a fence, enter the land of a neighbor, trample and consume crops, the owner of the animals is responsible for the damages. An owner of animals is also liable if he removes a fence and his animals trespass and damage another's land. In moving domestic livestock from one location to another down a road or path liability for trespass usually does not apply if the animals are lawfully driven and negligence does not occur. The privilege to use a road to move animals includes immunity to casual trespass on lands adjoining the road. (McElqunn 1986, Brownbach 1987, Thompson 1959)

A businessman was returning home with his wife and 2-year-old son. It was dusk and he suddenly spied a horse on the highway, struck it, killing his wife and injuring his son. The defendants were not the owners of the horse but pasturing it for them. The horse had wandered onto the road. The issue here is whether it was negligent for the defendant to pasture horses in an area of open range where they could wander onto the highway. The court said Montana has been an open range country before it became a state. The law that provides recovery for damages by trespassing livestock can only succeed if the trespassed property was enclosed by a legal fence or if there was willful and intentional driving of livestock onto another's land. In open range country the owner of livestock has no duty to prevent these from wandering and he is not negligent if such wanderings take the animals onto a highway which runs through the open range. The keeper of the horses had violated no duty owed to the plaintiff. (Bartsch v Irvine 427 P 2d 302, 1967)

In the state of Ohio by 1895 the courts recognized, with the growth and spread of the population and industry, animals had to be fenced in, rather than fenced out.. In Morgan v Hudnell, 52 Ohio St. 552, 1895, the court held that if an animal breaks onto the property of another and there damages real or personal property of the one in possession of said property, the owner of the trespassing animals is liable without reference to whether the animals were vicious and if such propensity was known to the owner. Today, the statutes of most states prohibit animals from running at large and make owners liable if damage is caused by the animals.

Liability for Animals,
Control of Dogs

Most states, cities or municipalities have laws or ordinances aimed at the control of dogs. These are directed to control disease, prevent the animals from becoming nuisances or injuring citizens. They provide for the quarantine, licensing, impounding and control of owned and stray dogs. Such statutes have been challenged by the public many times but the authority of the government to enforce such laws, along with the reasonable application of these, has been invariably upheld. For example, in one case this regulation of dogs under the police power of the state was sustained, the court saying, "Dogs are a species of personal property and are subject to the police powers of the state. (Crunk 1959)

Dog bites and injuries caused by dogs are of frequent occurrence and often of a severe nature; sometimes fatal. About 20 deaths occur each year in the United States from dog bites with about 70% of these occurring in children under the age of 10 years. Dog bites are a major medical problem. Five percent of all children between the ages of 1 and 9 years are bitten by a dog each year. The numbers of children injured in this way is greater than the cases recorded by health authorities for measles, mumps, chicken pox and whooping cough for this age group. One million dog bites are reported each year to the U. S. Public Health Service, but undoubtedly, an unknown number of minor bites go unreported. A more rational figure for dog bites is 5 to 10 million per year for the U. S population.

Legally the owner of an animal is responsible for its actions. Animals being items of personal property gives ownership certain rights but with these come responsibility. The owners of animals must control them in such a manner that they do not cause harm to other persons or their property.

Generally, at common law, if the owner of an animal has no prior knowledge, nor reason to believe, that the animal would become vicious or dangerous and injure persons or property, the owner is not liable unless he was careless or negligent. Legally, this has been called the "every dog is allowed one bite" rule. Once an animal has caused an injury and the owner is aware of this fact, he is responsible for any damage caused by the animal. The origin of the one bite rule may go back over 5,000 years to the Bible which says:

> If an ox gores a man or woman to death, the ox shall be stoned and its meat will not be eaten, but the owner of the ox will not be liable. But if the ox has been in the habit of goring before, and its owner has been warned but has not kept it under control, then should the ox kill a man or woman, it will be stoned and its owner put to death. If a ransom is imposed on the owner he will pay whatever is imposed to redeem his life. (Ex 21:28-29)

Prior knowledge of dangerous tendencies of an animal imposes absolute liability on the owner; the rule applies to dogs, cats, horses, bulls, goats, etc. The liability of an owner of a known ferocious animal for damages caused by it to another person is absolute when the animal is kept with the owner's knowledge of its dangerous tendencies and the injured person did not voluntarily and consciously act to bring about the injury. (Sibler 1958, Utzkuhn 1959)

A farmer was gored by a bull he had borrowed from a neighbor to breed his cow. The injured farmer sought to recover damages from the owner of the bull for his injuries. The court decided in favor of the bull owner because the animal had not previously shown any vicious behavior (Mann 1956)

The doctrine of strict liability means a person is liable without proving the occurrence of negligence in a duty owed to other persons. An individual who keeps an animal known by the owner and others to be dangerous assumes complete liability for continuing to keep the animal. Where a dog owner knew his dog had bitten several members of his family and a visitor on his premises, he was liable when his dog, without provocation, bit a boy peacefully walking along the sidewalk.

A tenant made out a check for his rent and asked his secretary to deliver the check to the landlord. In carrying out the assignment the secretary was attacked and severely bitten by the landlord's dog. The court said that one who knowingly keeps a vicious dog is liable to the person injured even though the injury occurred on the owner's land. Knowingly keeping such an animal constitutes negligence per se. (Turner 1941)

Biting is not the only type of injury caused by animals. A dog jumped out of a window, struck and injured a person walking on the sidewalk 16 feet below. Evidence showed the owner of the dog knew it was trained as a guard dog, was aggressive and made several attempts to jump out of the window. (Russo 1956)

When an animal that is known to be dangerous by it's owner is boarded or left with another person and this keeper of the animal knows of these dangerous tendencies, he as well as the owner becomes liable for damages caused by the animal he is keeping; liability for damages attaches to the keeper of the animals, as well as the owner. (Tidal Oil Co. 1941)

In a case involving an *invitee* a woman was injured when she was attacked by a dog when she was in the dog owner's home. Alleged that the owner failed to muzzle and restrain the dog since he had prior knowledge that the dog had previously bitten another person. The trial court decided in favor of the defendant dog owner, concluding the woman was in the dog owner's home as a social guest and had knowledge of the dog s aggressive nature. On appeal, it was decided the woman was an invites because the dog owner had asked her to come to his home for business matters to give him some tax advice, consequently he was liable for the injury as she was legally in his premises. (Phillips v Lindsay 1987)

A trailer park resident suffered contusions and injuries to her foot when another residents dog jumped on her, put his paws on her chest and knocked her down. The court found for the dog owner saying he owed no duty to the trailer resident and was not strictly liable since the dog had no known aggressive propensities. (Phillips v Lindsay 1967)

A husband and wife sued for personal injuries sustained by the wife. The couple were walking along on the sidewalk when a dog jumped at her, she caught her foot in the pavement and was injured. The court found for the husband and wife and on appeal it was held, 1. the dog had strayed onto the sidewalk in front of the owner's house and was not at large, 2. the owner had no knowledge of the dog's potential to rush or jump at people and was not liable under the strict liability rule for known dangerous animals. (Slack v Villan 1964)

A mother and her 4-year old child visited a friend of the mothers. When they knocked on the door the friend's 2 dogs began to bark loudly, the child screamed and was viciously attacked by one of the dogs. The child's lip was torn open and puncture wounds were inflicted on the face, neck and throat. On appeal the court found for the mother and child saying under an animal control act animal owners are liable for injury sustained if an animal, without provocation, attacks or injures any person who is peacefully conducting himself and is lawfully on the premises and this does not require proof of the dog's vicious nature or the owner's knowledge of such nature. The dog owner was liable for the injuries suffered by the child who screamed when the dog began barking and was attacked. Screaming was not a provocation for the attack. (Robinson v Meadows 1990)

The legal concepts of responsibility for damage or injury done by dogs equally applies to other species of animals. The principles of law are the same. A person who maintains a horse, bull, goat, cow or other potentially dangerous animal known to be vicious is liable for damages caused by such animal. In many cases the dog bite rule applies and if an animal owner had no reason to know or believe his animal was dangerous, liability does not attach to him, unless he is negligent in the keeping or handling of the animal.

This rule was applied where a horse was pastured adjacent to a school yard and reached over the fence and bit a child playing in the yard. The pasture's fence met the requirements of the municipality for an adequate one to contain a horse and there was no evidence the horse had bitten or threatened to bite anyone previously. The owner of the horse had not been negligent in keeping the horse and was not liable. (Liepske 1959)

The responsibility of an animal owner to those who come onto his land and there encounter a dangerous animal is primarily a question of the privilege of the visitor to come onto the land. Strict liability of the animal owner extends to social and business visitors who lawfully come onto the land. It does not ordinarily extend to trespassers or others who come on the land illegally or without invitation. However, courts have held that the owner of a known vicious dog may be held liable for injuries done by the dog to a trespasser and he is certainly liable for damage done to invitees. Even in wrongful trespass a dog owner is under the duty to exercise due care to prevent injuries to a trespasser. (64 ALR 3d 1039, 1972)

A company had a watch dog, usually tied, near the door of the business. A sign was posted on the time clock, Do not feed or pet the dog. Plaintiff employee was used to patting the dog on the head and found him friendly. One day the dog was in the middle of the doorway; as the employee reached to pet the dog he barked, jumped at her and inflicted severe hand and face wounds. The dog had bitten other persons on at least two occasions. Findings were for the employee plaintiff since the court found she did not provoke the dog, was in the habit of patting the dog and her actions did not constitute contributory negligence. (Ellsworth v Elite Dry Cleaners 274 P 2d 17, 1954)

Plaintiff was a customer in defendant's store where she was attacked and bitten by a dog. Unfortunately the dog had rabies requiring the plaintiff to undergo treatment. In her lawsuit the plaintiff contends the defendant storekeeper had a duty to keep the premises safe for customers. The animal was unleashed, diseased and dangerous. Defendant states the dog was a stranger, did not act abnormally, and no one knew of the animal's danger. Decision for the defendant; absence of evidence that the defendant knew of the dogs dangerous character (166 NE 71, 1933)

A case emphasizing the application of police power is one where dog owners attempted to reverse an order from a Commissioner of Health to destroy their dog. The court held that legal notice according to due process of law had been given to the owners, the dog had bitten 3 persons in 24 hours and this was sufficient to have the dog destroyed since the bites in each instance were severe enough to require medical treatment (Reda v NY City Health Dept. 1987)

The rule that harboring a known vicious dog renders the owner liable for injuries to human beings applies to damage done to other animals also. An ordinance prohibiting a dog of vicious nature to run at large, included dangers to other animals rightfully and peacefully on the streets as well as human beings. (People v Kay, 1989)

The current trend in the United States is toward the enactment of Dog Bite Statutes. These impose strict liability on dog owners even if they are unaware of an animal's previous viciousness. Under these statutes injury to a person or damage to property by a dog at large is the full responsibility of the owner or person responsible for the dog.

Most courts accept the view that dogs that attack and/or kill sheep or any livestock may be destroyed and this is a valid exercise of police power. Two examples of this are; a statute providing for the killing of any dog found, not on the premises of the owner, worrying, wounding, or killing any sheep or goats is valid. A statute providing for the killing of any dog found running, worrying or injuring sheep or cattle has been upheld (Johnson 1899, 98 P 2d 865, 1940)

When a dog injures or kills other domestic animals owners have been held liable because this is damage to another's property. Dog owners must control their animals in a manner that they will do no harm. In an action to recover damages for injuries and death to a chicken flock caused by a dog the court held that chickens are domestic animals within the meaning of a statute allowing for recovery from dog owners for domestic animals killed or maimed by a dog.

A person who kills a dog, or other domestic animals, that are doing damage to his property may be liable for the value of the animal killed. The right to destroy another's property depends on several factors. Even though a dog may be caught in the act of killing chickens it is not reasonable to shoot the dog if there are other means of stopping the animal's actions. The killing of the dog may not be warranted where it is obvious that the value of the dog is greater than the damage done to the chickens. (Chandler 1959, Tillery 1957, Smith 1959, Hill 1941)

Assumption of Risk

In tort cases this may be an affirmative defense used by a defendant in a negligence suit in which it is claimed the plaintiff had knowledge of a condition or situation which was obviously dangerous to himself and yet he voluntarily exposed himself to the hazard created by the defendant; this thereby relieves the defendant of any legal responsibility for any resulting injury in employer-employee relations. The assumption of risk is related to the express agreement of an employee to assume the risks arising out of his employment or occupation

Plaintiff's husband was killed by a bull on a dairy farm where he was the owner's tenant. The bull was mean and vicious and kept locked in a pen except when used for servicing. The plaintiff let the bull out for service and turned his back on the animal. The bull hit him full force in the back and killed the tenant. Findings were for the landlord. He is not liable for injuries caused by a vicious, mean animal where the tenant had full knowledge of the animal's character. (Hapke v Huston 22 NE 2d 124, 1939)

A husband and wife had a business training and boarding horses. Both were experienced with horses. They agreed to board and train an Appaloosa stallion for a friend while he was on vacation. The horse attacked the wife as she finished exercising it, knocking her over and biting her on the head, neck and shoulders and breaking her right index finger. It was later found the horse had injured 3 other persons. Judgment was given for the horse owner. The wife, a trainer of horses, assumed the risks of her job when she turned her back on the stallion. (Hardin v Christy, 1984)

A delivery man sued to recover for injuries sustained when bitten by a dog. The delivery man was on the property of the dog owner where there were signs posted warning of the presence of a dog; the dog was not known to be vicious and the delivery man assumed the risks of his job when he entered onto the property. (Benton v Aquarium Inc., 1985)

A receptionist employee of a veterinary hospital was bitten by a dog and the dog owner sued. The dog was brought into the hospital to be spayed, taken to the kennel and given a pre anesthetic sedative. Later the veterinarian asked the receptionist to bring the dog to the surgery. The dog was lying in the kennel, sedated but awake. The receptionist put a leash on the dog's neck and tried to bring it to the surgery but could not move the animal. She bent down to take the leash off and was bitten on the chin. The decision of the court was that the dog owner was not liable since the veterinarian's employee was performing her job and contact with and handling of dogs is an assumed risk of employment. (Tschida v Berdusco, 1990)

Horse Injuries

Horses are a source of pleasure, satisfaction, beauty and contribute to our agricultural and social economy. Nevertheless, they pose a potential danger to human health. The severities of human injuries range from minor cuts and bruises to death. There are about 12 million horses in the United States and each year 40 million persons ride a horse at least once. Contact with horses, including riding, cause about 250 deaths and 90 thousand injuries annually in this country. (Bixby-Hammett 1987) Next to boxing, horseback riding results in more serious head injuries than any other sport, including football. The injuries per number of hours engaged in this sport are larger than those occurring in motorcycle and automobile racing. (McGhee 1987)

Legally, owners of animals are responsible for an animals actions causing human injuries. In the case of horseback riding persons willingly, knowingly and voluntarily choose to ride a horse. In most cases the owner or renter of the horse is not liable unless negligence or carelessness is involved on the part of the owner, lessor.

Most injuries are the result of carelessness or faulty equipment. For example, tack failure, meaning poor equipment, is responsible for one-half of all injuries. Three fourths of riders receiving injuries to the head and neck do not use protective head gear (helmets). Safe equipment, proper instruction and supervision help to prevent injuries. (McLatkie 1979)

In the two year period, 1987-88, there were 92,763 hospital emergency room visits for injuries related to horseback riding, 14,120 of these involved a fracture of the upper extremities; arms, ribs, collar bone; ten percent of these required hospitalization. Soft tissue injuries, bruises and cuts, are the most common ones overall, next are fractures, sprains and concussions. The most serious injuries are those that occur to the head and neck. (Whitlock 1986)

Hospital reports on 305 persons treated for horse-related traumas showed 53% were due to falling off a horse with 44% of these having cuts and sprains, 30% head injuries, and 16% fractures. Several individuals had multiple wounds: franctures, sprains, cuts and bruises. (Seaber 1970-78-79-83) One who rents a horse to a person impliedly promises, or warrants, that the horse is suitable for the purposes for which it is rented, i.e., horseback riding, and the renter is liable for injuries resulting from viciousness or dangerous habits of a horse if he had knowledge, or should have had, of its dangerous habits. (Cohen 1957)

Riding stable owners or employees should attempt to determine the level of experience and expertise of the renters of their animals. If the owner or employee knows a horse is excitable or unsuitable for the casual rider, the renter is liable for injuries that occur to the renter. In addition to the horse's temperament the geographical area — hills, mountains, cliffs, vertical climbs, and the suitability of the equipment should all be considered by stable personnel.

Persons involved in fairs, exhibits and animal shows are also required to exercise reasonable and ordinary care in handling the animals to protect the public from damage or injury. Often, animals on exhibits or in contests become excited and aggressive. This fact should be taken into account by the responsible persons to prevent the occurrence of injuries to the attending public. (Darnald 1956, Weaver 1942, Mann 1956)

Prior knowledge of an animal's propensities, if these indicate potential harm to persons, render a horse owner or keeper liable for injuries. A riding academy patron was injured when his mount was frightened by the academy owner's dogs, causing the horse to rear up and throw the rider off. The owner's employee rented the horse to the customer and knew of the animal's tendency to become frightened and excited by the dog. Due to this prior knowledge the owner of the riding academy was responsible for the damages. (Collen 1957)

In another case, an owner of a dairy farm was deemed negligent in not foreseeing possible damage to an employee and giving him warning. A milk processing plant employee was trampled by a cow which became frightened by a photographer's exploding flashlight bulb. The court found the dairy owner and the photographer did not exercise ordinary prudence and care because they should have told the employee the cow was about to have its picture taken and the procedure could frighten the animal, since an exploding flashlight bulb is not a common occurrence in a dairy. (Darnald 1956)

An owner of a horse who is negligent in keeping and controlling an animal may be liable for its actions even though there is no evidence of prior dangerous tendencies. A 4-year old boy was kicked and injured by 2 horses running down a street in a populated part of the city. Evidence was presented showing the owner of the horses was negligent in allowing the horses to run loose in a crowded area. (Weaver 1942)

A horseback rider was injured during a fox hunt and sued the sponsor of the hunt. Due to the unique circumstances of a fox hunt, the sponsor had posted notices that the procedures were in compliance with the regulations of the 'Injuries from Equine Activities Act. In addition, the sponsor did not have to determine the riding ability of the participant to manage her animal in a safe manner since she furnished her own horse. The hunt sponsor's horse ran into and injured the plaintiff. The "Injuries from Equine Activities Act' provides that an equine activity's sponsor shall not be liable for injury or death to participants resulting from the inherent risks of equine activities. The finding was for the defendant sponsor. (Muller v English 472 SE 2d 448, 1996)

One who lets a horse for hire, although not an insurer of the horse's fitness and abilities, is under an obligation, sometimes called an implied warranty, to furnish an animal that is relatively safe for the purpose for which it is to be used and for a failure to use due care to discover dangerous propensities in rented animals, or to disclose these to the hirer, otherwise he may be held liable for injuries or death resulting from such negligence.

In Dam v Aliso Riding School (57 P 2d 1315) the court held it to be the duty of a liveryman to inform himself of the habits and disposition of the horses he keeps for hire. He must exercise reasonable care to ascertain such facts and if he fails to do this he may be held liable even though he did not know the horse was unsuitable for the intended use. The court said, "We agree that it is not always necessary to prove actual acts of misbehavior on the part of the horse prior to the accident, but in some way the plaintiff (injured party) must prove such facts as will justify a jury in finding that at the time and place in question the horse was unsuitable for the purposes for which it was hired.

Where the owner of a horse farm agreed to instruct a 14-year old girl in horseback riding and to provide an instructor to ride with her and to furnish a safe and dependable horse, he is not an insurer against every accidental injury which she might receive while riding the horse. (Smith v Pabst 288 NW 780; 1939)

Dangerous Animals

Dangerous animals are those which are known to be dangerous or those which the owner or keeper should know are likely to cause damage or injury to persons or their property. As previously indicated, in law animals are divided into two classes; those that are by nature wild and ferocious and domestic ones that are not usually dangerous. A wild animal, even if tamed, cannot be regarded as being safe. Unlike wild animals, domestic ones must be shown to be dangerous. Stallions, mules and bees, although at times dangerous, are classed as domestic animals while deer and raccoons are considered to be wild and potentially dangerous. The courts have not applied the rule of absolute liability for the keeping of wild animals to bees. Beekeepers are liable for damage done by their bees only if the owner or keeper was negligent in controlling the bees. Keeping wild animals imposes strict liability for damages on the keeper, as opposed to the keeping of domestic animals. The keeper or owner of wild animals, in spite of reasonable care and precautions in their management, is absolutely liable for any damage done by them to persons or property, hence, an act of negligence need not be shown to show them at fault.

A person keeping or boarding wild animals, even though not the owner, may be responsible if the animal inflicts an injury upon a person or their property. In an action brought to court for the loss of a finger, allegedly bitten off by a bear kept in a pen at the defendant's sale barn, judgement was given for the plaintiff who lost the finger. It was held that one who harbors a vicious and a dangerous animal, such as a bear, is responsible even though he is not the owner of the animal, for injuries caused by the animal to persons on his premises. (Corp Jur 1973)

States are given custody and ownership of wild animals as a part of their sovereign rights and they may regulate the taking, possession, capture or killing of wild animals. The property rights of an individual may occur in wild animals after they have been taken and kept in the possession of a private person. In the wild state they are not the property of any private citizens. (Crunk 1959)

The general rule for wild animals is that they are not the subject of absolute ownership while alive except in a limited form. They may be reduced to ownership by being taken into captivity and/or tamed until release or escape. Any animals that are in captivity, lions in a zoo or deer in an enclosed park, are subject to ownership while in captivity and are as much the subject of property of their owners as are domestic animals. (The case of Swans, 7 Co Rep 15b, 1592)

If a man brings into captivity wild animals and keeps them on his land he is liable for damage committed by them when they trespass on another's property. The rule is the same as for trespassing domestic animals and wild ones. Reclaimed animals are those of a wild nature but are useful for human food or for other reasons and have been tamed or are in captivity, such as deer, fish, ducks, bears, or buffalo. If these animals go to a neighboring land and trespass and do damage, the owner is liable for trespass. (Dewell v Sanders Cro Jac 490, 1618)

Plaintiff was riding his motor scooter on a Los Angeles street when the defendant's dog dashed onto the street, collided with the motor scooter causing rider to fall and receive serious injuries. The plaintiff claims this is in violation of an ordinance requiring dog owners to keep their animals on their premises or on a chain or leash when in public areas. The findings were for the plaintiff, the judge saying modern city conditions no longer permit dogs to run at large on the city streets. (Brotemarkle v Snyder 221 P 2d 992, 1950)

A motorist was driving on a highway when a deer leaped out and struck his car, injuring the driver and damaging the car. Driver of the car charges the state with negligence in not removing the underbrush along the highway so deer cannot jump out from under cover, unseen. The court said the protection of wild animals is a proper governmental function for the benefit of the general public and one cannot complain of incidental injuries from wild animals. (Anthony v State of New York 122 NYS 2d 830, 1950)

A motorist was injured when striking a bull that was on the highway. The court said there is no duty under the common law to keep domestic animals from being unattended on the highway. The fact that the animal was there and caused damage to a person's property did not make the animal owner liable for the injury, unless the owner was negligent in permitting the animal to be on the highway. It is the legal duty of a person having charge of animals to exercise ordinary care and the foresight of a prudent person in keeping their animals under control in a reasonable manner. (Pennyvan 1957, Gardiner 1940) An automobile, carrying passengers struck a mule on the highway and some passengers were injured. The court found that the owner of the mule exercised due care in the maintenance of the animal and was not negligent and therefore not liable. (Forier 1958)

Courts have classed dogs as potential dangerous weapons, taking into consideration the size, breed and disposition of the dog in question and if it has been handled in such a way as to cause injury to human beings or to property. Dangerous weapons have previously been considered by the courts to be inanimate items; guns, knives, clubs or brass knuckles. Recently a court held that a dog, used in a way as to constitute a threat to other persons, could be placed in the category of a dangerous weapon. (People v Kay 1989)

A class or breed of dogs known by the name of Pit Bull have been labeled by some authorities as being naturally dangerous and vicious animals. Pit Bulls have been responsible for one-half of all of the human fatalities from dog attacks recorded by health authorities in the past 15 years. Statutes have been enacted by several municipalities in the United States to require registration of these animals with animal control departments, requiring owners to carry insurance policies to cover the cost of any injuries that might result from an attack, with coverage as high as $50,000, and the keeping of these dogs in secure pens or cages. When taken from the owner's property the dogs must be muzzled and held on a strong leash. Prior demonstration of viciousness is not required to be demonstrated by injured persons to recover for injuries from the owner of a Pit Bull.

Pit Bull owners have objected to such laws as being contrary to the 14th Amendment of the U.S. Constitution, which says, "No state shall deprive any person equal protection of the law. Citizens rights are not to be abridged. All persons born or naturalized in the United States and subject to the jurisdiction thereof are citizens of the United States, nor shall any state deprive any person within its jurisdiction the equal protection of the laws."

Pit Bull owners and dog associations have recommended to law makers that breed neutral would be more acceptable than breed specific laws, i.e., applicable to Pit Bulls only. Such a law should include; 1 definition of a vicious dog, 2. why it is considered to be vicious and what actions make it so, 3. precautions that must be taken by owners to insure safe-keeping of the animals, 4. penalties to be assessed against owners of vicious dogs if they fail to abide by the regulations. Courts have ruled in favor of both breed specific and breed neutral laws, saying, "Dogs are subject to the full police powers of the state and may be destroyed or otherwise regulated in whatever manner the legislature deems reasonable for the protection of citizens." (Turnispeed 1988, Sentell 1897, Munn 1947)

A dangerous dog has been defined by legislatures as being a dog which has inflicted an injury, without provocation, a dog which has killed or injured a domestic animal, without provocation and any dog kept for the purposes of fighting. (Syracuse Law Rev. 1988)

The keeping or use of dogs for the purposes of fighting other dogs or animals is illegal in all 50 of the states of the U.S. It is a felony in most with fines as high as $100,000 and 5 years in prison. Transporting of dogs interstate for the purpose of fighting is also illegal. Similar types of laws have been enacted that apply to the keeping and use of game cocks (roosters) for fighting, (Ohio No. Law Rev 1988, 828 F Supp 196, 1986, Hoe 1986, Cal. Penal Code 597.5, 1983)

Dog fighting is barbaric and as a spectator sport sickening and one would believe a thing of the past. The following newspaper release shows this is not true.

Police broke into a warehouse and arrested 78 spectators at a Pit Bull dogfight contest, some spectators came from over 1,000 miles away to attend the spectacle. Over $50,000 in cash from bets placed on the fights was confiscated. Two dogs were already dead from fight wounds and 3 more seriously injured. The animal control officer said such dogfights are a common occurrence. (S.F. Chronicle 1995)

Laws similar to those that apply to dog fighting are in effect covering cock fighting, bullfights, fights between any animals and between a man and an animal. (USCA sec. 2156)

A case illustrates the why the public has reason to fear the dangerous potential of Pit Bull dogs: An individual raised and kept Pit Bulls and several of them had viciously attacked human beings. The dogs were kept in an enclosure which was not secure and the animals could come and go as they pleased. Eight of the dogs escaped from the enclosure and attacked and killed a woman lawfully walking along the street. The dogs knocked the woman down, stripped off all of her clothing except the shoes, tore her scalp off, inflicted numerous bite wounds and the woman died of the wounds and shock. The court said, "If an owner of a mischievous animal, knowing its propensities, shall willfully suffer it to go at large or shall keep without ordinary care any such animal and while at large it kills any human being, who shall have taken the precautions which circumstances may permit to avoid such animal, such owner shall be deemed guilty of manslaughter. (Munn 1947)

A number of governmental agencies in recent years have dealt with the perceived threat of Pit Bull dogs for the safety of citizens by enacting regulations aimed at these animals under the provisions of the police power of the government. The constitutionality of these laws have been challenged several times as improper use of the police power, as a deprivation of due process of law, or a failure to provide equal protection under the law. In Sharkey v Township (628 F Supp 198, 1986) a federal court held that a township could reasonably determine that Pit Bulls are dangerous animals. Invariably this type of restrictive legislation has been upheld. (U. Dayton 1988, City of Richardson 1990, Young 1990)

Restrictive animal control legislation must address three factors; 1. the protection of the public health and safety, 2. the protection of the constitutional rights of animal owners, 3. to respect the need for all animals to be treated in a humane manner. (Thorne 1988)

Injuries to Animals

As emphasized previously domestic animals are items of personal property and an animal owner has the right to bring a legal action and, if successful, collect damages if his animals are injured, killed or if their value is decreased due to the actions of another person. Liability of a person who injures or kills the animal of another person depends to some extent if the animal was damaged due to a lack of reasonable care, i.e., was the person committing the damage negligent? For example, a motorist cannot be considered negligent for damages when he injures a dog that dashes out onto a street in front of his car. The motorist does have the responsibility to stop when he strikes the animal and give or seek aid. Conversely, a driver of an automobile that is breaking the law, speeding or driving dangerously or on the sidewalk, and injures an animal, he is negligent and totally responsible, other mitigating evidence lacking. If an injured dog is not licensed and a local ordinance requires licensure, it has been held that the dog, being an item of personal property, the owner can still recover damages for negligent injury to the animal even if it is unlicensed. (Jones 1936. Scharfield 1942, Dalton 1940)

Negligence is usually the deciding factor in determining the liability for damage to an animal. In one case where a carrier, or transport company, did not properly care for an animal in their custody, they were held liable for damages. In Laridain v Railway Express Agency the carrier could not demonstrate the loss of a dog transported by it was due to negligence or lack of care by the owner, thereby making the carrier responsible for the loss of the dog. The court concluded that the defendant carrier failed to relieve itself of its obligation to the client by not taking proper care in the handling and delivery of goods entrusted to its care. The animal left its point of origin in apparent good health, with a veterinarian's certificate to this effect. On arrival at destination the dog was stumbling, uncoordinated and obviously in poor condition. It died in 3 weeks. Examination of the animal by a veterinarian led him to conclude the animal had suffered a severe blow to the head. The carrier was liable for the value of the dog. (Laridain 1951)

Most state statutes regulate the transportation of animals and require that transportation companies shall not allow any animal to be confined in any type of conveyance for more than 28 consecutive hours without being exercised, properly rested, fed and watered as necessary for the particular species of animal. The animals must also have adequate space in the primary enclosure in which they are transported. (Virginia Codes, sec. 3.1, 796.43)

Value of an Animal

The present concern for the welfare and rights of animals has influenced court decisions regarding the monetary value of pet animals. In a recent decision a judge said, "A pet may not be just a thing but it occupies a special place somewhere between a person and a piece of personal property." Usually, in law the value of an animal is judged by its market value: a 500 dollar dog is worth 500 dollars if injured, stolen or killed. In some special cases involving performing animals earning large incomes for their owners, recovery may be allowed for the loss of income generated by these highly trained and talented animals. A dog performing in motion pictures or a racehorse may, on the market, be worth thousands of dollars and in these cases the owner may recover an amount far in excess of the market or commercial value of the prized animal for its damage or loss.

Emotional stress is another recent concept where damages may be granted in excess of the commercial value of an animal if the emotional stress, in the view of the court, is real and damaging. In such cases punitive damages may be awarded. In one example a court decided a city had, through its fault and negligence, caused the loss of a dog by a city official. They allowed recovery for mental stress far in excess of the market value of the animal because it was a dearly loved family pet. Punitive damages have been awarded where an animal, in the care of another person, is severely injured or killed through the gross negligence and dereliction of duty of that person in caring for the animal of another person.

In a decision where that value of an animal was greater than that of its mere replacement, a defendant racetrack owner did not take reasonable and necessary precautions in the operation of his track and the plaintiff's horse was severely injured and had to be killed following a collision with another horse. It was shown in court that the accident could have been prevented through the use of due care on the part of the track owner. The horse owner was awarded over $100,000 for the loss of the horse. The legal argument in this case was that the measures of damages should be the value of this particular animal and not the value of an ordinary, non-racing horse. The decision shows a changing philosophy by the courts to examine the true value of an animal and not simply its market or replacement value. In this case the horse had the potential of earning large amounts of money based on its previous performances and its loss deprived the owner of a significant amount of income. (Trial Lawyers Guide, Feb. 1968, U. Hawaii 1982, NY Law Sch Rev 1988)

It has been decided that a person, not negligent, causing the death of a dog that he believed was about to do serious harm may not be liable for the killing of the dog. In this case the defendant struck and killed the defendant's dog with his car on purpose because he had seen the dog attack a boy standing on the street. The defendant was not held liable. (Devincenzi 1959))

If an individual places poison on his land with the intent of doing harm to another person's animal, he is labile for this action, even though he notifies the owner of the animals of his intent. Conversely, a property owner is not liable for the death of trespassing animals from poison consumed on his land when the poison was intended for controlling gophers and rats and he was not negligent in the use of the poison. A landowner's use of poisonous substances on his land does not make him an insurer against harm to trespassing livestock. (Bruister 1958 12 ALR 3rd, 1103, 1967)

The validity of an ordinance preventing the running of dogs at large was challenged. It was held by the court that a person who keeps a dog and permits it to run at large is responsible for its actions. The animal may be impounded without the filing of a complaint against the owner or giving him notice of its impoundment. This represents a valid exercise of a city's police power and does not deny the dog owner due process of law. Property is held by owners subject to the police power of the state and cannot be used or held in a manner that injures others or their property. (Thiele 1957)

Owners of dogs subject themselves to lawsuits if they violate statutes aimed at the control of dogs. Where a law required unlicensed dogs to be kept on a leash in the owner's yard and leashed at night, an owner was liable when his dog escaped and attacked a person lawfully on the street. (Duffy 1960)

Laws have been upheld requiring the licensing and vaccination of dogs against rabies. Some statutes require the vaccination of all dogs against rabies that reside in the city's limits, unless they are kept in an enclosure, on a leash or muzzled. Vaccination and the payment of a license fee have been challenged by the public many times and upheld by the constitution as being reasonable and not confiscatory. (State v Thule 1939, City of Birmingham 1938)

Law suits may result in cases where a dog is shot and killed by a police officer. If the officer was performing his duty and the dog was in violation of laws for the control of dogs, there is no liability on the part of the officer or the government. In Ruona versus the City of Billings the plaintiffs sought to recover damages for a dog shot by an officer while the animal was running at large. A statute for the control of rabies had been passed by the city authorizing the shooting of dogs running free in the city. The dog in question had chased a child and the policeman attempted to catch the dog but was unable to do so; as a result he shot it. There was no liability on the part of the officer or the city. (Ruona 1958) In a similar case a dog was intentionally shot and killed by an officer. The defense was that the dog was not licensed nor wearing an identification tag as required by a city statute for the control of stray dogs. The court held that the city has the right to enforce such a statute even to the extent of shooting dogs in violation of the law if there is no other means available for the control of the animal. (State 1946)

Notwithstanding the above cases, a police officer does not have the right to overextend his authority or take action against an animal where he has no legitimate reason to do so. A dog warden is not authorized to seize, kill, destroy or otherwise dispose of a licensed dog, not running at large or in the act of attacking or killing sheep. (Perkins 1958)

A policeman and the city for which he worked were sued for the wrongful killing of a dog. The policeman trespassed on the plaintiff's land without permission of the plaintiff with the apparent intent to unlawfully kill the dog. The court awarded the plaintiff several hundreds of dollars for mental pain and suffering due to the loss of the dog, saying:

1.   Dogs are items of personal property.

2.   A vicious dog, which is a public nuisance, may be lawfully killed when roaming at large, endangering the safety of persons and property, but the danger must be real and imminent and the animal must be running at large. (City of Garland 1963, Meekins 1963, Corp Jur 1973)

Guard and Police Dogs

A common practice is to use dogs for the purposes of protection or to guard property. One court has stated regarding the use of guard dogs that a person shall not permit the use of a guard dog on any premises unless a person or handler, who is capable of controlling the dog is present on the premises, and:

1. The dog is under the control of the handler at all times while it is being used, or:

2. The dog is secured so that it is not at liberty to go freely about the premises.

The use of police attack dogs has been a controversial issue for several years. How reasonable is it to use force and is the "find and bite" method used in the apprehension and arrest of a criminal suspect reasonable?

The use of police dogs results in reduced police search time, protects the safety of officers; they are less likely to lose the suspect, the risk of an ambush is low and the potential for being overpowered is reduced. The use of dogs may be better than the use of a deadly force; assault guns. However, persons suffering from dog attacks claim a violation of the 4th Amendment of the Constitution, unreasonable seizures, not being arrested in a reasonable manner, and the use of a greater than a minimum amount of force necessary for the situation.

The United States Constitution, Bill of Rights, Article IV states, "The right of the people to be secure in their persons, houses, papers and effects, against unreasonable searches and seizures, shall not be violated, and no warrants shall issue but on probable cause, supported by oath or affirmation, and particularly describes the place to be searched and the persons or things to be seized. (Whittier Law Rev 1992)

Statutes have been enacted by the states to protect the public from sudden unwarranted and surprise attacks by guard dogs when on premises lawfully and not in the act of trespassing. A person arrested filed a civil rights action against a city alleging his constitutional rights had been violated when a police dog injured him during his arrest. The district court said, "The law regarding the use of police dogs to find, seize and hold suspects was not clearly established at the time of the incident, but the use of police dogs to search for, find and seize a suspect, by biting if necessary, was reasonable under the circumstances." (Statute L.R. 1990, Chew 1990)

The estate of a burglary suspect, killed by a police dog brought a civil rights action against the officer involved and the police department for the death of the suspect. Judgement was given for the defendant police officer, the judge saying the use of a police dog to apprehend a suspected criminal does not amount to the use of a deadly force. (864 F 2d 1987)

The use of dogs to detect the presence of narcotics is a valuable aid in police work. Its reasonableness under the 4th Amendment of the United States Constitution depends on how this detection aid is used. The legality of the use of dogs to sniff one's luggage depends on the presence of strong suspicions that drugs in the luggage are probably present. In one decision the judge said the suspicious actions of a dog after sniffing justified the seizure of the plaintiffs bag. The plaintiff claimed his rights to privacy had been violated through the use of the dog. The court held for the defendant policeman saying, " a sniff of a piece of luggage is not a search in the traditional manner." (Colo Lawyer 1990)

The use of explosive and drug detecting dogs has been contested several times as being a violation of one's right to privacy under the 4th Amendment of the Constitution. A state court held the 4th Amendment does not apply to the use of dogs to examine inanimate objects and a canine sniff does not amount to a search. However, if an object must be removed from the possession of the owner this may amount to a seizure and this taking must be based on a reasonable suspicion of the presence of illegal material. (Pooley 1985, 482 U.S, 896, 1983)

U.S. Custom Dogs

The United States airports that have incoming international flights now use Beagle dogs to inspect the luggage of arriving passengers for the presence of food, animal products or plants prohibited from entry into the U.S. from foreign countries. The Beagle Brigade is now made up of 50 dogs that are the hardest working, lowest paid employees of the United States Civil Service Corps.

The beagles sniff luggage and packages brought into the U.S. for the presence of animal or plant products that may introduce agents of disease or plant pests into the country. For each discovery of an unlawful product the dog-finder receives a choice bit of food and a pat on the head. In one international airport two Beagles on duty will uncover an average of 200 pounds of contraband; this amounts to from 5 international airports over 1,000 pounds of potentially dangerous fruits, plants, meat and animal products discovered each day.

Beagles were chosen for the job by custom officials because they have a wagging tail, a sweet disposition, are not fierce or aggressive, and have a keen nose. They represent a breed that will not upset travelers when nosing their luggage and yet do a superb job. (The Penn Stater Sep/Oct 1994)

Control of Other Animals

In the past cats received no legal support such as that granted to dogs and domestic livestock; they held no legal status. In part this was due to the rarity of legal cases involving cats; their legal status had not been challenged nor clarified. In recent years cats have gone-to-court; a review of law suits involving animals produced 30 cases where cats were the subjects of litigation. (63 ALR4th, 1987)

The one-bite-rule described with dogs is not often enforced with cats and the demonstration of prior viciousness may not have to be shown with these animals. Today, many states have passed statutes that place total liability on owners of dogs, cats and other animals, regardless of previous knowledge of the animal's aggressiveness or viciousness. Still, in several instances prior knowledge of viciousness has been deemed necessary for the recovery of damages in the case of injury by animals to human beings. In one of these, the court said dangerous propensities in a cat with the owner's knowledge of these was necessary to place liability on the owner for damages done by the cat. (Lee 1976)

Cats, as items of personal property, are protected by law and stealing or injuring them gives an owner the right of recovery for their value or the damages inflicted. This may be the market value or, if proven, recovery for mental stress and sentimental value for the loss. (155 CA App 1976)

Municipalities have in recent years attempted to control the cat population by requiring the licensing of cats, similar to dogs. This is a legitimate exercise of the police power by the government but difficult to enforce with the cat population due to their wandering nature and difficulty and objection to capture to check for compliance with license law.

In addition to dogs and cats, all species of animals are subject to governmental control. The major reasons for this are the control of diseases transmissible to human beings and other animals, to protect the property interests and rights of individuals and the state and to control nuisances created by animals

The health departments of the states are given the power to control diseases of animals when and where they might endanger the health of the public. The government also has the powers to prevent adulteration of food and drink, prevent pollution of water supplies, abate nuisances that affect or may disturb citizens, and enforce programs for the maintenance of the public health, such as vaccination clinics for human diseases, rabies control and the disposition of animals and their wastes. (Ark Lawyer 1984)

Veterinarians are required to comply with laws and statutes dealing with animal disease control, sanitary and public health measures and anti-cruelty laws dealing with animals. Failure to do so may constitute culpable negligence. (Eau de Hog, 1984) Veterinarians should familiarize themselves with anti-cruelty laws because, 1. they may be called upon to testify in court in cruelty cases, 2. state statutes or laws may require the evaluation of a veterinarian as to what constitutes cruelty, 3. the veterinarian may be accused of cruelty in the handling or treatment of animals, 4. most practice acts make conviction of cruelty to animals by a veterinarian a cause for suspension of the license to practice. (Hannah, JAVMA 1997:211 47)

Sales of Animals

In previous times the rule of Caveat Emptor, let the buyer beware, applied to all sales of goods, including animals. Due to untrustworthy and unscrupulous sellers, buyers have become protected by the law. The sale and purchase of animals are subject to the same principles of contract as other goods and come under the Sale of Goods Act of 1979 and allied legislation.

For a binding contract of sale there must be an offer, which has been unconditionally accepted based on an intention to enter into legal relations between parties with the ability to contract in law, and there must be some consideration which is usually the price, not necessarily the actual value of the animal, usually in the form of money. The seller surrenders the animal and the buyer payment in some form.

A contract for the sale of goods need not be in writing, oral contracts for the sale of animals are valid, e.g., animal auctions where the agreement to buy may be the nod of the head, but the more valuable the animal(s) sold are the better to have a written contract. The parties to the sale of an animal may include whatever terms they wish into their agreement, so long as they are not illegal. Terms usually included into an agreement are known as conditions or warranties. If a term is of fundamental importance to the contract, it becomes a condition, if it is peripheral it will be a warranty. Generally, stipulations as to soundness of an animal or its ability as a breeder or racing horse are treated by the courts as warranties. The Sale of Goods Act provides the basis for matters as the time of payment, (on delivery), and the place of delivery (seller's premises) and remedies when things go wrong; failure to deliver the animal or failure to pay for it. It is implied that the seller has the right to sell the animal and any warranties applying to it, and the buyer has the right to quiet possession of the animal. In all these transactions there is an implied condition that the animal sold will be suited for the purposes for which it is sold.

 In the sale of animals most courts place liability on the seller if the animal was diseased and if there was no valid health certificate issued by a veterinarian and the seller knew of the animals diseased condition. If the seller did not know of this and had no reason to know, he is not liable. (Hannah, JAVMA 1995:206:36)

 A veterinarian may be involved in the sale of animals. If the veterinarian fails to make a proper examination of the animal(s) for sale which would meet acceptable standards of care and to issue a proper health certificate and to notify seller or buyer of the presence of a zoonotic disease dangerous to man and other animals, the veterinarian would be liable for malpractice and negligence.

 A plaintiff sued the defendant for alleged fraud in the sale of one-half interest in a dairy herd of cows. The defendant told the plaintiff the herd was free of Bang's disease, but it was not. The court held this was not an expression of opinion but a fraudulent misrepresentation on which the plaintiff relied and he was entitled to recover damages resulting from the loss of milk production and the value of the animals for dairy purposes as opposed for sale as beef. The herd had been under quarantine for Bang's disease at the time of sale. (Cloakley v Bouslog 234 P 2d 880, 1951)

Warranties

Express and implied warranties apply to the sale of goods. Legally, goods shall be fit for the purposes for which purchased. The word goods is broadly interpreted to include tame and other domestic animals and their sale is protected by the rule of implied warranty (Uniform Commercial Code 1991, sec. 2105.1)

When an auctioneer acts as the agent for an animal owner and sells livestock and the name of the owner is disclosed, the auctioneer is not personally liable for defective animals; if the identify of the owner is not given the auctioneer is liable if defective animals are sold. Generally, in the absence of an express authorization from an animal owner, an auctioneer has no power to warrant the goods he offers at an auction so as to bind the seller. His agency does not carry with it by implication the power to warrant for the owner. (Drake Law Rev 1982, Ark Law Rev 1984, Iowa Law Rev 1985)

An animal feed manufacturer sued a family farm corporation on their alleged open account to buy feed. The farm filed a counter suit claiming the feed was defective and dangerous and the warranty as to the quality of the feed was breached. Recent purchases of feed had a large amount of fines, which separate the feed components, and as a result the cattle overeat ingesting toxic substances such as urea and rumensin, develop acidosis and rumen damage. Following a complaint on this condition the next batch had even more fines. The farm's losses were $182,363 and with undisputed evidence that the feed was defective, an award of $166,363 was given to the farm. (Cargill Inc., v Elliott Farms 363 NW 2d 212, 1985)

A thoroughbred horse owner sued a grain retailer for the loss of 11 horses which died from eating moldy grain. The court found the owner of the horses was guilty of a degree of contributory negligence by using the feed and was awarded $22,500 which amounted to 15% of the horse owner's total loss of $150,000.

A pig breeder sued a feed producer for breach of an express warranty claiming the feed sold to him did not contain the promised nutrients and medications and his pigs died as a result of this lack of ingredients. The plaintiff pig owner seeks to recover for damages to his business, recovery is denied due to lack of proof of lack of ingredients. (Drew v United Product and Consumer Corp. 778 P 2d 1227, 1989)

A cattle feed operator brought an action against a manufacturer of a synthetic growth hormone because his cattle gained weight more slowly than expected. The ruling was that the cattle owner could not recover for the economic loss due to the slow weight gain of his cattle since this fact could not be proved with certainty. (Tomka v Hoechst Celanox Corp. 528 NE 2d 103, 1995)

In a case against a seller of hay for a breach of warranty the seller did sell a product not fit for a particular purpose. The feed was not fit for livestock consumption and the seller did not inform buyer of the defective feed. (Lester v Logan 893 SW 2d 570, 1994)

The central issue in warranties is an animal's fitness or suitability for a specific use or purpose. Did the animal fulfill an implied promise on the part of the defendant (seller) that the animal would satisfy the buyer's expectations? Such a promise is a warranty and was this breached?

A television actor was rehearsing a scene where he was required to crawl under a horse. After the first trial the actor complained that the horse moved and on the next one it moved and stepped on the actor's hand, crushing 2 fingers. In court the plaintiff actor claimed the defendant had assured him the horse was a veteran performer and guaranteed the animal to be safe for the TV production. Defendant horse trainer claims the horse had never showed any signs of aggression or viciousness. Decision was for the defendant horse trainer because evidence was insufficient to show he had failed to exercise reasonable care in determining that the horse was safe for the purpose intended. (Baum v Central RR Co. 175 NE 2d 828, 1958)

A plaintiff signed an agreement before riding a rental horse, "I the undersigned assume all responsibility for horse and equipment and it is understood that the management is not liable in case of an accident." The plaintiff claims a friend told the renter of the horse that she was not an experienced rider. She had difficulty handling the horse and on the trail the horse suddenly spun around, broke loose and threw the rider against a tree trunk causing severe head damages. Testimony showed the horse had tried to throw an experienced rider, and the plaintiff contends the defendant had given her a horse that was not suited for an inexperienced rider and had therefore breached an implied warranty of fitness of the horse for the purpose intended. Finding was for the plaintiff since the defendant did agree to furnish a gentle and easy to ride horse. (Estes v Smith 282 P 2d 534, 1955)

Defendant sold to the plaints 16 milk cows and some land and falsely and with the intent to defraud, orally told the plaintiff the cows were not infected with Bang's disease and he had never had Bang's disease in his herd. The cows were infected with Brucellosis (Bang's) prior to the time of the representations. The plaintiff had relied on the statements of the defendant and due to this suffered losses (damages) of $10,256.60. Three cows were infected with Brucella at the time of the sale and 4 more became infected subsequently. Damages awarded to the plaintiffs.

The plaintiff bought 1500 white leghorn chickens and later purchased another 1900 and agreed to pay $1.25 per chicken within one year. At the time of delivery all of the chickens suffered from chronic respiratory disease (CRD), complicated by coccidiosis and a generalized secondary bacterial infection. Plaintiff was assured the chickens only needed antibiotic in the feed. This was done but did not control the disease. An award of $7,761.80 plus fees to plaintiffs. (Hawkins v Jackson 103 SE 2d 634, 1958)

Warranty of Soundness

Consistently, in European countries the shaking of hands was used to bind a bargain, this was true with horse sales, called a hand sale or *vendito per mutiam*. It is difficult, without the use of negatives, to explain the meaning of the words sound and unsound as applied to horses. One judge held the word sound meant perfect, another said sound means the animal is free from disease at the time it is warranted. It may be defined that a horse is sound when he is in possession of his natural and constitutional health and in such bodily perfection as is consistent with his natural formation. (Kiddel v Elurnard 9M and W 67, 1836-97)

In the English Common Law of the 1600 and 1700's it was already recognized that in the sale of horses a warranty of soundness, or the presence of unsoundness, presented problems for the seller and buyer of horses or other animals. Soundness, or the presence of disease or an abnormality, is often a matter of opinion, even with the use of an expert on horse flesh. A warranty of soundness has been a continual question for the veterinary profession, especially when a horse warranted sound turns unsound. A warranty is in the nature of an insurance regarding the condition of the animal and when a person warrants a horse sound he insures that of which he knows very little. Unlike the warranty of manufactured goods, a horse is warranted on a matter of opinion. If an action is brought on a breach of warranty of the soundness of a horse, the owner or the seller is entirely in the hands of the veterinarian. (Oliphant GH, The Law Concerning Horses, London, 1647, Sweet and co.)

Product Liability

Product liability is related to the law of warranty in that it is a breach of a manufacturer's guarantee of the usability of a product. A major difference being that in warranty a product, or an animal, may not be useful for the purposes for which it was bought while in product liability a product placed on the market has a defect which causes injury to human beings or animals. For example, a cattle prod is faultily made with 100 times the accepted electrical charge and thereby kills animals when used by the purchaser. The manufacturer would be liable for death of animals due to a defective product.

A manufacturer is strictly liable when an article is placed on the market, without inspection, that has a defect that causes injury to man or animals (377 P 2d 897) A breeder of thoroughbred horses sued a grain dealer to recover for the loss of 11 horses which died from eating moldy grain. The judgement was that the owner of the horses was guilty of a degree for contributory negligence because he knowingly used the moldy feed. He was awarded $25,000, which was 15% of the horse owner's total damages of $150,000. (Adkins v Burns Mill and Feed inc., 844 So 2d 839, 1994) In Lester v Logan (893 SW 2d 570, 1994) A seller of hay was sued for a breach of warranty over the farmer's cows who ate the hay purchased from the dealer and died. The hay was not fit for livestock consumption.

Auctioneer

An auctioneer in selling property for another is the agent of the seller, or owner and represents all of his rights and liabilities. These, in the absence of any statutes changing them, are governed by the law of agency. Where the auctioneer, or agent, has disclosed his principal he becomes the vendor himself and is responsible for the title to the goods auctioned. When a contract has been completed the auctioneer is personally liable on the contract unless prior to its formation he has disclosed the principal for whom he is acting, if the principal is disclosed, he is the person who then has the contractual relation with the bidder. (Williston on Sales)

Wills

Various types of trusts or the willing of property and money to animals, or for the purposes of their care or memory, have been recorded over the years. These may be enforceable depending on their intent, extent of the coverage, and the feasibility of carrying out the wishes of the donor.

A woman bequeathed $30,000 for the erection of a suitable fountain for the benefit of thirsty birds and other animals to be placed in a prominent place in the city, accessible to all animals. The heirs contested the will and the court ruled that a charitable gift to benefit man through animals is a good and acceptable charity. (Coleman Estate 138 P 992, 1914)

A gentleman left $150,000 to a state Board of Child and Animal Protection Agency with the request that the Agency use the money to provide protection and relief to hungry, thirsty and abused and neglected cattle, horses, dogs and cats and to use the income to prosecute those who neglect and abuse animals. The heirs said the gift was too vague and indefinite to enforce. The court said the bequest was valid as a public charity. (Forrester Estate 279 P 721, 1929)

A Chicago citizen left $40,000 for the erection of a drinking fountain for horses in a Chicago park and a statute of a horse named Cook with a plague giving the donors name, the name of the horse and its time for a race at Garden City Park race track in 1856. The court said a charity is defined as benevolence, kindness and this gift satisfied this definition.

A charitable trust, which neither law or public policy forbids, may be applied to almost anything that tends to promote the well-being of social man. Gifts or benefits for the general preservation or protection of animals are usually sustained as fitting a charitable purpose. (Ould v Washington Hospital 95 US 303, 1877)

A trust for the support of a dog is valid under a statute providing that gifts for humane purposes shall be valid. In ones last will and testament it was provided that the sister of the testatrix should have a life interest in all her property except for the sum of $1000 which was to be set side and used for the continued care of the pet dog of the testatrix. The will was upheld. (Willet v Willet 31 ALR 426, 1923)

Insurance

Animals, being items of personal property, are as insurable as an automobile, diamond ring or a fur coat. Any item of personal or real property can be insured, depending on the insurer's willingness to take the risk on the property to be protected and the willingness of the insured to pay the required fee. One difference in insuring animals is that they are living things subject to injuries, disease, accidents and damage by careless or mischievous persons. This makes insurance of animals more precarious due to the uncertainties of the future of living things.

The owner of a horse sought to recover under his insurance policy which covered destruction of the animal in case of an incurable illness or injury providing that a written certificate from a qualified veterinarian was first obtained certifying that destruction of the horse was necessary to relieve incurable suffering. A veterinarian found an insured horse was totally blind from periodic ophthalmia which rendered the animal useless as a saddle horse. The horse was not suffering from acute pain. On the advice of the veterinarian the horse was destroyed. The insurance company maintained that destruction of the horse was not necessary to relieve incurable suffering. The judge said suffering and pain are matters of interpretation in their meanings. Blindness can certainly result in a degree of suffering and pain due to contact with unseen objects and from the fear of the unknown. (Abraham v Ins Co. No Amer 84 A2d 670, 1912)

A horse apparently had a broken leg, the bone was splintered, shattered and protruded through skin of the animal. It was suffering pain and misery and a veterinarian recommended disposal of the animal. It was held that the killing was justified and the insurance was collectable. (Livestock Ins Co v Edgar 105 NE 641, 1914)

A horse had a disease from which it could not recover and the plaintiffs claimed as an act of mercy, and to prevent suffering, that a veterinary surgeon direct the horse be killed; this was done. The court ruled, in denying liability on the part of the insurance company, that it was not shown that the horse was suffering or in pain . (Tripp v Northwestern Livestock Ins. 59 NW 12, 1894)

Most cases in law reports on insurance for animals seem to involve horses, but almost any kind of animal can be insured; prize bulls, purebred dogs, performing animals, rare and exotic ones, and even for sentimental reasons depending on the insurance company and the insurer.

Patents, Copyrights and Trademarks

The purpose of the United States Patent Act is to protect one who conceives of and develops a new product from being copied by other persons and to insure the developer that the time, interest and money spent in making the product ready for marketing will not be wasted or lost for specified period of time; long enough for the inventors to recover monetarily for their effort. Patent protection is usually for 17 years. Under the Patent Protection Act of 1988 this may be extended for several years to remunerate originators for their time in the development of a product.

The U. S. Supreme Court said, "The patent system is designed to undergird the investment in pushing technology forward. It functions most effectively in the expensive, breakthrough technologies where uncertainties of success or payback abound. The patent system offers the innovator a temporary respite from copying." (206 Q 1980, 595 E 2d 1979)

Section 101 of the U. S. Patent Act states, "Whoever invents or discovers any new or useful process, machine, manufacture, or composition of matter, or any new and useful improvement thereof may obtain a patent therefore, subject to the conditions and requirements of this title. (35 USC 161, 1983)

Non-patentable items are principles, laws of nature, mental processes, intellectual concepts, ideas, natural phenomenon, mathematical formulae, methods of calculation, fundamental truths, original causes, motives, the Pythagorean theorem, and computer implementable claims.

The grant of a limited but exclusive property right in a human being is prohibited by the Constitution. (U.S Constitution Art. 1)

A patent application was submitted to the U. S. Patent Office in 1972 for a genetically engineered bacterium capable of breaking down (digesting) the components of crude oil. Such organisms would have significant value for the cleaning of oil spills from tankers when they occur in oceans or waterways. Such a property (oil ingestion) was not possessed by any known, naturally-occurring bacteria. The patent office refused to grant a patent on the grounds that the application was for a living organism, a product of nature, therefore not patentable.

On challenge, the application reached the Supreme Court for decision. This review produced some basic and essential conclusions relative to the patentability of living organisms.

1.   Although the Plant Protection Act excludes bacteria from its protection, this does not mean that Congress intended to exclude al living things from section 101 of the Patent Act.

2.   In the claim for a patent entitled, "Microorganism having multiple, compatible, degradative, energy-generating plasmid and the propagation thereof," application should not have been rejected on the sole ground that the claim was for a living organism.

3.   The purpose underlying the patent system would require the court to include microorganisms and cultures in the terms, "manufacture and composition of matter," found in the Act and the fact that the subject matter is alive is a distinction without legal significance and it should be treated under this section no differently than chemical compounds.

4.   A live man-made microorganism is patentable subject mater under section 101 of the Patent Act. The applicant's microorganism constitutes a manufacture of composition of matter within the statute (49 Bench Bar Minn, 1996)

In 1991 a group of farmers, animal welfare and animal protective associations filed suit against the U.S. Patent Office challenging the rule that non-natural occurring, living organisms are patentable matter. The court of appeals ruled that the decision was an interpretive one exempt from the notice and comment requirement of the Administrative Procedure Act and, secondly, the farmers and animal groups did not have standing to seek a declaration that animals are not patentable subject matter and an injunction against the inssuance of animal patents was out of order. (932 F 2d 920, 1991)

Prior to the above patent court decisions living cells and whole animals were placed in the category of natural phenomenon and were not patentable. An exception to this rule of living things being excluded from patenting was the acceptance by Congress in 1930 for the patenting of asexually produced living plants, "Whoever invents or discovers and asexually produces any distinct and new variety of plant, including plants varying from the normal, mutants, hybrids and newly found seedlings, other than a tuber-propagating plant or a plant found in an uncultivated state, may obtain a patent therefore, subject to the conditions of this title." Luther Burbank, the famed botanist, was a major force in promoting this legislation to protect and encourage agricultural research. (35 USC, sec 161, 1988)

The Plant Protection Act and the decisions in the Chakrabarty and Bergy cases prompted the U.S. Patent and Trademark Office in April of 1987 to announce it would consider applications for non-naturally occurring, nonhuman, multicellular living organisms: i.e., genetically altered whole animals. The case influencing this decision was an application for a patent of a genetically manipulated Pacific oyster, made sterile through genetic engineering and therefore edible throughout the year, unlike naturally-occurring ones. The first patent given for a whole mammal was in 1988 for a mouse susceptible to cancer that was produced through genetic manipulation. "Last month the government granted the first patent on something that can look you in the eye."

Persons against the patenting of living organisms say:

1.   The availability of patent protection for animals will foster excessive interference with the natural world.

2.   The patenting of animals will de-value human life.

3.   The issuance of a patent on animals will contribute to the suffering of animals in research and agriculture

4. The patenting of animals will lead to a decline in the genetic diversity in commercial species of animals and will accelerate the trend toward commercialism of academic research.

5. The patenting of animals will undermine the family farm. (Vermont Law Rev 1993)

When government actions have been challenged, not only for the patenting of animals but with the Marine Mammal Protection Act, Endangered Species Act, Wild Horse Act and others, the courts have often raised the question of standing with respect to the challengers of these acts. To have standing a plaintiff, or the challenger of a law, must show to the courts that he or she has a personal interest, or stake, in the outcome of the controversy and show an injury to them that is protected by the Constitution. (Memphis 1991, Creighton 1991, UMKC 1990)

Copyrights cover creations by individuals or groups that include books, articles, music scores and the like. Many veterinarians write scientific articles, books or stories for popular consumption. If published by a recognized company or organization these are copyrighted to protect author and publisher from plagiarism or duplication of material for gain without permission. Some types of copyrights may extend for the life of the author plus and additional 50 years.

Trademarks are signs, logos, pictures, drawings or other types of symbols that identify a company, manufacturer or business with a particular activity, product or profession. Sometimes veterinarians desire to have an identifying symbol or mark on their place of business on cards or on a vehicle used for business purposes. Such items can be protected from being copied by the registration of the trademark with the proper authorities. This is best done by an attorney familiar with the Patent and Trademark Office.

As evidenced in this section the public has become more concerned about the position of animals in our society, their legal and moral rights as living creatures. The patenting of living things is another legal and moral question which has aroused concerned opposition as well as keen support. The U.S. Office of technology predicts several million applications for the patenting of genetically engineered living organisms in the next decade. On patenting, Adam Smith (political economist) in 1776 found that patents are a good way of rewarding the risk and expense of inventing. In 1785 Jeremy Bentham (Utilitarian) praised the patent system concluding that it had an infinite beneficial effect and costs little. John Stuart Mill (political economist) opined that to deny patent protection would be a gross immorality.

GLOSSARY

ABROGATE: to repeal, to cancel or repeal by authority, to annul.

ABSOLUTE LIABILITY: the state of being bound or obliged by law or justice to do, pay, or make good something that is free from all restrictions or qualifications, unconditioned liability.

ABSTAIN: to refrain from, to do without something as food, water, to do without voluntarily.

ACCEPTANCE: the act of voluntarily receiving something, or a voluntary agreement to certain terms or conditions. In contracts acceptance is to consent to the terms of an offer which creates a binding contract.

ACCUSATION: a formal charge against a person that he or she is guilty of a punishable offense; the charge is placed before a court or magistrate having jurisdiction to inquire into the alleged offense.

ACTIONABLE: subject to or affording ground for an action, meaning litigation or a lawsuit.

AD LITEM: for the purposes of litigation, i.e., a guardian ad litem is a person given the power and duty to act on behalf of another, usually a legally incapacitated person, for purposes of a lawsuit.

ADVERSARY: an opponent, the opposite party to a lawsuit.

AGENCY: a relation created by express or implied contract, or by law, whereby one person (principal) delegates to another person (the agent) the authority to transact some lawful business or to do certain acts for him or her with more or less discretionary power.

AGGRESSOR: one who engages in aggression; one who initiates an offensive or unprovoked assault or act.

AGISTER: one who is hired to feed and care for cattle, sometimes other animals.

ALLEGED: asserted, claimed, stated, charged.

AMENABLE: responsible, answerable, accountable, liable to punishment.

APPREHENSION: seizure, taking, or arrest of a person on a criminal charge, fear, anxiety, dread.

ARBITRATOR: an unofficial person chosen by parties to a lawsuit who investigates the matter and makes a determination.

ARREST: to seize or to take into custody by legal authority; to stop, to check, hold.

ARSON: the malicious burning of real or personal property of another.

ASSAULT: unlawful attempt or threat to commit battery with the ability to inflict injury on another person.

ASSERT: to state positively, to affirm, to state as true, to put into effect.

ASSOCIATION: a society formed for transacting business or carrying on some business or pursuit for mutual benefit or advantage of a group of persons.

BAILMENT: delivery of personal property in trust for some special purpose with a contract, express or implied, to conform with the object or purpose of the trust.

BONA FIDE: in good faith, with integrity, honest, sincere, authentic.

BURGLARY: the breaking and entering into the place of another in the night for the purpose of committing a criminal act.

CARTE BLANCHE: complete authority or freedom of action or judgment.

CAUSE OR CAUSATION: that which produces an effect.

CAVEAT EMPTOR: let the buyer beware, a rule of law that a purchaser buys at his or her own risk

CHARTER: a document issued by the government establishing a corporate entity.

CHATTEL: any tangible, moveable thing, personal properly as opposed to real.

CIVIL LAW: the part of the law concerned with non-criminal matters, contracts, property etc.

COMPENSABLE DAMAGES: payment for damages awarded as compensation.

COMPENSATE: to make suitable or equal return or payment, reimburse, remunerate.

COMPLAINT: the first or initial pleading on the part of a plaintiff in a civil action; the court document that alleges certain misconduct of the defendant and the request of redress or compensation.

CONDITION PRECEDENT: a condition that must be fulfilled or an act that must be performed before some right can be gained.

CONSIDERATION: the cause, motive, price or influence that induces parties to enter into a contract, the reason or cause for a contract, the promise to act or forbear that is given by one party to an agreement and accepted by the other as an inducement to the other's act or promise.

CONTRACT: a promissory agreement between 2 or more persons that creates, modifies, or destroys a legal relationship, an agreement on sufficient consideration to do or not to do a particular thing.

CREDIBILITY: worthiness of belief, the quality in a witness that renders his or her evidence worthy of belief.

CRIME: an act which the government has deemed contrary to the public good. A wrong injurious to the public.

DEFENDANT: a person against whom a civil or criminal action is brought in a court of law

DOCTRINE: a rule, principle, theory, or tenet of the law.

DUE CARE: a concept used in tort law to indicate the standard of care or the legal duty one owes to others.

EASEMENT: the right of one owner of land to make a lawful and beneficial use of the land of another, created by express or implied contract, may occur through continued uninterrupted use of property or by custom.

EMPLOYEE: one who works for an employer, a person working for salary, wages or compensation who is authorized to act in some capacity for the employer.

ESTOP,ESTOPPEL: to stop, bar, impede, an impediment raised by law.

ETHICS: the system or code of morals of a particular group, religion, or profession

EVIDENCE: all the means by which any alleged matter of fact is established or disproved.

EXPRESS CONTRACT: an actual agreement of the parties the terms of which are stated in explicit language, orally or in writing, at the time the contract is made.

FEE: in real property law a condition of complete ownership which can be sold by the owner or given to heirs.

FELONY: crimes such as murder, rape and burglary, graver than misdemeanors.

FRAUD: a deceitful practice or willful device resorted to with the intent to deprive another person of his or her right or in some manner to cause harm or injury.

GOOD SAMARITAN LAWS: laws that protect from liability a rescuer or one who pities and selflessly helps another, unless the rescuer is grossly negligent.

GRAND JURY: a jury of inquiry summoned to sessions of the criminal courts whose duty is to receive complaints and accusations in criminal cases and issue bills of indictment where the jury is satisfied that a trial should be held.

HEARSAY RULE: a statement made by other than a witness to prove a truth of the matter being tried, usually inadmissible in court

HEIR: a person who succeeds by descent and the right of relationship, according to the rules of law, to an estate in land or personal property on the death of an ancestor or other person.

HUMANE: having the best qualities of mankind, tender, merciful, considerate, etc.

IMPLICATION: that which is implied, hinted at or suggested, not directly expressed.

IMPLIED CONTRACT: an agreement between 2 or more persons that creates an obligation to do or not to do a specific thing which arises by implication.

INCOMPETENT: lacking in ability, fitness, legal qualifications to discharge a duty.

INDEMNIFY: to compensate for loss or damage or expense incurred, to compensate a defendant in a lawsuit.

INDICTMENT: an accusation in writing presented by a grand jury charging the person named has committed some act that by law is a public offense.

INFORMED CONSENT: informing a patient or animal owner of the risks of a medical procedure before its performance with permission relieving the professional of liability for an uninformed client.

INJUNCTION: a court remedy given for the purpose of requiring a party to refrain from performing an act or activity liable to be harmful to citizens.

INJURY: any wrong or damage done to another, to his person, rights, property, a violation of a legal right.

JURISDICTION: the power to hear and determine a case at law, the geographic area in which a court has power.

JURY: a certain number of men and women selected by law to inquire into certain matters of fact and declare the truth based on the evidence presented to them.

LIABILITY: an obligation to do or refrain from doing something, bound or obliged by law to do something, pay a fine, make reparations

LEGAL DUTY: that which the law requires to be done by a person, this may be created by contract.

LIBEL: a false and malicious publication printed for the purpose of defaming one.

LITIGATION: a judicial controversy for the purpose of enforcing a right.

LOCALITY RULE: a rule holding a practitioner of a profession to the standards of care, responsibility and training of those of the same profession in the same general area.

MALFEASANCE: the wrongful or unjust performance of an act that the person has no right to perform, the doing of an act that is totally wrongful.

MALICE: the doing of a wrongful act intentionally, without just cause or excuse.

MALPRACTICE: any professional misconduct, unreasonable lack of skill, evil practice, illegal or immoral conduct that causes injury to a person.

MISDEMEANOR: an act committed or omitted in violation of a public law.

MORAL TURPITUDE: an act or behavior that violates moral sentiment or accepted moral standards of the community and is morally culpable.

NEGLIGENCE: the failure to do something a reasonable person would do, the doing of something that a reasonable person would not do, the failure to use ordinary care.

OMISSION: neglect or failure to do something, not doing something the law requires.

ORDINANCE: a local law applying to persons and things subject to the law locally.

OWNERSHIP: one's exclusive right of possessing, enjoying, and disposing of a thing.

PENALTY OF PERJURY: the penalty for knowingly and willfully giving false testimony.

PARTNERSHIP: a contract between 2 or more persons to place their money, effects, labor and skill in lawful commerce or business and to divide the profits and bear the losses in agreed proportions.

PLAINTIFF: the party in a civil lawsuit who brings the action into a court of law.

POLICE POWER: the power of the government (states and local) to impose restrictions on private rights for the promotion and maintenance of the health, safety, morals and general welfare of the public.

PERSONAL PROPERTY: things moveable as opposed to real property (land).

PRICE-FIXING: a combination of persons or businesses for the purpose of raising, depressing, fixing or establishing the price of a commodity for their benefit and to the detriment of others.

PRIMA FACIE: sufficient to establish a fact or facts, at first sight, before further investigation.

PRIVILEGED COMMUNICATION: communications which occur within a professional relationship and under professional confidentiality.

PROBABLE CAUSE: facts sufficient to cause a person of reasonable caution to believe a wrong has been committed.

PROXIMATE CAUSE: an event which produces a result without which the injury could not have occurred.

PRECEDENT: a previously decided law case recognized as the authority for the case in question and for the disposition of future similar cases.

PRODUCTS LIABILITY: the strict liability of a manufacturer when he knowingly places an article on the market without inspection for defects which may cause injury to the user.

RECIPROCITY: a relationship where a state favors the privileges granted by another state and returns the favor, i e., recognizing a professional license from another state.

SALE: a contract by which real property or personal property is transferred from the seller (vendor) to the buyer (vendee) for a price agreed upon by the parties.

SCIENTER: knowledge, previous knowledge of an operative state of facts, frequently implies guilty knowledge, or fraud.

SERVANT: one who works for and is subject to the control of another, an employee.

STANDARD OF CARE: the degree of care and skill associated with a profession in handling, treatment and care of a patient.

STATUTE: an act of a legislature under its authority which becomes law governing specific conduct within the scope of the statute.

STATUTE OF LIMITATIONS: a law which fixes the time in which parties must take legal action to enforce their rights or thereafter be barred from enforcing these.

TENANCY: a tenant's right to possess an estate by lease or title, usually a landlord/tenant relationship.

TESTIMONY: a statement made by a witness under oath regarding a legal proceeding.

TITLE: ownership, the right to possess a thing, real or personal property.

TRADEMARK: a mark, word, letter, number, design, picture or combination thereof used by a person or business to demonstrate ownership of the thing.

TORT: a wrong, a private or civil wrong or injury, independent of a contract, which results from a breach of a legal duty owed another.

VENUE: a neighborhood; synonymous with the place of a trial; a change of venue means to move the place of a trial.

WARRANTY- an assurance given by one party to a contract or the existence of facts upon which the other party can rely and depend upon.

ZONING: separation or division of a municipality into districts to regulate, control, or limit the uses of real property.

REFERENCES

CHAPTER 1
HISTORICAL BACKGROUND

Cuschan S, Socio-Juridic condition of the individual in Roman culture. vol. 43 The Jurist, wtr. 1983, p. 125

Edmunds PD, Law and civilization. Public Affairs Press, 1959, Washington D.C.

Evans EP, The criminal prosecution and capital punishment of animals. London 1906, William Heinemann Press.

Magna Carta and our law. vol. 23 Tenn. Bar Journ., Jul/Aug 1978, p. 40

McConnell B, They shoot horses. vol. 143, New Law Journ. June 5, 1992

Student Lawyer, vol. 9, Feb 1981, p. 19

Van Wernelo P, An introduction to the principles of Roman Civil Law. Cape Town 1976, Juta and Co. Ltd.

CHAPTER 2
MALPRACTICE AND NEGLIGENCE

61 Am Jur 110, 1972

38 ALR 2d 523, 1954

71 ALR 4th, 811, 1981

Ardoin v Hartford Ins Co. 360 So 2d 1331, 1978

Barney v Pinkham 45 NW 694, 1890

Bartless v MacRae 635 P 2d 666, 1981

Beck v Henkle Craig Livestock Co. 88 SE 865, 1916

Bekkemo v Erickson 242 NW 617, 1932

Bellance v Dunnington 57 ALR 2d 267, 1928

Branks v Kern 348 SE 2d 815, 1986; 359 SE 2d 780, 1987

Breece v Ragan 138 SW 2d 79, 1940

Brochett v Abbe 206 A 2d 447, 1964

Brown v Bleiburg 178 Cal Rep 454, 1981

Brousseau v Rosenthal 443 NYS 2d 285, 1984

Brune v Belinkoff 235 NE 2d 793, 1968

Carter v Louisiana State Univ. 520 So 2d 383, 1988

Conner v Winton 8 Ind 315, 1856

65 Cor Jur 2d 413, 1966
Corso v Crawford 415 NYS 2d 182, 1979
Dodd and Dodd v Wilson and McWilliams 2 All England 16, 1943
Erickson v Webber 58 So 446, 60 ALR 914, 1931
Eastep v Vet Med Exam Board 539 P 2d 1144, 1975
Fredeen v Stride 525 P 2d 166, 1974
Hannah HW, JAVMA 1989; 195:1220
Hannah HW, JAVMA 1990; 197;337
Hannah HW, JAVMA 1990; 197;834
Hannah HW, JAVMA 1991; 198;1531
Hannah HW, JAVMA 1993; 202:1066
Hanners v Salmon 288 SW 307, 1931
Hohenstein v Dodds 10 NW 2d 23, 1943
Johnson v Wander 592 So 2d 1225, 1992
Jankoske v Preiser 510 NE 2d 1084, 1987
Kelliher v Pinkham 45 NW 694, 1890
Kerbow v Bell 38 ALR 2d 500, 1953
King JH Jr, The standard of care for veterinarians in malpractice claims.
        v 58 Tenn Lw Rev 1990, p. 1-71
Kuehn v Wilson 13 Wisc 116, 1860
LaPort v Associated Independent Inc. 163 So 2d 267, 1965
Lyford v Martin 82 NW 479, 1900
Massa v Dept Registration and Education, 487 NE 2d 392, 1985
Moreland v Lowdermilk 709 F Supp 733, 1989
Nichols v Jacobsen 298 P 505, 1931
North Miami General Hospital v Goldberg 520 So 2d 650, 1988
Pendergraft v Royster 166 SE 285, 1932
Prahl v Gerhard 25 Wisc 466, 1870
Ramiro and Restrepo v NY State 550 NYS 2d 536, 1989
Smith v Guthrie 557 SW 2d 163, 1977
Snow v Allen 151 So 468, 1933
Southall v Gabell 277 NE 2d 230, 1971
Staples v Steed 52 So 646, 1910
Turner v Benhart 527 So 2d 717, 1988
Turner v Sinha 582 NE 2d 1018, 1989
Williams v Gilman 71 Maine 21, 1891

CHAPTER 3
VETERINARIAN-CLIENT RELATIONS

Bolles v Linton 236 P 26, 1928
California Jurisprudence 2d, Liens, sec. 5-8, 1952
Carpenter v Walker 54 So 60, 1933
Cazalet E, Equine Vet Journ 1977; 9:183
Connecticut Med. Editorial, 1975; 42:595
Corboy PH, Jacobsen AJ, Trial lawyers guide. 1968, Callaghan and Co.
Corpus Juris vol 65, p. 413, 1966
Deering California Codes, sec 1834-1836.6, 1973
First National Bank v Silva 254 P 262, 1927
Georgia Statute 50-17 (a), 1986
Hannah HW, Legal briefs, JAVMA 1991; 198:1148
Hannah HW, Legal briefs, JAVMA 1993; 203:976
Hannah HW, Good Samaritan laws and veterinarians. JAVMA 1995;
    206:977
Hannah HW, Legal briefs, JAVMA 1991; 198:67
Hannah HW, Legal briefs, JAVMA 1991; 199:1576
Hendershot v Western Union Telegraph Co. 76 NW 828, 1898
Julian v DeVincent 184 SE 2d 535, 1971
Kelliher JC, Vet Med Small Anim Pract 1977; 72:1148
Kuhn v Brownfield 12 SE 519, 1910
Ladd v Witte 92 NW 365, 1902
Levine v Knowles 197 So 2d 329, 1967
NE Kansas Prod Credit Assn v Ferbrache 693 P 2d 1152, 1985
Patton GW, Bailments in the commonlaw, London 1953, Stevens
Price DA, JAVMA 1979; 175:426
Public Act 78-1106, sec 91-124, 1973
Quist v Sandman 99 P 204, 1908
Scott v Simpson 167 SE 920, 1933
Small Claims Study Group, Quincy House, MA. 1972
Southall v Gabel 283 NE 2d 891, 1971
Weinrub v Harlem Bakery 197 NYS 833, 1923
West California Civil Code, sec 3051, 1988
Wills v Knowles, District Court of Appeals, Florida June 1978

CHAPTER 4
VETERINARY PRACTICES

Ackerman v Roberston 3 NW 2d 723, 1941
8 ALR 4th, 223, 1981
8 ALR 4th, 223, 1981
11 ALR 3d, 1399, Nuisance 1967
1 ALR 4th 994, Nuisance 1980
9 ALR Digest, 1995, Worker's Comp.p. 479
54 Amer Jur 54z., 1971
Areen J, et al, Law Science and Medicine, Mineola NY, 1984, Foundation Press
Atherley G. et al, Biomedical surveillance, J Occupat Med 1986:28:958
Baram M, The right to know, Am J Pub Health 1984; 74:385
Berlew DE, Hall DT, The socialization of managers, Admin Sci Quart, Sep 1966, 208
Beck v Henkle-Craig Livestock Co. 88 SE 865, 1916
Blair v Dumond 108 NYS 2d 738, 1951
Bloecher and Schoof Inc. v Penn RR Co. 160 A 281, 1932
Bond v Berson 146 A 773, 1929
Boyer R, Biomedical monitoring in the work place. J Occup Med 1986; 28:935
Bradley v Consolidated Silver Mine Co. 289 P324. 1934
Breecher V Brown 17 NW 2d 377, 1945
Burt v St. Mary's Hospital, Ind App Ct 1978
29 CFR 1910 et seq, 1990, 1993
City of Rome v Mac Williams 52 GA 251, 1875
City of Birmingham v West 183 So 421, 1938
v 19 CO Lawyer 1990, 92429
Cooper v State Board of Vet Med 178 A 178, 1934
66 Corp Jur 2d 727, 1950
70 Corp Jur 2d 551, 1987, sec. 5
70 Corp Jur 2d 918, 1987, sec 7
Crawford LM, A tribute to Liautard, JAVMA 1976; 169,:35
Curran WJ, The doctor as a witness, Philadelphia 1965, WB Saunders Co.
DeVincenzi v Faulkner 344 P 2d 322, 1959
Doake v Farmer's Coop. 94 NW 2d 115, 1959

Dorney RC, Making time to manage, Harvard Bus Rev Jan-feb 1988, 38
Dorland Medical Dictionary, Philadelphia 1974, WB Saunders Co.
Drucker PF, The effective executive, New York 1967,
Harper and Rowe
Ellos WJ, Ethical practice in clinical medicine, London 1990, Roetledge
Field R, Barram M, Screening and monitoring data as evidence in legal
    proceedings, J Occupat Med 1986; 28:946
FFDCA, 21 CFR, 351, 1995, 352, 1995
Garlick SH, The Whys and wherefores of corporate practice, New
    Jersey, 1982, Medical Economics Books
72 Georgetown Law J. 1231, 1984
Getty MG, Enforceability of non-competitive covenants in physician
    employment contracts. J Legal Med 1986;7:235
Gillon R, Medical ethics, Brit Med J 1994; 309:184
Goldfarb v Virginia State Bar 421 U.S.773, 1975
Haase v Morton and Morton 115 NW 921, 1908
Hadley J, Vet Rec 1977; 101:269
Hall MC, Ethics in veterinary medicine, JAVMA 1931, 79:13
Haluska v Univ of Saskatchewan 52 AWR 608, 1965
Hannah HW, JAVMA 1977; 170:802
Hannah HW, JAVMA 1978; 172:236, 886
Hannah HW, JAVMA 1989; 194:650
Hannah HW, JAVMA 1990;196 and 197;1384, 50
Hannah HW, JAVMA 1991;198: pages 67 and 788
Hannah HW, JAVMA 1992; 201:702
Hannah HA, JAVMA 1993; 202:384
Hannah HW, Pointers on liability of Public veterinarians. JAVMA 1994;
    205:1280
Hannah HW, Veterinarians and waste disposal. JAVMA 1995;205:308
Hartford Ins Co v Thompson 175 F2d 10,1949
Hausman v Geiman 252 NW 857, 1934
4 Univ Hawaii Law Rev. 1982, p. 207
Herzberg F, How do you motivate employees? Harvard Bus Rev
    Sep/Oct 1987;109
Hood J, Worker's compensation and employee protection laws. West
    PUbl Co 1984, St. Paul MN.
Hewitt v State Medical Examiners 814 P39, 1906
Hyrne v Erwin 55 Amer Rep 15, 1896

Judd v H.S. Coe and Co. 117 Conn 510, 1933

Joint Conference on Public relations and ethics. JAVMA 1952; 126:107

JAVMA 1974; 165:1974

JAVMA Judicial Counsel, Principles of veterinary medical ethics, JAVMA 1979; 174:25

JAVMA 1993; 269:915

JAVMA Extra label use of drugs, JAVMA 1994; 205:1231

Kerbow v Bell 38 ALR 2d 723, 1953

Kramer v State Board of Veterinary Examiners 55 So 2d 93, 1952

Krames Commun., Managing employee productivity, Daly City, 1988, CA 94015

Leake v Venice 195 P440, 1920

Lawrence v Board of Registry in Medicine, 132 NS 174, 1921

Laude KJ, New Eng J Med 1936; 215:826

Lauritzen v City of New Orleans 503 So 2d 580, 1987

Livingston JS. Pygmalian in Management, Harvard Bus Rev Sep/Oct 1986, 121

Lorsch JW, Mathias PF, When professionals have to manage. Harvard Bus Rev Jul/Aug 1987; 78

Levois MA, Walden CA, Law and ethics in the medical office Philadelphia 1988, F. A. Davis Co.

Marmot v State 45 Ohio State 14, 1831

Mason JK, McColl-Smith RA, Law and medical ethics, London, 1991, Butterworth's

McLean SAM, A patients' right to know, Brookfield VT, 1989, Gauer Publ Co.

Merillat LA, Code of ethics of the AVMA, JAVMA 1940; 96:92

Miller F, Biological monitoring, Am J Law Med 1984; 9:387

Mintzberg H, A managers's job. Harvard Bus Rev. Mar/Apr 1980, 163

Morbidity Mortality Weekly Reports (MMWR), 26(5) 37, 1977

MMWR, 26(26);377, 1977

MMWR, 27 (23);192, 1978

MMWR 28 (28);333, 1979

MMWR 34 (26); 402, 1985

MMWR 34 (30); 464, 1985

MMWR 35 (35); 561, 1986

Mintz B, Medical surveillance of employees J Occupat Med 1986; 28:913

Missouri State Vet Med assn v Gilsan, 230 SW 2d 169, 1950
Morganstern F, Deterrence and compensation, WHO International labor
   orgn., Geneva, 1982
Nebraska Constitution, art 3, sec 18, 1927,
Nat'l Labor Relations Act, 29 USCA 1975, sec 151
Occupational Safety Health Act, 29 USC 651, 1970
Office Technol Assessment, U.S. Congress, April 1983, p. 224
Parkinson, the law, Boston 1980, Houghton-Miflin Co.
Peet Stock Remedy Co. v McMullen 32 F 2d 669, 1929
People v Love 131 NE 809, 1921
People v Witte 146 NE 178, 1925
Perkins JA, The university as an organization, New York, 1973,
   McGraw-Hill book Co.
Peters TJ, Waterman RH Jr., In search of excellence, New York 1982,
   Harper and Row
Presidential report on occupational health and safety, 1976, p. 111
QRB Communique, Protecting health care workers,
QRB 1988; 14:14406
Raines L, Biological testing, J Occupat Med 1986; 28:921
Reid v Robertson 200 SW 2d 900, 1947
Richardson JR, Text on evidence, Cincinnati, 1974, WN Anderson and
   Co.
Richardson JR, Text on testimony, Cincinnati 1974, WR Anderson and
   Co.
Robinson JC, The rising long term trends in occupational injury rates,
   Am J Pub Health 1988; 78:276
Rosenthal K, Jacobsen L, Pygmalion in the classroom. New York 1968,
   Reinhart-Winston
Rumbaugh GE, Ardans GS, Vet Med Small Anim Pract 1978; 73:1321
Sanborn v Weir 112 A 229, 1921
Simmons M, Danger, experimental animals, J Occupat Health 1982;
   51:30
Seligman J, Corporations, New York 1995, Little Brown and Co.
Stapleton J, Disease and compensation debate, Clarendon Press 1986,
   Oxford
State v Hopkins 166 P 304, 1917
State v Gazlay 5 Ohio 14, 1831
State v Haughton, Rankin and Co. 6 Louisiana Ann 783, 1847

State v Dickens 1 SE 2d 837, 1939
State v Tule 8 A 2d 17, 1939
State v Moresi 24 So 2d 370, 1946
13 Stat Law Rev , Sum 1992, p. 50
Stout-Weigand N, Fatal occupational injuries, Amer J Pub Health 1988;
    78:1215
726 SW 2d 723, 1987
Thiele v City and County of Denver 312 P 2d 786, 1957
Trial Lawyers Guide, Feb. 1968
Vesley D, Hartmen H, Laboratory acquired infections. Amer J PUb
    Health 1988; 78:1213
Wall St. J. 5-1-92, B5, 1-13-93, p. 34
Wisconsin Bar J., April 1994, p. 3
42 USCA 4332 et seq.
West's Annotated CAlifornia Codes, 1991, St. Paul, MN. West PUbl
    Co.
Wilkinson v Colley 30 A 26, 1894
90B Yale Law J. 1981, p. 1792

CHAPTER 5
PROTECTION OF ANIMALS

Ames BN, Identifying environmental chemicals causing mutation and
    cancer. Science 1978; 204:587
Bartlett EA, Medical regulation of the CAlifornia horseracing industry.
    vol 27 San Diego Law Rev 1990, p. 743
Biggerstaff v Vanderburgh Humane Soc. 453 NE 2d 363, 1983
CE America Inc. v Antinori 210 So 2d 443, 1960
Commonwealth v Gonzalez 588 A2d 529, 1991
Douglas WHJ, Tissue culture models in experimental medicine. EXP
    Med Biol 1981; 7:196
Fliegel RM, vol 23 Golden Gate Univ Law Rev, Apr 1993, p. 599
Glantz SA, Financial impact of animal regulation. Science 1989;
    244:1531
Goss LB, Sabourin TB, Utilization of alternative species for toxicity
    testing. J Appl Toxicol 1985; 5:193
Hatch OG, Biomedial research. Am Physiol 1987; 42:591

Holden C, Industry toxicologists keen on reducing animal use. Science 1987; 236:252

Jori A. Sharp decline in animal use in a pharmacological research laboratory. Lancet 1984; 2:229

LaRue v State 478 So 2d 13, 1985

Mahiai v Suna 742P2d 359, 1987

Martinex v Sommonwelath of Pennsylvania, 472 A2d 1180, 1984

Miller JL, In vitro methods not likely to replace animal testing of drugs. Clin Pharm 1986; 5:351

Morris RK, Fox MW, On the fifth day; animal rights and human ethics. 1977, Washington D.C., Acropolis Press

National Academy of Sciences, Inst Lab Anim Rsources. Toxicity testing, 1984, washington D. C.

Parson RM, In vitro techniques. Human Reproduct 1986; 1:559

Regaldo v U.S. 572 A2d 416, 1990

Rose JC, Animals in research. Pharos 1985; 48:19

Rowan AN, The concept of the three R's. Devel Biol 1980; 45:175

Ryan T, Progress without pain. vol 31 St. Louis Univ Law J, 1987; p. 13

Schmidt-Nielson B, Research animals in experimental medicine. Exp'l Biol Med 1981; 7:46

Sabourin TD et al, The efficacy of three non-mammalian test systems in the identification of chemical tetratogens. Appl Toxicol 1985; 5:227

Singer P, Animal liberation, New York 1976, Avon Press

Sinclair U, The Jungle, New York 1906, New American Library

Smyth DH, Tissue culture as an alternative. J Roy Soc Med 1980; 73:229

Soave OA, Alternatives to the use of animals for research. Lab Anim 1982; 7:23

State v Flynn 687 P 2d 596, 1984

State v Tweedie, 444 A2d 855, 1982

State v Wilson 464 So 2d 667, 1985

State v Gaines 580 NE 2d 1158, 1990

Tuch v U.S. 477 A2d 1115, 1984

U.S. v Hayashi 22 F2d 859, 1993

U.S. v Mitchell 553 F2d 996, 1977

CHAPTER 6
PROTECTION OF THE PUBLIC

64 ALR 3d 1039, 1975

41 ALR 3d 888, 1972

64 ALR 4th 817, 1987

26 Arkansas Lawyer Apr. 1992, p. 36

Bauman DE, Vernon RG, Effect of exogenous bovine somatotropin on
        37 Arkansas Law Rev , 1984, p. 119 lactation, Ann Rev Nutr
        1993; 13:437

Bender v Welsh 25 A 2d 182, 1942

Blair v Dumond 108 NYS 2d 738, 1951

Bixby-Hammett DM, Accidents in equestrian sports. Amer Family Pract
        1987; 36:122

Braunback S, Kansas fence laws, v. 56 Kans Bar Assn 1987, p. 15

Briley v Mitchell 110 So 2d 169, 1959

Bruister v Haney 102 So 2d 806, 1958

Bixby-Hammett D, Brooks WH, Common injuries in horseback riding,
        Sports Med 1990; 9:36

City of Birmingham v West 183 So 421, 1938

City of Garland v White 368 SW 2d 12, 1963

City of Richardson v Responsible dog owners of Texas. 794 SW 2d 17,
        1990

Chandler v Vaccaro 334 P 2d 998, 1959

Chew v Gates 744 F Supp 952, 1990

Cohen v Rodenbaugh 162 F Supp 748, 1957

v 19 Colo Lawyer 1990, p. 2429

Corp Jur 2d Animals, sec 16, 1973

v 24 Creighton Law Rev , June 1991, p. 1515

Crunk v Glover 95 NW 2d 135, 1959

Dalton v Dean 136 SW 2d 721, 1940

Darnald v Voges 300 P 2d 255, 1956

DeVincenzi v Faulkner 344 P 2d 322, 1959

Dinkem v Weinberger 162 NYS 2d 465, 1957

Detroit Coll Law Rev 1984, p. 757

v 31 Drake Law Rev. summer 1981-2, p. 637

Duffy v Gerhart 157 A 2d 585, 1960

503 F 2d 953, 1974 854 F 2d 909, 1987 v 26 Land and Water Rev, 1991, p. 511

Gardiner v Black 217 NE 573, 1940

Hannah HW, JAVMA 202; 1993

4 Univ Hawaii Law Rev 1982, p. 207

Hill v Scruggs 2 So 2d 543, 1941

v 47 Iowa Law Rev 1983, p. 803,

Johnson v McConnel 80 P 2d 545, 1899

Jones v Craddock 187 SE 558, 1936

Laridaen v Railway Express Agency 47 NW 2d 727, 1951

Liepske v Gunther 95 NW 2d 774, 1959

Litzkuhn v Clark 339 P 2d 389, 1959

Mann v Stanley 296 P 2d 921, 1956

McElgunn CA, Injuries by animals. v 24 Washburn Law J 1986, p. 676

McGhee CNJ et al, Horse riding and head injury. Brit J Neurosurg 1987; 1:131

McLatckie MB, Equestrian injuries; a one year prospective study. Brit J Sports Med 1979; 13:19

Meekins v Simpson 96 SE 2d 893, 1963

Meyer KG, Animal branding, v 12 J Agric Taxat and Law. Summer 1990, 2. 179

MMWR Injuries associated with horseback riding, May 25, 1990

v 21 Memphis State Univ Law Rev, Summer 1991, p. 791

Niday v Jenkins 136 NE 2d 447, 1955

v 34 New York Law School Rev 1988, p. 411

Oakley v State 214 SW 2d 298, 1948 Palmer LL, Liability of ranchers and farmers for injury caused by fencing or not fencing rangelands, 14 J Agric Taxat Law 1992, p. 25

Pennyvan v Alexander 91 So 2d 728, 1957

Perkins v Hatteny 155, NE 2d 73, 1958

Pooley v State of Alaska 705 P 2d 1293, 1985

Porier v Spirey 102 SE 2d 706, 1958

Ruona v City of Billings 323 P 2d 29, 1958

Russo v Scheiber 175 NYS 2d 188, 1958

San Francisco Chronicle Mar 13, 1995

Scharfield v Richardson 145 ALR 980, 1942

Seaber AV, Chronicle of the Horse, 1970; 34:53, 1983; 46:44 1979; 42:12

Sentell v New Orleans and Carrollton RR C. 166 U.S. 698, 1897
Silber v Siedler 188 NYS 2d 111, 1959
Smith v Riedinger 95 NW 2d 65, 1959
State v Tule 8 A 2d 17, 1939
State v Moresi 24 So 2d 370, 1946
v 13 Statute Law Rev, summer 1992 p. 50
v 39 Syracuse Law Rev 1988, p. 1445
Thiele v City and County of Denver 312 P 2d 786, 1957
Thorne JA, v 39 Syracuse Law REV 1988, p. 1445
Thompson v Matuschek 333 P 2d 1022, 1959
Tidal Oil Co. v Forcum 116 P2d 572, 1941
Tillery v Crook 297 SW 2d 9, 1957
Turnispeed v State 367 SE 2d 259, 1988
Turner v Shropshire 147 SW 2d 388, 1941
Tynlan v Harlan 159 NE 2d 769, 1959
v 59 UMKC, wtr 1990. p.409
35 USC 161, 1988
206 USPQ 193, 1980
U.S. v Algon Chem. 879 F2d 1154, 1989
U.S. v KG Containers 674 F Supp 1394, 1987
U.S. v Colahan (IBA) 811 F 2d 287, 1982
Vaughan v Miller Bros. 153 SE 289, 1931
Weever v First National Bank of Limon 330 P 2d 142, 1958
Weaver v National Biscuit Co. 125 F 2d 463, 1942
Whitlock M, Horse riding accidents, Lifeline Ambulance Mag. 1986
v 13 Whittier Law Rev 1992, p. 515
Young v Broward Co. 570 So 2d 309, 1990

ANIMAL RIGHTS REFERENCES

Bender DL, Leone B. Rohr J. Animal Rights, opposing viewpoints.
    1989, San Diego, Greenhaven Press
Blackman DE, et al. Animal Welfare and the Law, 1989, Cambridge U.
    Press
Clark SRL, Animals and their moral standing. London, 1997, Routledge
Carruthers P. The animal issue, 1994, Cambridge U Press
Clarke PAB, Linzey S. Political theory and animal rights 1990,
    Winchester MA, Pluto Press

Francione GL, Rain without thunder. 1996, Phila. Temple U Press

Francione, GL, Animal rights and welfare 49 Rutgers Law Rev 397, 1996

Garner R. Animal rights, the changing debate 1996, NY U Press, NY

Jasper JM, Nelhim D, The animal rights crusade. NY 1992, The Free Press

Palmer C, Animal liberation. 1995, in Ethics and Society Paper #1, Oxford U Press

Rollin BE, Animal rights and human morality, 1992, Buffalo, NY, Promethus Press

Silverstein, H. Unleasing rights, 1996, Ann Arbor, U Michigan Press

INDEX